FREEWHEELING

THE FEUDS, BROODS, AND OUTRAGEOUS FORTUNES OF THE BILLES FAMILY AND CANADA'S FAVORITE COMPANY

IAN BROWN

Harper & Collins

TORONTO

First published in 1989 by
Harper & Collins Publishers Ltd.
55 Avenue Road
Suite 2900
Toronto, Canada M5R 3L2

Canadian Cataloguing in Publication Data
Brown, Ian, 1954-
   Freewheeling

ISBN 0-00-215977-5

1. Canadian Tire Corporation Limited – History.
2. Billes family. I. Title

HD9745.C34C3 1989   338.7′6138112′0971
C89-094885-2

Printed and bound in Canada

To my mother and father

Kernaghan's boarding house used to be the last house – last building – on the edge of town. It's still there, still close to the sidewalk. But the town has spread a little at all its edges. A Petro-Can gas station. A Canadian Tire store with a big parking lot. Some new, low houses.

– Alice Munro, "The Moon in the Orange Street Skating Rink"

Oh, we are travelled and educated enough to realize that the limits set to our ambition are small and petty enough, looked at from outside and above. But everything in this world is comparative, Uncle Gotthold. Did you know one can be a great man, even in a small place; a Caesar even in a little commercial town on the Baltic? But that takes imagination and idealism – and you didn't have it, whatever you may have thought of yourself.

– Thomas Mann, *Buddenbrooks*

To my mentor Fronto I owe the realization that malice, craftiness, and duplicity are the concommitants of absolute power; and that our patrician families tend for the most part to be lacking in the feelings of ordinary humanity.

– Marcus Aurelius, *Meditations*

▼

ACKNOWLEDGMENTS

This book would not have been possible without the help of literally dozens of past and present employees of Canadian Tire and their many associates. They should not, however, be blamed for the final result.

I am particularly grateful, for the many hours they spent talking to me, to Alfred J. Billes, the co-founder of Canadian Tire; Martha Billes; Alfred Dickson Billes and his wife Norma and their children; Gwen Billes; and John and Betty Billes. They had little to gain from this book, but considered it important anyway.

I am grateful, as well, to Hugh Macaulay, Dean Groussman, Allan Goddard, and others at the company, too numerous to mention; the dealers, notably Arch Brown, Denvil Brown, Reg Quinn, Peter Montgomery, Ron Mann, Grant Wallace, Don Graham, Vern Forster, and the incomparable Walter Muncaster; Mayne Plowman, Dean Muncaster, John Kron, William Dawson, Richard Hobbs, Barry Setnor, Gary Philbrick, Robin Law, Joseph Groia, John Stransman, R. B. Matthews, Peter Dey, and Larry Wright.

I would also like to thank Charles Macli and Kathleen Richards, my editors, and Peter Livingston, my agent, for their friendship, help, and encouragement; Edwin O'Dacre and Shirley Sharzer, my former bosses at *The Globe and Mail*, for giving me time away from my regular duties to write this book; and Phil Jackman, my editor at the *Globe*, for his suggestions.

Finally, my deepest thanks to Johanna. Her tireless patience, sharp eye, and endless support during the two years it took to complete this book are, in the end, the reason it exists.

Toronto
February 1989

Some of the characters in this book

John William Billes ("J.W."): founder and first president of Canadian Tire; the great patriarch.

Gladys Maude Billes: J.W.'s long-suffering wife.

Alfred Jackson Billes ("A.J."): J.W.'s younger brother; self-professed co-founder, second president and board member of Canadian Tire Corp. Ltd.; marketing genius.

Barbara Billes: Fred's wife, and one of his greatest supporters.

Muriel Billes: A.J.'s wife, less long-suffering.

Alfred Dickson Billes ("Dick"): younger son of J.W. Billes; aspirant to his father's throne; board member of Canadian Tire Corp. Ltd.; Canadian Tire dealer.

Alfred William Billes ("Fred"): A.J.'s eldest son; aspirant to his father's throne; owner-dealer of Canadian Tire's main store at Yonge and Davenport; controlling shareholder and board member of Canadian Tire Corp. Ltd.

Martha Gertrude Gardiner Billes: A.J.'s daughter; aspirant to her father's throne; controlling shareholder and board member of Canadian Tire Corp. Ltd.

David George Billes: A.J.'s younger, least involved son; chairman, Performance Engineering Ltd.; controlling shareholder and board member of Canadian Tire Corp. Ltd.

Dean Muncaster: son of Walter Muncaster, Canadian Tire dealer; graduate, Western Business School; first non-Billes to run Canadian Tire Corp. Ltd; third president and chief executive officer, Canadian Tire Corp. Ltd., and a member of its board. The whiz-kid.

Alex Ethelred Barron: chairman of Canadian Tire Corp. Ltd.; formerly chairman of Fry & Co. Muncaster's greatest ally.

Robert Law: board member, secretary and general counsel to Canadian Tire.

Richard Hobbs: graduate, Western Business School; Canadian Tire dealer; vice-president and board member, Canadian Tire Corporation Ltd.

John Kron: graduate, Western Business School; vice-president and board member, Canadian Tire Corp. Ltd.; later president, White Stores Inc.

William Dawson: Canadian Tire dealer; vice-president merchandising, Canadian Tire Corp. Ltd.

Gary Philbrick: consultant; friend to Dean Muncaster; responsible for Canadian Tire's computer systems.

Alan Warren: former Canadian Tire counterman; Canadian Tire dealer; chairman, Canadian Tire Dealer Holdings Ltd.; member of the point team that tried to buy control of Canadian Tire Corp. Ltd. from Fred, Martha and David Billes in October, 1986.

R.B. "Biff" Matthews: lawyer, McCarthy & McCarthy, Toronto law firm; counsel to Fred Billes.

John Stransman: lawyer, Stikeman Elliott; counsel to Martha Billes.

Peter Dey: lawyer, Osler, Hoskin & Harcourt, Toronto law firm; counsel to Gordon Capital and Dealer Holdings Ltd. during takeover atempt of Canadian Tire in October, 1986; former chairman of the Ontario Securities Commission.

William Biggar: vice-president, Merrill Lynch; hired by Fred and David Billes to find a buyer for Canadian Tire.

Stanley Beck: The no-nonsense chairman of the Ontario Securities Commission.

Joseph Peter Paul Groia: assistant general counsel, Ontario Securities Commission.

Jean Pigott: president, Morrison Lamothe Ltd., board member, Canadian Tire Corp. Ltd.; director, National Capital Commission.

Hugh Macaulay: chairman (following Barron), Canadian Tire Corp. Ltd.; chairman, Ontario Hydro; member of the Big Blue Machine, and friend to William G. Davis, former premier of Ontario.

Dean Groussman: fourth president and chief executive officer, Canadian Tire Corp. Ltd.

THE BILLES FAMILY

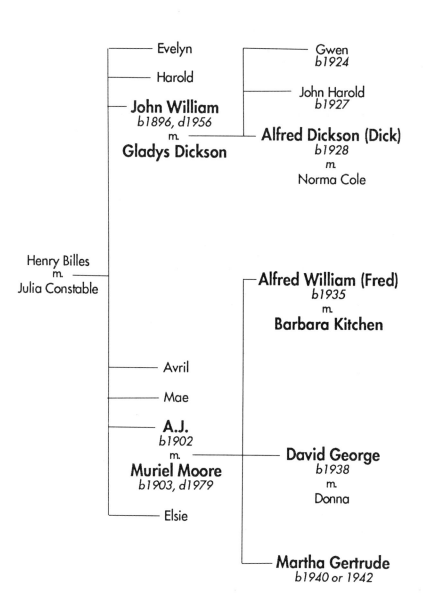

Henry Billes
m.
Julia Constable

- Evelyn
- Harold
- John William
  b1896, d1956
  m.
  Gladys Dickson
  - Gwen
    b1924
  - John Harold
    b1927
  - Alfred Dickson (Dick)
    b1928
    m.
    Norma Cole

- Alfred William (Fred)
  b1935
  m.
  Barbara Kitchen

- Avril
- Mae
- A.J.
  b1902
  m.
  Muriel Moore
  b1903, d1979
  - David George
    b1938
    m.
    Donna
- Elsie

- Martha Gertrude
  b1940 or 1942

CONTENTS

▼

PART I

THE FIRST SPOKE

1

AN ARGUMENT

THIS WAS BEFORE anyone knew how sad or how absurd the entire situation had become.

It was an evening in the fall of 1986. Alfred Jackson Billes had called his children together at his modest condominium in the far north end of Toronto. He wanted to try, one last time, to stop his children from selling the family store – for he loved the store as much as he loved the children. His children knew that, but his sons, Fred and David Billes, wanted to sell it anyway. Their sister Martha Billes disagreed; she wanted to keep the store in the family, and she wanted a hand in steering it.

A modest enough problem, surely – an easily resolved family squabble. Everyone arrived at A.J.'s condo in time for dinner. Fred, A.J.'s eldest, largest son, was there; so were David and Martha. Marjorie, A.J.'s second wife – who also happened to be the mother of Fred's wife Barbara – had cooked dinner. Martha didn't like lasagna, but that was almost predictable. Martha could be a difficult woman to please.

No one was drinking; Marjorie was a strict Baptist, and didn't serve alcohol. Several members of the third generation of Billeses had come as well. Fred's eldest son, Alfred, Jr., was there with his wife Sue; so were Heather, one of Fred's daughters, and David, her husband, who hoped to make a career for himself in the company. Dennis Gardiner Billes, Martha's husband, was in attendance, and so was Fred Sasaki, a longtime employee of the store, and one of A.J.'s most trusted associates. Marjorie ran in and out, serving refreshments.

3

With everyone in the room, the old man's condo felt packed. Fred and Heather and her husband were sitting next to the piano; David occupied the peach-colored armchair by the fireplace; Martha sat alone the other side of the hearth: "All alone on a seat for two – which is how I like to sit in meetings anyway," Martha remembered. "It was a love seat." Her husband, Dennis, was across the room. Behind her, next to the humming heating vent, a window overlooked the city.

A.J.'s condo took up a corner of one of the "luxury towers" that had sprung up like fads on that verge of Toronto just east of Yonge Street to the north of Sheppard Avenue. The old man had never cared much for luxury; he chose the building because it was close to the subway, which he took to work every morning at half-past six. For a man worth in the neighborhood of $500 million, the condominium was decidedly modest.

The fact that the Billes family was worth half a billion dollars came as a surprise to everyone who didn't know who they were. They didn't act the part. To look at them, to listen to them, you thought: maybe a marina in some small northern Ontario town – sure, they might own that. Or maybe a string of convenience stores. And that was just as the Billeses intended. It was part of the big joke they liked to play on the Canadian public. For the store in question was no mere Mom-and-Pop operation, even if the Billeses liked to think of it that way. At stake in the conversation that evening was nothing less than Canadian Tire Corporation Limited, the most successful retailing company in Canada.

After everyone had settled in, A.J. kicked off the conversation. "Now," he said, his old voice thin as paper. He was eighty-four. "Who will start our discussion?"

To outside ears it might have sounded formal; but the Billeses worked hard to separate family matters from affairs of business. This was business, and business required distance, discipline, rigor. They never were much for talking to one another, in any event.

Fred mumbled; no one seemed to want to say anything.

"Well, Fred," A.J. said, "you're the eldest of my kids. Why don't you start?"

SO Fred began to review the situation. The family owned sixty percent of Canadian Tire's common shares, divided three ways among Fred, David, and Martha. That gave them control of the corporation. Fred and David wanted out because running the company in conjunction with their sister had become too difficult.

Martha, on the other hand, took her father's side. She had no interest in selling what she considered her birthright. She had only recently taken a part in the affairs of Canadian Tire. For twenty years after Fred, David, and Martha inherited their share of the company in the early 1960s, the company had been run by Dean Muncaster, an outsider appointed by A.J. Martha had waited impatiently until 1980 for her father to give her a seat on the company's board; it was 1985 before she and her brothers finally disposed of Muncaster. Martha was only just beginning to grasp the power she had. She was no idiot, and she brought a lifetime of frustrated ambition to Canadian Tire's boardroom, tightly wrapped in her own special brand of feminist principles. Martha and her big brother Freddy hadn't seen eye-to-eye on the operation of the company for almost a year. Still, she wanted to run it as a family. But running a huge corporation as a family was proving impossible. There were too many hidden agendas, too many secret wishes, and too many intra-family conflicts for the empire to run smoothly. The question, then, was who was going to give up what to whom? Would Fred let Martha run it? Would Martha back down? The answer on both counts was no.

BUT Freddy wasn't talking about any of that. His "review" of the situation was barely on its legs when he began to insult Martha. "Freddy said something he shouldn't have said,"

Martha later recalled. "Something like, Martha's sleeping around. Something on that level." Martha didn't take it as an insult, but Dennis, her husband, certainly did. Dennis got on his high horse. "Take that back," he said.

This was unacceptable. Dennis was Martha's second husband (and not long for the world as such, either). Or at least he was Martha's spousal equivalent: some of the Billeses – Fred's wife Barbara, for instance – weren't quite sure what Dennis's marital status was. Even though, or perhaps because, Dennis had taken Martha's last name, the family considered Dennis an outsider. Still, Dennis was not one to step down quietly.

Fortunately, at that very moment, Martha and Dennis suddenly noticed a tape recorder taking in their interchange. "Who the hell authorized a tape recorder?" Martha said. "It's against the law."

A tape recorder: that was charming, at a family discussion. But the crisis was again defused. Everyone would receive a copy of the tape.

Fred picked up his summary of the situation before the family. His description was so one-sided, however, Dennis could no longer contain himself. "Speak up, Martha," Dennis said.

"I'll wait," Martha replied.

But Dennis wasn't having any. "Speak up!"

That was when David Billes, normally the meekest of men, told Dennis to shut up, and the trouble started. It was a hot, intense moment, and when Martha recalled it afterwards, she remembered pushing and shoving and Dennis landing on his backside in his chair.

No sooner was he down than he was up again, with Martha on his arm, heading for the door. The meeting had lasted exactly six minutes. It was the last time Martha Billes talked directly with her brothers for nearly three months.

In that time, the Billes family conflict would be spread out for all to examine on the front pages of newspapers across the country, culminating in one of the most controversial Canadian business tug-of-wars of the postwar era. That wasn't quite what the Billeses had planned, but it certainly made for entertaining reading.

THE Billeses are, without reservation, the strangest clan of wealthy people I have ever met. I had first encountered Fred and his sister Martha at a securities commission hearing in Toronto, shortly after the shoving match in A.J.'s apartment. The hearing had been convened because the Ontario Securities Commission (OSC) suspected the Billeses were trying to avoid paying off their fellow shareholders, and the press was going nuts. Still, very few Canadians knew the Billeses by sight, or even by name and reputation. The family had owned Canadian Tire for sixty years, but the Billeses' presence in national life was so invisible that a lot of people in the hearing room mistook Fred's wife Barbara for his sister Martha. Barbara wasn't flattered by the comparison. Later during the hearing, when a photographer tried to take her picture, Barbara made a spectacle of herself in the course of trying to remain "anonymous." Then, when her behavior was written up and published for all to see, she was offended.

Eventually I came to understand that this was fairly standard behavior where the Billeses were concerned. They behaved in unusual ways, and were shocked when someone noticed. They seemed to have a fluctuating sense of who they were. They wanted to be thought of as ordinary people, and couldn't understand why, suddenly, they now occupied a special place in the public imagination – the place average people reserve for figures of great wealth and power. Most rich and famous Canadian business families understand this dilemma, and work within it. The Eatons, the Richardsons, the Bronfmans – they've always understood their "royal" status, and they maintain a reserve that reinforces it. They never disappoint their public, even if it means revealing very little about themselves.

But the Billeses – they were a different story. Whenever the

Billeses emerged in the public eye, they starred in a Canadian version of Dogpatch. I had never seen the members of a patrician business family behave the way the Billeses did, at once afraid and disdainful of public attention. The Billeses were a phenomenon: a family of great but recent fortune that did not understand its own wealth, or the consequences of it. They weren't used to having money, however much they enjoyed it. The Billes family, in other words, were a walking, talking, squabbling microcosm of the Canadian middle class. For sixty years from the day it was founded, Canadian Tire and its owners said everything there was to say about the practical, modest dreams of Canadians in the twentieth century.

Even before the securities hearing ended, I realized I had a uniquely bizarre story on my hands. Study Canadian Tire, I told myself, and you study Canada. This book is the result – a book about a chain of "automotive-hardware specialty stores," as the phrase has it, owned by three of the greatest eccentrics in the history of Canadian capitalism. But it is also, I hope, about the only possible culture in which that combination could exist: the world of workaday aspirations, the world we all inhabit.

BUSINESSES operate on the presumption that they can accurately predict the future; to predict the future, they pretend they are rational beasts run by rational men. If the story of the Billeses and Canadian Tire offers any insight, it is the opposite lesson: that even the most successful companies are brimming with craziness, political machinations, wacko emotions, and heaven knows what else.

Canadian Tire was anything but the paragon of rationality its executives pretended; indeed, given the way the Billeses and some of their colleagues behaved, it was a miracle the company didn't blow apart at the seams a lot sooner. And the most amazing thing was that all this inner madness at Canadian Tire was the biggest single secret in Canadian business! On

Bay Street, Tire was touted as the stuff of corporate greatness, a leader in its field, a maker of millionaires. Behind the scenes, however, the company's executives tore their hair out and battled daily with the ruling family. In theory Tire was Winsville; in practice it was Bananatown. . . .

The company was amazing enough, of course: a huge, fast-moving, brilliantly organized, vastly profitable sixty-year-old sales machine, a retail monument to the single most glorious ideal of middle-class Canada: Self-Improvement. And very few people on the outside knew anything about it. For nearly a century, Eaton's was the most famous retailer in Canada. Everyone shopped at Eaton's, and everyone figured Eaton's was the best retail company in the universe. The Eatons never denied it, at any rate. But Eaton's – at least according to insiders – can barely claim more profitable years than losing ones. Canadian Tire, on the other hand, was and is one of the most successful corporations of all time, anywhere. Not the biggest, but the most successful.

Even the company's dealers – a band of 400 self-made men whose material greed had been harnessed to the collective good of the corporation – were legends in their hometowns across the country, shining embodiments of one of the most important and least understood heroes of twentieth-century Canadian culture – the small-town millionaire. With their help, Canadian Tire – or Tire, as it was known to insiders – had never once shown a year-end loss since the company was founded in 1922. For more than sixty years, until 1985, Tire never lost money in any of its operations, either – and when it did, following a disastrous foray into Texas, the company had a collective nervous breakdown of such proportions that one of the finest executives in Canadian corporate history was blasted out the door on a rocket.

Oh yes, Tire was a story. For beneath the workings of a company hailed as a model of capitalistic progressiveness lay countless tales of intrigue and woe: the struggles of two brothers to create a company of their own in the raw early

years of the century, when the automobile was still a play-
thing; the jealous younger brother's attempts to control the
show; intra-mural corporate sex; inter-family rivalries; greed
and demolished hopes; a son and a daughter vying to impress
their father, and each other; the hidden power of wives; an
outsider who tried to steal the company away from the family;
the byzantine politics of a corporation; the effects of inherited
money, and the self-defining, self-protecting, self-distorting
world such money creates; the way it distorts ordinary ethics,
the decline of monolithic family wealth; a group of creative
securities lawyers and their clients, the Billes children, who
concocted a scheme, the effect of which was to deny their
own shareholders hundreds of millions of dollars; the huge,
swollen material enthusiasms of the dealers and the middle
class they served; and, of course, the story of a house divided
against itself.

It was all there, for all to see, if only someone looked
closely enough. The strange thing was that hardly any of the
players ever did. But then, self-examination has never been
the strong suit of the Billeses or the age of populism. For all
the wealth created in this country in the past sixty years, we
still misunderstand money and its human consequences. We
glorify money, we disdain money, and sometimes we do both
at once; but we seldom apprehend its deepest, vilest, most
inspiring, most valuable meanings. In building the empire of
Canadian Tire, the Billes family put those lessons on full
display. The question, for those who watched the family
empire shudder and crumble, was whether to laugh or cry.

And now, thanks to Dennis Gardiner Billes and his interfer-
ing, they weren't talking to one another. Perfect. As Tolstoy
could have written so famously, all happy families resemble
one another. But an unhappy family that owns a business is
unhappy in its own peculiar way.

2

A VISION ON WHEELS

MARTHA BILLES was A.J.'s most loyal child. That, Martha realized, was a handy irony. Growing up, Martha had played in the aisles of her father's Canadian Tire store; but because she was a woman the company was off limits to her professionally. It was predictable, then – as it often is when people are forced by unnatural circumstances to become spectators to power they feel is rightfully their own – that Martha became the company's most dedicated student. Her home on Lake Simcoe, her parents' old country place, was packed with Canadian Tire memorabilia: photographs, records, accounts, fragments of what the company and the family had been. Tire's glorious past became Martha's present. In the speculative orgy that followed Fred and David's announcement in October, 1986, that they planned to sell Tire, the search for the cause of the disarray that surrounded the Billeses became a game. Some pointed to Fred's relationship with his sister Martha; others, to Fred's relationship with his father, A.J. Billes. There was a third faction that blamed the chaos on Dean Muncaster, who had run the company for twenty years as Canada's star chief executive officer before Fred and Martha grabbed control and fired him in 1985. There were a thousand different theories. There were even those who said the seed of the crisis at Canadian Tire in the fall of 1986 lay in the ambitions of certain young lawyers at the Ontario Securities Commission, and maybe there was something to that as well.

During the months after the hearing Martha pondered it all, sifting it through, reinterpreting the history that had made her. Oftentimes, as the family squabble intensified, Martha retreated in her Jaguar to her sprawling home on Lake Simcoe, an hour and a half north of Toronto. There, overlooking the water, she could ponder the record of Tire's past, for in it lay the roots of her family's obsession.

HENRY BILLES, Martha's grandfather, was one of twenty-two children of Benjamin Billes, a wealthy thrice-married soap-maker in London, England, whose family extended back, according to Billes legend, to the French Huguenots. Henry had grown up in London and in baronial splendor in the Billes ancestral home, Eridge Green, on the estate of the Marquis d'Abegaveny near Tunbridge Wells in Kent. But the life of a younger son well down the ladder of inheritance didn't appeal to him, and he ran away as a teenager to Toronto. There he married Julia Constable, the daughter of an innkeeper in the working-class neighborhood of Cabbagetown. By 1896, the year John William, his second son, was born, Henry Billes had attained the station of a butcher employed by a wholesale meat company in Riverdale in the eastern flank of Toronto. Riverdale had once been an upper-middle-class English neighborhood, but streetcar lines built across the Don River had imported distillery and foundry workers who made the neighborhood a working-class one. For those with sufficient imagination to conceive of an escape, Riverdale was a place to leave: friendly enough, family-centered, practical, but cir-cumscribed in its hopes.

Henry and Julia Billes weren't wealthy, but they were comfortable working class. Julia made all the clothes for her four daughters and three sons, and Henry was fortunate enough, thanks to his job, to have all the meat his family could eat. They were also devout members of the Anglican All Saints' Church, where Henry taught Sunday school, and equally devout anglophiles.

Bill Billes, as John William was known, had always been treated as the eldest: his older brother Henry, who later qualified as an electrical mechanic, suffered from periodic depressions (the "whimwhams," he called them) and was considered "irresponsible." Bill was more serious, even as a child. As a young boy he was torn between travelling (he often wandered down to Lake Ontario to watch the boats at anchor) and an equally intense desire to conform. Julia, his mother, managed to channel him into church: Bill, who was fond of music, was a choirboy. Torn between a life of duty and a life of freedom, he compromised and became a capitalist.

His brother Alfred Jackson Billes was six years younger, and even more devout. Alf wanted to be a missionary, thanks to some clerics who had visited All Saints' from South America. "I guess it was the idea that the missionaries were there uplifting people, trying to make something better of these people," he told me recently. "It wasn't the idea of going overseas. It was the idea of helping these dark people. I recognize today, however, they're very different people. They're great people [when they are] kept under control."

With six years between them, the younger boy automatically deferred to his older brother. Their working relationship had been forged on Bill's paper route. Alf would sit on the back of a wagon folding papers, for which Bill paid him six cents a week. Or so Alf claimed later when the two brothers were running the largest automotive supply company in the world. By then John William's newspaper route had become a patented legend at Canadian Tire: as late as 1970, Tiremen maintained any man could qualify for a Tire dealership if he told the selection committee he'd had a paper route as a boy. The newspaper story was useful too because it subtly set out the pecking order in Bill and Alf's relationship: Bill was boss, Alf was the junior employee. Bill insisted on that.

By 1913 Bill had earned $1,000 (the equivalent of two years' wages in a store) selling seeds to his fellow students at Dufferin Commercial School, where he studied accounting.

He ditched school shortly thereafter (he finished third form, or the equivalent of grade eleven) and went to work as bookkeeper for both the Seeger Plumbing Company and Mack Truck. He also worked as sales manager at The Hamilton Tire & Garage Ltd., a Ford dealer at the corner of Gerrard and Hamilton streets just west of Broadview Avenue in Riverdale. The firm had been founded in 1909 and specialized in buying surplus tires from manufacturers in the winter – snow removal was non-existent in the country and unreliable in the city, and drivers still put their cars up on blocks for the season – and selling them at discount prices in the summer to a local clientele.

J.W., as Bill came to be known, had been obsessed by cars since the day as a young boy he had been permitted to steer the automobile of a family friend. He bought his first car, a 1910 Model T flivver, in 1914. He loved its mechanics, its shimmies and stops and tappets. The Hamilton Garage was too small for a young man of his ambitions, however.

By the fall of 1913, at the age of seventeen, J.W. had saved enough money for "a fling" on the West Coast. Such a trip was the working-class equivalent of a tour in Europe. Thirty years later, whenever he remembered the trip, his face would soften up as it did only when he ran into someone he felt comfortable with, which wasn't often. The western trip was his last taste of real freedom, for while he was in Banff his father died of a heart attack after trying to break up a brawl between two immigrants.

J.W. was eighteen years old, and broke. Back in Toronto there were two brothers and four sisters and his mother waiting to be fed. Alf, the youngest, was twelve, and in ninth grade. His father's death forced him to quit school (he too had studied bookkeeping), and he began work at the Dominion Bank. "I was [still] in knickers," A.J. remembered.

The brothers struggled to support their family. In 1922, luck came their way: the owners of The Hamilton Tire & Garage Ltd. in Riverdale offered to sell J.W. their business for

$1,800. The operation consisted of one room and a mechanical shop. Bill, then twenty-six, convinced twenty-year-old Alf to leave the bank and become a minority partner. As prime mover and older brother, J.W. controlled seventy-five percent of the shares, even though Alf put up most of the money: Alf was a penny-pincher, whereas J.W. spent a lot of his spare cash on girls. He always had a thing for girls. Alf knew nothing about the tire business, but agreed to do as his big brother said. It wasn't the first or the last time he would.

AUTOMOBILES had been slow to catch on in Canada. In the early years, Canadian farmers hated them because they frightened cattle and horses. Farmers often booby-trapped roads with nails and glass, and charged motorists $5 to pull their cars out of the mud. Motoring was considered a fad that would quickly die out. In 1901, only one in a thousand Canadians had even seen a car, and the ones who had them were wealthy. John Eaton, Timothy's son, built the first "house for cars" – otherwise known as a garage – in 1899, the same year the first car appeared in Montreal. Canada's most eager motorists were its prominent capitalists. Gradually, ordinary Canadians started to emulate the rich folks. Cars represented The Future and Progress – concepts that had previously not enjoyed much popularity among Canada's cautious rural population.

The automobile "fad" soon took on a more durable life. Even farmers became enthusiasts, having discovered that a car's engine could run a log-splitter and a grain-dryer and a generator. By 1913, when Bill Billes bought his first batch of tires as an employee of Hamilton Tire & Garage, there were 23,700 motor vehicles in Ontario – half the cars registered in the country. In 1922, when the Billes boys bought the Hamilton Garage, 210,333 passenger cars were backfiring their way around the province. By then, Canada's automobile population was second only to that of the U.S. In 1920 and

1921 in Toronto, disease took 403 lives, 67 people were murdered, and 2,183 were killed or injured by automobiles. Modern life was evolving.

A car was becoming an attitude, the badge of the "automotively-minded," of the progressive, *self-improving* person. Cars were a harbinger of a new way of life and a new mentality that the Billeses and Canadian Tire would track and serve for the next sixty years. Canadian Tire's specialty – the automobile, and later articles for home repairs and sporting goods – always lay at the heart of whatever experience the masses were having at any given time, whether it was automobile travel, home ownership, or "leisure life."

The first and greatest of these mass experiences was automobiling. As cars became more common, the collective consciousness of Canadians was transformed from one dominated by the land and the weather, by the wilderness and seasonal time, into an urban, and later suburban, consciousness dominated by company rhythms, punch clocks, urban life. In 1901, when J.W. Billes was five, sixty-two percent of Canadians lived in the country – and well over half the "urban" population lived in towns of fewer than 10,000 people. By 1921 – twenty years later – half the population lived in towns, and more than half of that in cities larger than 10,000. In 1921, Toronto and Montreal both hit the half-million population mark for the first time. Canadians were becoming less interested in the land and more interested in one another – and thus in comparisons and status and keeping up.

J.W. Billes saw cars catching on with a vengeance – the vengeance peculiar to the middle class when it decides to appropriate for itself yet another bauble of the rich. Cars weren't as yet very comfortable or fast, but they were an improvement on the horse and buggy – and *self-improvement*, as J.W. instinctively understood (as only a poor boy with wealthy ancestors and huge and unwanted responsibilities can understand), was becoming important to postwar Canadians. *The Canada Year Book* of 1922 noted that "now [the car] ranks as a comfort to those in moderate circumstances and it may even become a necessity . . . to the masses." The masses! Yeah! And J.W. Billes would be there to serve them.

ON September 15, 1922, the Billes brothers went into business. "Our money was being made on cars," A.J. later remembered. "In those days cars weren't very good. You always had trouble starting them. So, if you had money, you parked it in a heated garage. (Parking cars) was how I learned to drive." In addition to parking twenty cars a night, the brothers performed repairs. "What I didn't know about an automobile," A.J. admitted. "People would come in, and they wanted information. It was free information. And that was probably what it was worth."

The first year was difficult: the Gerrard Street bridge was out for repairs, and traffic by the garage was thin. J.W. had also managed to lose the pair's savings on the stock market. The brothers took day jobs in the summer, and that winter worked days at the garage, taking turns sleeping in the one-room office at night to guard the cars.

The following year they closed the garage, and after a brief stay at Yonge and Gould streets opened a retail outlet at 639 Yonge Street at Isabella Street, on the edge of downtown Toronto. Eglinton Avenue, two miles to the north, was still a corduroy road in places.

But there were 40,000 cars in Toronto, and what stock the brothers carried comprised a small range of repair parts for Fords and Chevrolets, the two most popular makes of car in the city; batteries; a homemade antifreeze that Alf mixed in the basement; toolboxes; radios; transmission bands that needed replacing every 10,000 miles. That year, the city's first Closed Car Show introduced windshield wipers, an improved car heater, and an automatic starter, and the Billes brothers carried those items too.

But tires remained the brothers' stock in trade, their

philosopher's stone, a reminder to everyone in the company of the enduring glory of the mundane and the essential. "Having been connected with the rubber business," A.J. recalled, "Bill knew of specials. We could usually buy seconds or some line that they wanted to get rid of. We were very, very fortunate – or maybe it wasn't just fortunate, because Bill really knew tires. And we never got stuck with a bad lot of tires. In those days the guarantee on tires was only for defects and workmanship. When we moved into that store, I took over the adjusting. And that was a very tricky job. And after a year, I said, well, I can't go on fighting. Because that's what it was. A customer would come in with a shard of glass or a stone bruise, saying, well, I didn't do that. So I introduced the first one-year unconditional tire guarantee. People came in looking for a fight, and there wasn't one."

Tire quality was a big issue, even in magazine editorials. Before the introduction of the balloon tire in 1929, a man – it was generally a man driving a car – was lucky if his tires lasted 1,000 miles, which was also the total number of miles of paved road there were in Canada in 1922. The other 422,942 miles of byways fell for the most part into the "unimproved earth" category and remained that way until the burgeoning $100-million "auto tourist" trade from the United States made Ottawa decide to do something about improving the nation's highways.

The old tires had been only four and a half inches wide, high-pressure jobs as frail as a raincoat, holding back fifty-five to sixty pounds of pressure per square inch. Even using lower-pressure "balloon tires" a motorist could expect at least one blowout, and more likely one each way, on a day trip between Toronto and Newmarket, twenty-five miles north. Drivers took to filling their tires with milk and molasses to try to strengthen them; these, of course, made for a fine stench when the tires blew.

The Billeses' unconditional guarantee didn't make tires any more reliable, but it was good publicity for their store and earned them a heap of business. By 1927, they had moved south across Isabella Street to larger premises at 637 Yonge Street, where they incorporated. The new venture was to be called Canadian Tire Corporation Limited. "We used Canadian Tire because it sounded big," A.J. admitted. The company wasn't big at all, but it was developing a sturdy mail-order business. "You don't start these kinds of things," A.J. later said, as modest as ever. "They start themselves. We were advertising mainly in the *Star*. And people began to write in. We didn't do anything deliberately. It just happened."

A.J. may have been willing to pass the young company's success off as fate, but in fact its growth was the result of J.W.'s methodical, utterly rational business acumen. His brainwave was to realize that automobiles were about to transcend their luxury status and become an indispensable human tool, much as computers would sixty years later. J.W.'s father had been too poor to own a car, but J.W. was going to make it cheap to run one.

IN the same spot on the corner of Yonge and Isabella streets sixty years later, Leather Boys and Peroxide Girls dye and preen to AC/DC and Motley Crue played at anvil-shattering volume and pose like the most advanced orchid hybrids of Leisure Capitalism . . . but we're getting ahead of ourselves. In 1928, the fifty-foot Canadian Tire store bore a "Super-Lastic" trademark on its window. Next to the trademark was a picture of a tire on legs running away with a silver dollar, also on legs. Next to them was a slogan: "We Give You a Longer Run for Your Money." The company's name was plastered onto the store in ten different spots. Inside, J.W. Billes and his brother A.J., as Alf now called himself, were reinventing principles of mass merchandising sanctified sixty years earlier by the patron saint of Canadian retailing, Timothy Eaton.

Timothy Eaton had established The T. Eaton Company Limited as the Great Source, a central "department store" at which Canadians could satisfy all their needs at once rather than resorting to specialized and therefore less convenient merchants. J.W. Billes chose instead to become one of Canada's earliest specialty mass merchants by concentrating on a single category of products – car parts, and later hardware and sporting goods – which he would supply to grateful Canadians at cut-rate prices. If Canadian Tire was the offspring of a growing urban population and the burgeoning Machine Age, it was also the first company to market a state of mind – that of the self-sufficient do-it-yourselfer. J.W. Billes had discovered psychographic marketing.

J.W.'s theory of retailing was simple. If he could buy in bulk from a factory jobber or wholesaler, he could undercut the prices of smaller salesmen and middlemen, thereby appealing to ever greater numbers of customers. In this he helped to bring about one of the most important shifts of power in the history of Canadian business, from wholesalers, who dominated nineteenth-century Canadian merchandising, to retailers, who call the shots to this day. The big picture – the wide-screen notion of a nation as a single huge entity, as a macroeconomic oneness – was being focussed down to the ever-more-fragmented level of the individual and the personal. If that meant the diminution of Canadians' sense of what life was all about, such theoretical considerations did not exactly weigh heavily on the minds or consciences of the incessantly practical Billes boys.

In ten years of working for rubber companies, J.W. and A.J. Billes had come to understand the dirty little secret of the automobile business. Automobile companies, intent on protecting their markets, insisted on "individualizing" their parts. (They still play this game: according to Ford, you shouldn't repair a Ford with non-Ford components.) The brothers realized, however, that once they'd seen one carburetor, they'd seen them all. So, the Billes boys bought huge quantities of auto parts directly from the manufacturers and undercut the car companies. This marketing strategy – though J.W. wouldn't have thought to call it that – reinforced the idea that Canadian Tire was there to help the little man who was willing to help himself. Needless to say, car companies found the new boys distasteful, and they waged an intense campaign to discredit the quality of Tire's products. In fact, the brothers sold the same products Ford and General Motors did, just as today GM and Ford sometimes sell parts manufactured by Canadian Tire.

To circumvent charges of stealing, the lads sold factory-made goods under Canadian Tire's name. Dunlop manufactured Canadian Tire's first Super-Lastic Tires, for instance, in 1931. The tires were considered inferior to Dunlop's established brand, but they were cheaper because J.W. bought them in bulk. For every low Canadian Tire price, there was a lower one still, because the company sold "seconds" as well. Canadian Tire's rock-bottom bargains attracted more customers, which in turn allowed J.W. to buy in ever-greater bulk at ever-lower prices. Sixty years later, business-school trained directors of Canadian Tire would refer to the system – and it is unchanged – as "order of magnitude" marketing. To J.W., it was known as cornering the market.

In the adjusting department, A.J. was known as Mr. Jackson, so no one could tell he was the owner of the store. "I guess the tire business was no rougher than any other," he later said, "except at the retail end you were more subject to the wrath of the customer, who never knew anything about automobiles, but who tried to pretend he knew everything. And you were always trying to reverse that. I had my experiences. But the worst one was a fellow who was bigger than I was. And we went through a window. . . . Of course, the fact was, our parts weren't poor quality. In those days, if you were a price-cutter, you were a dirty Jew. And that's what they called me, a dirty Jew. And that's all they had to say, because my fuse was very short."

A classy couple of guys! By the 1920s, John David Eaton, in spats and a top hat, was accompanying his mother, Lady Eaton, to the opening of Eaton's College Street store. The Billes boys were still rolling in the gutter on Yonge Street, defending their turf. Local gas stations refused them credit, for fear they wouldn't pay. Then again, the Billes boys never wanted to belong to the Establishment. Tire was the Kingdom of Average Folks. "We feel that we have a definite duty to perform," J.W. explained in a catalogue in the mid-thirties. "While we number among our valued customers men in all walks of life, still the vast majority are hard-working people who must necessarily get the most for their dollars by buying intelligently."

THE first Canadian Tire catalogue was completed in the fall of 1928. J.W. wrote it himself, and it became Tire's bible, a tome fat with J.W.'s specialty, paternalism. Canadian writers and academics have always tried to understand "the Canadian national character," whatever that is, by examining Canadian literature and history. They ought to look instead at the only books everyone actually reads – catalogues. Anyone who wants to know where the middle class's head was at in post-Depression Canada need only gaze at Canadian Tire's catalogue.

Tire's original price list, or flyer, appeared in the spring of 1926. The company's mail-order business was growing, and J.W. had been impressed by the number of Pharis tires being delivered each day for Eaton's from the radial car (electrical-powered streetcar) that ran west from Toronto. If Eaton's could sell from its "wish book," so could Tire.

Tire's first flyers consisted of a single sheet. Besides listing prices, it featured a road map of Ontario on one side, and an inset of the Maritimes, Tire's other main market, on the other. Maps were rare in 1926. In addition to mailing them J.W. liked to give the catalogues away free to the working-class crowd (who took the radial car because gas was expensive) on its way back home to suburbia. This was the perfect Canadian Tire market: steadily employed people who had enough money to afford a car, but who also were financially careful enough to know the value of a dollar. By 1928, the flyer was sent to every car owner in Ontario.

J.W.'s catalogue which evolved from the flyer, retained the form of a road map and was intended as a semi-annual publication. Its sales pitch was dead on from the beginning. He advertised Canadian Tire as a "direct factory distributor," and emphasized the company's product testing – which he in fact did in his office. J.W. never sold a tire without pointing out what a customer would pay for it elsewhere. If Super-Lastic balloon tires went for $8.30 regularly, Canadian Tire had them for $5.20 – "six-ply tires at four-ply prices." New inner tubes were $1.45; "specials" and "seconds" sold for 99 cents.

He could write, too. Before 1932, inner tubes were manufactured by stitching two ends of a sleeve of rubber together. Because the inseam was the same length as the outer edge, it buckled. When tire manufacturers finally made inner tubes on a circular mould for the first time in 1932, J.W. went cautiously berserk: "Super-Lastic 'Moulded to Fit' New Process Black Tubes," he wrote: "Something entirely new . . . a crowning achievement in rubber chemistry. A tube that practically eliminates ALL seepage – a tube that is not affected by heat or cold – a tube that laughs at old age. Laboratory tested to strains ten times greater than in ordinary service. A truly remarkable product but costing even LESS than our former regular lines."

The catalogue's power lay in its ten-decibel promise that it could provide an affluent lifestyle – *pleasurable leisure* – for all men, whatever their station. Eaton's may have made more goods available to more Canadians for the first time, but Canadian Tire made them *affordable*. Tire, as much as any other force in Canadian society between 1920 and 1960, aided in the democratization of middle-class affluence. A new ragtop for a roadster, for instance – now known as a convertible – could be had for $5.95, about half a week's pay for a Tire employee.

In later years, when the company had expanded into the
leisure market, the catalogue became a paradise of affordable
diversions. In 1944, the chain's selection of hockey gloves
started at the Professional De Luxe Gauntlet for the "Top
Notch" player, horsehair-padded with an eight-inch cuff, for
$6.75. (The cheapest model, of Pigtex – nice name – cost
$2.15.) Anyone could afford to play. Ski boots ranged from
$4.49 to $11.98, while skis cost from $3.98 to $8.95 for
"supreme quality hickory" boards. Tents, boats (a twelve-
footer for $28, a sixteen-footer for $85.50), motors, fishing
gear, sporting goods, camp supplies . . . all were available
from Canadian Tire at low, low prices. Even golf, that
traditional obsession of the upper middle class, appeared in
the catalogue's pages by the late 1930s: $1.99 for a cloth
"Traphagen" golf bag, $3.45 for a set of irons, $4.25 for a set
of woods ("Good clubs improve your game"), and three balls
for 79 cents. And of course J.W. carried notions, attachments,
and options galore, from the King Bee Attach-O-Wipe, which
allowed a motorist to convert any air or electric windshield
wiper into a twin wiper, to the fuzzy dice of 1939, the Fooey
Face: "Give the bird to the horn-blowing Nuisance. Tongue sticks
out! Eyes illuminate! Gives out a Razzing Sound! $2.89."

J.W. also used the catalogue to sermonize to his many
children in Consumerland. He deplored debt, having had to
put his house in his brother's name for fear of having his assets
seized after he defaulted on some monthly payments for a set
of books he agreed to buy in the 1920s. "Easy terms?" J.W.
wrote in the spring and summer catalogue of 1939. "Debt is
easier to get into – than out of. . . . Credit means buying tires
the hard way . . . the costly way . . . the worrisome way. . . .
Buy with Cash . . . the easy way."

As for the covers. . . . In the spring of 1941, having evolved
through several sizes and formats, a new Canadian Tire hero
showed up on the catalogue cover: a chubby, white-haired
Scotsman who always appeared with two young sons. At first
the catalogue depicted the old man as the butt of the young

men's jokes, but within three years a girl had been added and the story the covers told was always the same: the old man having the last laugh at the expense of the two lads, let's call them Dick and Fred, to win the favor of a young woman with blonde or red hair and large, large, savings. Consider a few scenarios: Dick and Fred and a muscular lifeguard are looking on astonished as the old man struts out of the surf with a gorgeous blonde in a low-cut bathing suit in his arms; or the lads' new car has broken down by the side of the road, leaving the old man free to pick up the little blonde number in his ancient Model T; or, in a backyard setting, the old man is accidentally painting Dick's face as he ogles a blonde with a trowel in her hand. The old man was the forerunner of Sandy McTire, the thrifty Scotsman who first appeared on Canadian Tire money, and who on the catalogue consistently outlasted his youthful sons because he shopped at Canadian Tire.

Perhaps the all-time classic cover illustrated the spring and summer catalogue of 1961. This was the famous hot dog cover. Years later, as the Ontario Securities Commission and the rest of Canada watched Fred and David battle Martha and her father for the right to sell Tire, the hot dog cover would come to mind as a parable. Of course, no one knew that back then, in Barbecue Season, 1961 . . . a Merc in the carport of the split-level in the background . . . a low-priced motorized barbecue with a king-sized twenty-four-inch bowl with coppertone finish in the fore . . . Dick and Fred – just like the real Dick and Fred Billes, the sons of J.W. and A.J. Billes, respectively, come to think of it, both of whom were gunning for A.J.'s job as president at the time – are each proferring a hot dog in a bun to a cute blonde sitting at the picnic table. Let's call her Martha. But is Martha interested? No way! Her eyes are on a gigantic T-bone steak the old man is holding up in front of her on the end of a long sharp fork. Sandy the septuagenarian, who, incidentally, looks a lot like A.J., has a look on his face that says, "No Competition!" He's wearing a white chef's hat inscribed with the question, "*Wot'll it be*?"

Suggestive covers were a potent marketing ploy that worked for more than twenty years before the old man and A.J. retired at virtually the same time, in the mid-sixties. Tire's catalogue was more than a wish book: it was material leisure-life happiness. When J.W. wasn't hyping Canadian Tire's years of service (by dating the founding of the company to 1913, he made Tire older than General Motors, which had been created in 1918), he boasted *choice*. By the mid 1950's, material choice rivalled the intellectual freedom to choose as the guiding spirit of North American democracy. *Features* and *options* were what choice and Tire-style democracy were all about. How about the "electrical servant," the "famous" Hamilton-Beach Food Mixer with a choice of ten speeds, from "extra-slo to high-whipping," complete with a choice of "at the stove" or "on the stand mixing," or this Super-Deluxe Toaster ("just as practical to use as it is lovely to look at, with its shimmering mirror chrome with attractive wide base and mar-proof feet"), or perhaps a lawnmower to give your lawn that carpet-cut smoothness, or fifty pounds of gro-koted lawn seed for twenty-five percent thicker growth, or (sigh) this Dog-O-Matic hot dog steamer?

Oh girls or boys, sons and daughters, Moms and Dads, listen to me, Sandy McTire, for I can show you the road to affluence, the easy, straight road to the great modern dream of contented materialism.

3

FAMILY BUSINESS

NO MATTER HOW other people interpreted the family split-up of the fall of 1986, the longtime employees of Canadian Tire viewed it as nothing short of cataclysmic. They had been part of the company – part of the family, as they preferred to say – since the beginning. The old guard who made up the Canadian Tire corporate family – the likes of Mayne Plowman, who had run the automotive parts department, or Bill Preece, who founded the brake-bonding subsidiary, or Tommy Rye, one of the buyers, or even Myrel Pardoe, who had toiled as a secretary for more than fifty years and was *still working there*, at the age of seventy-five – the old guard figured the end of the world had arrived. They considered that by selling out, Fred Billes and his brother had committed a sacrilege. Some, like Preece, put it down to the natural course of things, to Fred being tired of running the company; others, like A.J., said it was downright greed. Even so, they didn't like to think about it. Canadian Tire meant too much to them, for starters; and anyway, such matters were family business, and private. If there was one lesson they had learned from the Billes brothers, it was that you don't go airing your filthy laundry in public. The old-timers' faith in Canadian Tire was a religion of its own, a private faith that was spreading to the company's customers as well.

The brothers who had installed this dream in three-quarters

of a million customers' heads by the early 1930s were radically different men with completely separate responsibilities within the company. From his office above the floor of the main store, J.W. bought everything the store sold, with the exception of tires, batteries, and oil, which A.J. handled. Because he determined what the company would sell, J.W. effectively controlled it. He had an unparalleled knack as a buyer. He could pick up hundreds of thousands of army-surplus snow shovels after the war, and sell them at a profit for ten years. Early in the 1920s, Toronto had suffered two consecutive mild winters. When a local manufacturer of tire chains decided it was never going to snow again, J.W. bought his inventory. The chains were being hauled into the store as it started to snow, and it didn't stop for three days.

A.J. was the front man. He ran the sales counter and the two-car service bay at the rear of the store, and supervised shipping. Whenever the countermen had a spare moment, they headed to the back to fill mail orders.

The Billes brothers also were adept at inventing new consumer needs. There were, for instance, the radiator shutters the brothers had bought cheaply from a local supplier. Shutters could be closed across a car's radiator by means of a lever in the dash. Closing the shutters helped an engine heat up faster in winter. The only problem was that the driver often forgot to reopen the shutters, whereupon his radiator boiled over. That in turn created a need for Glycerol, Canadian Tire's radiator coolant, which Alf made in the basement for twenty-five cents a gallon and sold for forty-nine cents.

But the brothers' greatest talent was their ability to hire people who would remain loyal to the corporation for life. This is not to say there weren't dismissals and firings; there were, often because of A.J.'s temper. But Tire attracted a consistent breed of employee. Perhaps it was the brothers' knack for running the company as a small family business that was so attractive, or perhaps it was their desire to help the little man beat the Establishment that made Tire a magnet for the eager and the dispossessed. Whatever the cause, Canadian Tire early on developed a unique corporate culture, as Mayne Plowman made quite clear.

Like many first-generation employees at Canadian Tire, Mayne Plowman grew up on a farm – in Plowman's case, three-quarters of a section in western Manitoba. He had come east at fifteen with his parents in 1927 as part of the rural exodus into urban Canada. The city fascinated him. "You have to picture," he said one morning in the fall of 1987, remembering his first days in Toronto, "being on a three-quarter section farm in Manitoba, on which your light was an oil lamp. And we come down to the east and it's all electricity and movies and all the rest of it. . . . It was quite a big deal as far as the Plowman family were concerned."

His education had been amputated after the eighth grade – another common occurrence among Tire's early employees. Often, sales was the only prospective employment for an uneducated man. In 1931, Mayne Plowman became the second employee in the service department at the back of the Canadian Tire store at Yonge and Isabella, and the eleventh in the company as a whole. The Depression was everywhere. He couldn't afford a tie.

A.J. Billes was twenty-nine. "Course, when you're seventeen, that's an old man," Mayne said. "I kinda liked him. I can't explain why. I felt so free talking to him. And he seemed to talk to me that way." A.J. had a great talent – an instinctive talent, which some store executives would later call deviousness – for gauging a situation. "Damn few men would ever be able to match him in being able to size up a situation," Plowman asserted. "And he's got enough of 'let's take a chance' in him that if he sees anything in what he's thinking about or you're talking about, he's ready to, as they say today, go for it. . . . This is the way his mind worked. I suppose he thought of your track record and that sort of thing, but nevertheless he wasn't afraid to give you a chance to try it."

This wasn't to say A.J. was an easy touch. Plowman's first job

as a mechanic included washing the garage floor. A.J. was
tight, too: the sawdust used to sweep the floors was used
several times. But Plowman often found A.J. on the floor
beside him, washing away. Or, A.J. would sell a customer a set
of tires, and then change into a pair of overalls and race
Plowman to install them.

The lads in the store worked hard. For ten dollars a week in
the early 1930s, a counterman worked from eight in the
morning to ten at night three days a week, and eight to six the
other three. Inventory was done on New Year's Day – there
were no customers in the store – for no pay. It was one's due
to the family. (J.W.'s wife was a Methodist, but unlike
Timothy Eaton, who for years dictated that Eaton's close at six
and that its curtains be drawn on Sunday, he separated his
religious beliefs from his business habits.)

If you worked hard, you got promoted. By the mid-thirties
Mayne Plowman was a salesman earning $50 a week in
commissions – a fortune. The main work in the service department in those days was changing tires and relining brake shoes
with Chrysotile, an asbestos compound riveted onto the brake
shoes. But the company kept abreast of new parts, even
carrying some of the first hydraulic brakes to come out on
Chrysler cars in 1928. "They were quite a sensation,"
Plowman remembers. For one thing, they actually worked.

J.W. never had A.J.'s sense of ease with his employees. Most
of the salesmen didn't know the tall, thin man whose head
emerged from his shirt like a paper bag with a string around
its neck. "The strange thing was," Plowman was amazed to
discover, "Alf wasn't the head of the organization. His brother
J.W. Billes was. I didn't know J.W. But the strange thing was,
there used to be a fella come in, he was always late getting to
work, he'd get in about ten o'clock. What I didn't know was
that he was there at twelve o'clock at night. And I remember
saying to my manager in the service department, 'This guy's
gonna get caught one of these days coming in late.' I was
changing a set of tires one day a few weeks later, and a

pair of feet – I was down on the floor, because you didn't have hoists in those days – and I was taking the wheels off the car. Or at least the rims, because it wasn't wheels then. You took the rims off, and the tires. And a pair of feet showed up in front of me, and stood there for a moment. I looked up. It was this chap. He said, 'How much are you making a week?' Well, I had always been taught through my parents that you didn't discuss those things with others. And I didn't know that he was the big cheese. So I was tempted to say, 'Well, that's really none of your business.' But I didn't. So I said, 'Fourteen.' He said, 'Starting next week, you get sixteen.' " Plowman had been on the job three weeks. The tall man, of course, was J.W. Billes.

Only occasionally, on Saturdays, would J.W. step out of his office to help on the counter. A customer would ask for a set of piston rings. J.W. would dive into the order book on the counter, and then disappear into the back of the store. Several minutes later he would reappear at the other end of the counter. That was his signal that a new salesman should take on the abandoned customer. J.W. couldn't handle personal encounters. Tommy Rye, who went to work as a buyer's assistant for J.W. after the Second World War, put J.W.'s reticence down to the old man's insecurity over his lack of education. "I don't think he wanted to be involved with all the highly educated people."

Recklessness wasn't unknown to J.W., but it was rare. He had owned a racehorse, had taken an early $2,000 flyer on the King Edward Hotel Co. Ltd., and in 1922 had picked up 100 shares of Oak Tire and Rubber Co. Ltd., which later folded. But that was the past, a life he had closed down when he returned from his whirlwind tour of Banff as a young man. Otherwise he was as reticent as a moose. If J.W. had to speak in public, he typed his speech word for word on a piece of canary copy paper, and trembled while he read it. Whenever he actually broke down and made conversation, he slapped the side of his leg with his papers and hemmed and hawed and

stuttered and generally behaved like a rare species of giraffe
that had inexplicably wandered into a cocktail party.

But J.W. knew his business inside out. During the day he
bought merchandise and wrote catalogue copy; most nights
he dictated a hundred letters to tire jobbers from Halifax to
Saskatoon, trying to persuade them to sell Canadian Tire
products. In 1934 he had his master stroke, and franchised
the company's first associate store outside Toronto, in Hamilton. Originally J.W. and A.J. planned to open a chain of
satellite stores, run by branch managers. Their experience
with two unsuccessful branch stores in Toronto in the 1920s,
however, not to mention their lack of capital, had convinced
them that a man would run an operation more vigorously if he
were its owner. And so Dealerland was born. Dealers owned
their own stores – there was no franchise fee, as was the case
in other organizations – but they had to buy all their merchandise from J.W. in Toronto, who set all prices. The system was a
marvel of participatory capitalism. It also guaranteed that the
Billeses would always have customers.

From the very start, J.W. maintained strict control through a
system of field men who appointed dealers and handed out
"good boy" bonuses, as the dealers dubbed them, according
to performance. "We had a market out there," A.J. later said,
"through the amount of advertising we had done. We had
been advertising mainly in Ontario and the Maritimes. And
entrepreneurs out there had seen the success we had, and we
had a lot of letters inquiring about becoming – they weren't
called franchises then – becoming dealers. We saw that we
couldn't run a mail-order business forever. J.W. picked
people who obviously didn't have money. And we knew why.
Because if they didn't have money, they'd have to do things
the way we wanted them done." Mayne Plowman sat on the
dealer-selection committee well into the 1970s, and interviewed dozens of prospective dealers. His specialty on the
committee was to ask a prospective dealer how he got along
with his father. It was psychology, a subject Plowman had

read a lot about in night school. He figured if the dealer liked his father, respected him, he'd make a good dealer, and a good member of the Tire family. He looked for someone who was strong, but obedient, a Son who saw that the way of the Father was righteous, and who believed that the Faithful would be rewarded.

BY 1937, the brothers had expanded again, and moved their headquarters and main store to an abandoned supermarket at 837-847 Yonge Street, on the northeast corner of Yonge and Davenport in midtown Toronto. J.W. moved reluctantly: he preferred to invest his profits in merchandise, rather than illiquid real estate. While J.W. tended his flock of dealers, A.J. ministered to his employees at the main store.

Already factions were taking root. You were J.W.'s man, or A.J.'s, but you were seldom both. The dealers mistrusted A.J., who seemed to put the interests of head office's employees (most of whom reported to him) ahead of the interests of the dealers. For their part, A.J.'s countermen considered the dealers hicks, prima donnas, thieves from the country. The split between the two camps was a mild one, a source of good-natured competition, but within it lay the seeds of an important separation of Church and State.

A.J. was impatient. "He could blow his stack and the roof shingles would rattle," Plowman remembered. "Every once in a while, you'd have to go out and cool him down." But his anger was erratic, unpredictable. If an employee admitted a mistake, A.J. was tolerant and forgiving, brimming with largesse and wisdom toward the unavoidable frailty of all men. If he came upon the mistake himself, or if someone tried to cover it up, he erupted.

A.J. seldom held grudges, but he had prejudices. He wasn't above taking oil home from the company stocks (the prerogatives of ownership), but if he caught an employee doing so he fired the guilty party instantly. A.J. claimed that thieves betrayed the Canadian Tire family. In the same way that he loved "systematizing" everything – one of his retrieval systems in the company's new headquarters at Yonge and Davenport would have done Rube Goldberg proud – he needed to keep tabs on everything, as if the organization might run away from him. Discoveries that threatened his sense of control set him to ranting.

He seemed to mistrust Jews, a view J.W. shared. God's Chosen People dominated the automotive-parts business, and J.W. and A.J. used their anglophile Anglicanism to set themselves apart from that crowd. They tended not to hire Jews – even in the late 1980s there were still relatively few Jews among the dealers' ranks. The homogeneity of the company's racial makeup only enhanced the sense its employees had of Canadian Tire as one big Christian family.

A.J.'s racism was in part practical: like all retailers, he was petrified of unions. European immigrants had been exposed to unions in their home countries, and were considered dangerous. Racism was also standard competitive procedure in retailing, especially in the mid-thirties, when Hitler's presence in Europe was heating up xenophobia around the world. The inside front cover of the 1937 Canadian Tire catalogue, which depicted the company's new location at 837-847 Yonge Street, was a full-page color advertisement for the corporation. It featured a photograph of the company's fifty employees (ten of whom were women) inside the store, plus insets of the two owners – J.W. Billes, president, and A.J. Billes, vice-president. A.J. looked particularly tall and thin and dark-haired and handsome. "Who Are We?" the advertisement's headline asked:

> While the vast majority of motorists know our firm through many years of business contact, others have been incorrectly informed as to our personnel. Every day some new customer tells us that he had been informed that we were Yankees or a subsidiary of an American firm; others are told

that we are Jewish, still others that we are Germans, Italians and almost every other nationality under the sun. ALL OF THESE STORIES ARE WRONG.

The Canadian Tire Corporation ownership, management, and staff are Canadians of Anglo-Saxon descent and the vast majority are natives of this city.

While nationality or creed should not, in our opinion, enter into business matters, we are proud of the fact that we are an out-and-out Canadian organization and feel that our customers should have any false impressions corrected *once and for all.*

A 100% CANADIAN ORGANIZATION

THE most valuable asset the brothers created with their consistent emphasis on hard work and like-mindedness, however, was loyalty. By the mid-eighties, twenty percent of Tire's head office staff had worked at the company for more than twenty-five years. Their devotion was understandable, but strangely masochistic. Both brothers were secretly generous, but their Anglo-Protestant ethics prevailed: an employee earned their generosity. Three months after he started work in 1931, Mayne Plowman was given a $50 bonus. He personally thanked A.J. Six months later, in December, he received $100, and thanked A.J. again. The following June, in 1932, his bonus was $150, and he dropped by A.J.'s office to thank him. Mayne Plowman was nothing if not grateful. The third time, A.J. took his glasses off. "Mayne," A.J. said, "when you first came here, we gave you $50. Then $100. Then $150. And each time you thanked us." A.J. looked at Mayne. "Don't thank us anymore. Because if you don't earn it, you don't get it."

This one-two punch, a hard-soft combination of high expectations and generosity, set up a Pavlovian work ethic that fueled the entire company. Having been raised in the uncertain Depression, Tire's employees were particularly susceptible to any promise of security, especially if getting it meant a personal sacrifice. *Beat me! Pay me!* Even in the early 1940s, Tommy Rye, working as Tire's seventeen-year-old office boy, was earning $12 a week, only two dollars more than the company had paid a decade earlier. But Rye considered himself a wealthy man compared to a private in the armed services, who was earning roughly $1.30 a day. Service to the company was as good as service to your country. "Everyone worked like crazy," Tommy Rye said. "But everyone did, or you starved to death. Because there was no social services."

By 1945 the Pavlovian bonus system had evolved into the first stage of Tire's famous profit-sharing plan. Ten percent of an employee's earnings were withheld by the company; any portion of these earnings could be traded for Canadian Tire common shares, which had first been issued in 1944 when the company went public. The bad news was, no employee could touch those retained earnings until he or she retired. That could be forty years. The good news? Between 1945 and 1987 Canadian Tire's shares split 350 times: one common share worth $8.50 in 1944 was worth $4,900 in 1987. The Billeses thereby created a generation of millionaires within the ranks of the staff. Tales of vast wealth abounded, as A.J. never tired of reminding his employees. There was, for instance, the little floor sweeper, an Irishman named Jimmy Douglas, an orphan from a council home in London who had grown up adopted on a farm in Saskatchewan and had worked at Canadian Tire for twenty years. When he finally walked into Plowman's office in 1968 and announced his intention to retire and fulfil his lifelong ambition, which was to travel to New York and see the Metropolitan Opera, Jimmy had $320,000 in the company's profit-sharing plan.

And yet these new millionaires seldom left the company for a life of ease. That wasn't what Family Tire was all about. In 1986, ten years after he retired, Mayne Plowman still lived on Poyntz Avenue, where he had bought his first house, a tiny two-bedroom matchbox, for $1,995, cash, in north Toronto. A strange land, to be sure, where the street names ranged from the sentimental (Neighbourly Lane) to the bizarre (an entire subdivision named after composers, Liszt and Ravel and their like). Mayne Plowman was still wearing a thin, pencil mustache, though by now it matched his white hair: it looked good on him. (A.J. had one too.) Plowman was thicker-set than A.J., though, solid, as if his body had settled from years of rocking on his heels, hands in his pockets, listening to people describe the turmoil in their engines.

Mayne's life had been successful by any measure. From the position of mechanic he had been promoted to manager of auto parts, and was eventually made a director of the corporation. But success had not changed his material aspirations. The trim little house on Poyntz had been fine for Mayne: it had Ps carved into the shutters, but otherwise it was like all the others on the street. The lawns looked as if they came in a kit. He finally sold it for $128,000 after his second wife died in 1984, and moved, but not very far. Just across the street, to a house that was every inch the same. He married the widow of his late next-door neighbor. He figured he was lucky. "There's always been someone looking after me," Mayne would say, and that was true enough. He could have been wealthier, had he become a dealer – A.J. had offered him the Burlington store, in 1958 and 1961 – but such a move would have been disloyal. "I think I had a bit too much of what we had been and where we were. It would have been a bit like cutting off half of my arm." He had been part of the Home Office family, and he couldn't leave.

Even his new-found wealth left him uneasy. (By the time he retired, thanks to the company's stock plan, Plowman was a millionaire several times over.) Mayne had gone in for a little jewelry – he now wore a diamond pinky ring, a gold bracelet, and a gold chain around his neck, hung with a fancy script P – but he restricted his indulgences to the odd trip, to spoiling his son and daughter. And of course there was his Hammond organ, a huge monster packing the power of an orchestra, sitting in the corner of the living-room like the instrument panel of a jumbo jet. The organ was a fascinating thing: Bill Preece had one too, and so did Tommy Rye! Strange, up there on the rim of the city, where life seemed so normal: having been raised in the hard center of the Depression, in the arms of Tire, where you received as much as you gave, Mayne and his generation considered a Hammond organ to be one of the few "practical" extravagances you didn't have to feel ashamed of. At least you could play it.

Profit-sharing had made Mayne Plowman a wealthy man. The plan had been A.J.'s idea – the perfect combination of capitalism as he described it, which rewarded individual initiative and saving, and socialism, which shared the wealth. But profit-sharing at Canadian Tire wasn't just a bonus. To the staff, their share of the company's profits was their proof that they were owners, and part of the Family. Yes, Daddy *likes* me!

UNLIKE their children, the Billes *pères* had no trouble getting along. The reason was obvious. J.W. was the undisputed boss. A.J. might disagree, but he always deferred to his older brother. "A.J. had a lot of flair," Tommy Rye observed in retrospect. "And there were a lot of things J.W. wouldn't let him do. The staff all knew that A.J. ran the store. And that J.W. ran the business. It was a foregone conclusion."

"There was never an argument," A.J. remembered, "and we never, ever quarrelled. Now, that wasn't my fault. Communication was really important. There was rarely a night when we didn't get together and discuss something. And if J.W. picked up his pen, I knew I had to get out of the office. But I never didn't get what I wanted. I guess he was just testing me, to make sure I knew my own mind." A.J. was more outlandish, the promoter, the expansionist. It was A.J. who put his countermen on roller skates (at his wife Muriel's suggestion), when the company moved into the enormous new store at Yonge and Davenport. A.J., who ran the store, and knew how merchandise moved, wanted bigger warehouses; by the mid-fifties, mail-order deliveries were a month behind schedule. J.W. thought the company's money was better invested in merchandise. A.J. threatened to buy a new warehouse with his own money. The next morning J.W. capitulated, and A.J. purchased the building before his brother changed his mind.

A.J. didn't always prevail, however. "My father was a very strong individual," Dick Billes, J.W.'s younger son, later pointed out. "And he ran his business like a dictator." A.J. wanted to try the gas business, and he wanted to develop profit-sharing more than J.W. thought was necessary. He also wanted to move into Quebec, which J.W. considered unwise: Quebec was out of J.W.'s direct control, and used another language. "In many respects he was right," A.J. later admitted. "Quebec gives us more trouble. If you know Frenchmen, then I don't have to tell you anything more. They're great people, and great fun, but they don't show the profit."

The quiet, demanding, perfectionist, patriarchal, parsimonious beanpole who seldom emerged from his office stuck to simple principles. None of the departments – which were known by letters (E for Electrical, T for Tires, and so on) operated at *anything less than an eighteen-and-a-half-percent profit margin*. Today such numbers are almost unheard of, except at Canadian Tire. J.W. rationalized everything, even the decision to sell bicycles: if the store could make loyal customers out of boys, they would be more prone to think of Canadian Tire when they bought their first cars. Fifty years later that same notion – get 'em while they're young – would be taught as standard retailing theory in the country's business schools.

For all their success, however, A.J. and J.W. had both feet firmly planted on the ground. Until the early 1950s, J.W. Billes and his brother paid themselves $10,000 a year each, drawn from their stock dividends. Neither man had any time for clubs or high life: J.W. ate his lunch at the Pilot Tavern or

the Morrissey Hotel, for a quarter. The brothers stayed away
from the Toronto business establishment, and the establishment returned the favor. Whatever contact the Billeses had
with Bay Street was managed through their underwriter, Alex
Barron, who had founded Fry & Company (later Burns Fry
Limited, the brokerage firm) and would later become chairman of Tire's board.

The brothers' mutual regard, which their children showed
so little of thirty years later, paid off. In the thirty years
between 1927 and J.W.'s death in 1956, Canadian Tire *never
lost money*. Nor would it do so until 1981. Until 1945, a year
after the company went public (at which point it did $2.1
million in annual sales), J.W.'s business records consisted of
two filing cabinets; the company's books were virtually
nonexistent. He kept everything in his head. Business prospered anyway. In 1933, Canadian Tire had sales of
$790,769.97, half in mail-order sales, 28 percent to dealers.
The next year the company beat $1 million in sales. In 1939 it
did $2 million. J.W.'s dream was to do $1 million a month. By
1953, Canadian Tire was hauling in more than $18.5 million
a year in annual sales, 84 percent of which was sold to the
dealers.

In the end, of course, it was success that bound the
Canadian Tire family together, united their aims, and
rewarded their dedication. It was not to last. The children of
the founders, having grown up in the age of material privilege, were a different generation, for whom service and
authority were relative notions, and no longer sacrosanct.
Choice was not a dream for them, but a right. By the fall of
1986, the notion of service that had bound Mayne Plowman
and his generation of Tiremen was almost extinct, killed by
the germ of affluence. That, at least, was the way Mayne
Plowman saw the childrens' desire to sell Tire. Freddy Billes,
Martha, David, they were all victims of their age. In Mayne's
opinion, "afflooency" (pronounced with the accent on *flu*,
like a sneeze) lay behind the Billes kids' problems: they

hadn't had to earn their patrimony. Or maybe it was just that they'd gone "off track." They could have waited until A.J. had died. "I feel sorry for people who've grown up since 1955," Mayne would say. "They've grown up in a different society, at a time when Mum and Dad were more than likely to throw a kid ten dollars than sit down and chat with him. The bad thing is, no one does a good enough job leading kids through their younger years, because no one thinks they have the time."

Big Daddy J.W., the Great White Father, as his employees referred to him, looked after everyone. Never mind that the Billes brothers made sure the shares never cut into their own control position within the company: control was not the issue. Security was. "You could never be partners with them," said Bill Preece, who worked in the company's first machine shop, and later ran its brake-bonding company. "They drew the line there." But who wanted to be partners, or to control anything? That was not within the boundaries of the Canadian dream. Control worked against the notion of security, for control meant you could suffer losses. Better to forsake independence and great winnings for safety, dependability, the warmth of bureaucracy. Better to be Canadian.

When Tommy Rye married in 1948, he still didn't feel he knew J.W. well enough to invite his boss to the wedding, even though J.W. asked where the service was to be held. When Tommy and his bride ran out of the church several weeks later, rain was sheeting from the sky. Standing at the foot of the church path, huddled apart from the crowd, was J.W. Billes. "He was there," Rye always remembered. "We were part of his family."

Yes, the Canadian Tire corporate family was a wonderful thing. At home, however, when the Billes brothers went their separate ways at night . . . well, that was another story, and it wasn't *Father Knows Best*.

4

COVETING

THE CEREMONIAL LUNCH held on March 25, 1953, in the banquet hall of the Park Plaza Hotel was intended as a celebration of everything that was right with the world. The Canadian Tire Corporation Limited was forty years old, for starters, while across the country Canadians were sitting on the single biggest explosion in middle-class wealth in all of economic history – an event known as the North American postwar boom. Between the end of the Second World War and 1959, the population of Canada grew by more then 43 percent; disposable income, on the other hand, blew up 167 percent. Canadian Tire was right in the middle of it. In 1944, the year Tire went public, its shares were worth $8.50 each; by 1952, they were fetching $90. The number of Canadian Tire stores across Canada had grown from 116 to 171. Within the company, one reign of Billeses was about to be succeeded by the next.

Most of the 230 employees in the banquet hall had assembled to pay homage to the company that had been their security blanket for nearly forty years. A cloud of blue cigarette smoke hung over the room, warm and reassuring.

The luncheon had been the dealers' idea. They had a lot to be thankful for. Since Canadian Tire's formal incorporation in the 1920s, the Billes brothers had transmogrified a fifty-foot-wide automotive-parts discount store into a web of

42

dealerships that dominated the auto supply business in 120 pint-sized and not-so-pint-sized towns throughout Ontario, Quebec, and the Maritimes. The company earned $907,000 for itself in 1953, nearly twice the profit of the previous year. The company's net profit before tax had grown by roughly three hundred percent between 1946 and 1953 – whereas profits for the wholesale and retail trade in general remained flat. Even in 1943, in the middle of the war, with goods in short supply and tires rationed according to need to the likes of the police and doctors, Tire paid out more than $20,000 in Excess Profits Tax.

First Walter Muncaster, the tall, bespectacled dealer who had begun his career as a clerk in a hardware store, presented Gladys and Muriel Billes, the founders' wives, with two dozen roses. Within five years, Walter would be the first dealer to do $1 million worth of business a year. Then A.J. and J.W. were each presented with a Golden Ruler, a gold-plated straight-edge with the Golden Rule itself inscribed on its back.

But then Walker Anderson, who had become the company's first dealer in 1934 in Hamilton, rose to present a brace of gifts from the dealers. From the very beginning of his speech, Anderson seemed to take A.J.'s side against J.W. Anderson was resplendent in a rich navy-blue six-button double-breasted suit, four buttons on each sleeve, and a navy blue and white polka-dotted bow tie. His dark eyebrows, set off against his high forehead, intensified his piercing eyes: he had the look of a man with a hidden agenda. He had a speech too, a monster that employed a ship-of-state metaphor that Anderson was beating to death at that moment.

"These voyagers were determined men, who were able to battle the storms of high seas, even though they like all travellers must have been exposed at times to the travellers' malady, sea sickness, however, they remained at the helm even though the work was hard and the hours were endless and" – Anderson didn't seem to have to breathe at all – "in so doing they sighted their objective and entered the ocean of success."

The ocean of success! A wonderful phrase! A phrase of greatness!

"Like many other successful men they gave first of themselves and we should learn from this that we too must give before we receive. . . ."

Anderson then presented J.W. with a painting called *The Farm Pond*, by Henry J. Boddington, and jokingly called it *The Pause that Refreshes*. But J.W. had no intention of retiring. A.J.'s picture was a schlocky Woolworth's Nostalgic Period number of a doggy and a kitty sipping some milk together and called, of all things, *Your Turn Next*. Interesting title!

But the surprises weren't over. Next, Muriel stood up, to thank the dealers. Not Gladys, the president's wife: *Muriel*, the vice-president's wife. Gladys was sitting on the other side of the podium, dressed elegantly but somberly, the height of good, conservative taste, a 400-watt smile pasted across her face as she listened to Muriel showboat her way to prominence in front of the entire company, resplendent in a double-breasted peplum and a lace collar, wearing a spring hat that looked like a perfectly cooked omelet.

Whatever Gladys thought of Muriel's wardrobe or speech was shunted aside as Muriel delivered her coup de grâce: an open invitation to everyone in the room, all 230 of them, that very night to her slate and limestone mansion at 24 Old Forest Hill Road, in the heart of Forest Hill, Toronto's wealthiest neighborhood. Next to Muriel's Forest Hill home, Gladys's shack in Lawrence Park looked like a . . . a gardener's shed. And now the entire company was going up there, to *her* house, the house of the wife of the vice-president. "I will expect you all up to our home tonight to see the picture in its place," Muriel concluded cheerily. However subtly, however unconsciously, A.J.'s wife was challenging Gladys's and J.W.'s role as the spiritual leaders of Canadian Tire, as the mater and pater of the Tire Family.

For the trip that evening to Muriel's home, J.W. changed into one of his navy-blue double-breasted suits while Gladys hauled out the notch-collared, full-length natural brown mink J.W. had given her years before. It was a stylish coat, but she seldom wore it: mink offended her deep-seated Methodist sensibilities, contradicted her belief in the fleeting nature of worldly possessions, her conviction that there were others in the wide, poor world who needed money more than she did. But Gladys Billes, for all her modesty, was capable of playing company politics as well as anyone. Muriel's challenge to the pecking order in Canadian Tire at the Park Plaza luncheon demanded that Gladys parade her possessions, because possessions, the outward manifestations of wealth and power, spoke loudest in the ranks of the Canadian Tire family, and expecially among the dealers, whose entire lives were dedicated to material improvement, to the getting and spending of money and all it could buy.

Muriel's mansion would impress the dealers no end. It embodied her own up-to-date sense of the "new Toronto" and the new importance the city attached to visible affluence. To Gladys, such ostentation was out of character for a Billes; it offended the values J.W. stood for, his ethic of modesty and self-sacrifice and private pleasure. Still, if Muriel intended to flex her power by *flaunting* her possessions, Gladys was ready to fight gems with gems, and mansion with mink.

In the four years since A.J. had bought Muriel her Forest Hill bauble, J.W. hadn't visited once, even though the house was only ten minutes by car from his own. By the time Gladys and J.W. arrived that evening, the mansion was full of employees, drinking and playing the piano. The house was brimming with freshly cut flowers that stood out against the heavy brown of the oak panelling. The entire place emanated permanence. A photographer snapped shots of A.J. and Muriel in the foyer, arm-in-arm and drinks in hand. Gladys's house didn't have a foyer. J.W. permitted the man a few group shots – though he never took Gladys's arm, and neither of them drank – and then, once he was in earshot of the dealers and the company men in the front hall, he let a single zinger fly.

"Gee, Alf," he said. "I wish I could afford a house like this."

J.W. Billes, the all-time genius of Canadian Tire, could buy ten such homes and not miss the money. Well: that wasn't true. He could afford ten of them, easily; but he missed every penny he spent. J.W.'s point was, *I don't need to buy this sort of home. I don't need to show off. I'm the boss.* Gladys said nothing at all. But she never forgave her sister-in-law for upstaging the president's wife.

Of course, when Fred Billes and his brother and sister appeared before the Ontario Securities Commission in December of 1986 to explain why they wanted to sell Canadian Tire, one unmentioned irony was that the battle royal between Fred Billes and his sister was merely a continuation of this earlier conflict between the wives of the founders. It was a conflict that reflected two very different marriages; two ways of looking at the world and material goods; and two families, and how they grew – and grew apart.

IN 1928, a year after he published the company's first catalogue, J.W. Billes moved into a new house at 177 St. Leonard's Avenue in Lawrence Park, in the north end of Toronto. He needed the space for his children: Gwendolyn Myrtle Billes, the eldest; John Harold Billes; and Alfred Dickson Billes, known as Dick, who had been named after Alf, J.W.'s brother. J.W. had purchased the house at 177 St. Leonard's in a distress sale, for $1 and the assumption of a $9,000 mortgage.

The neighborhood of Lawrence Park had been developed after the turn of the century by Colonel Wilfred Servington Dinnick, an Englishman from Surrey. Dinnick died in 1920 at the age of forty-one, but while he was alive he tried to recreate in Lawrence Park his beloved English countryside.

He named the new suburb's streets after his favorite English locales, and insisted its houses all resemble English country homes – even though downtown Toronto was only twenty minutes away. Dinnick was also a strict Anglican, and didn't encourage Catholics to move in.

The new house at 177 St. Leonard's fit the Lawrence Park mold perfectly. The exterior was off-white stucco, in the modest English-cottage style popularized by the architect Eden Smith, who built his kitchens in the front, rather than the back, of his houses. With its spacious corner lot, its broadly sloping, asymmetrical roof, its fieldstone front door border, its gracious bay windows, leaded panes, marble fireplace, and one-car stable-style garage, the genteel four-bedroom house was perfect for an up-and-coming Anglophile like J.W. Billes. The poor boy from Riverdale had risen as high in Canadian society as he ever wanted to go.

The house was also perfect for Gladys Maude Dickson, whom J.W. had married in 1924. He had been twenty-eight, Gladys twenty-six. She was a tall, slim, pretty flapper with sloe-black eyes, a modest manner, and a passion for gardening and quiet, individual pursuits. Gladys's father had run off while she was a girl, leaving her mother to raise her in a cramped house in Riverdale, Toronto's grittiest working district. There Gladys found consolation in Methodism: she disapproved of drinking and smoking. But she was a warm person. J.W. married her, he said, for her red hair.

He first met her skating at the Old Orchard rink in Toronto's west end, and courted her at church, where they discovered a common love of music: J.W. sang for the Mendelssohn Choir, and Gladys played the piano. The couple honeymooned briefly in Bermuda after Gwen was born, within a year of their marriage – J.W. claimed he couldn't afford it until then – but after she moved from Davisville Avenue to the St. Leonard's house, Gladys set to work to create the home she never had. She planted a rock garden thick with perennials that flower to this day in the front of the house; a maple tree in the back beside a goldfish pond; and even lined the side of the road with lily-of-the-valley for her neighbors to enjoy.

She was to stay at 177 St. Leonard's for forty years, with her plants and her birdhouse. She lived most of that time alone. Gladys quickly discovered her husband was as absent as her father had been: J.W. worked six days a week and most nights at the office. Gladys tended to her children and her garden and slaved for the Red Cross and Mothercraft and other charities that had been taken up by the long-forbearing wives of Toronto's capitalists.

For all Canadian Tire's success – in 1933, in the midst of the Depression, the company had sales of nearly $800,000 and doubled its size over the next five years – Gladys and J.W. lived like Spartans. Money was Not Discussed. Dick Billes was a teenager before he knew his father owned Canadian Tire! The house on St. Leonard's was imposing on its corner, but its kitchen was minute, and there was only a single finished bathroom. The bedrooms were plain and unadorned.

In 1936, when her youngest son was eight, Gladys wrangled enough money out of her husband to enlarge the kitchen, and add maid's and butler's quarters to the side of the house, under which J.W. then added a two-car underground garage. Gladys's only other extravagance, beyond leaded-glass window panes and solid brass hardware throughout the house, was a new upstairs bathroom. It was lined in light green vitriolite set off by forest green vitriolite trim, the same tiling material used in some of Toronto's older subway stations. The bathroom also boasted a pedestal sink as well as a bathtub.[1] The bathroom, and the light-filled sunroom off the formal living-room, the public rooms, where Gladys's tastes ran to

---

[1]The bathroom! That great *objet* of contemporary concern, with its faucets and tiles and toilets and sinks and showers! Here again, the Billeses displayed an instinctive feel for the concerns of the middle class. Today, of course, we've once again turned the bathroom into a display case for our personal taste, income, and artfulness.

Oriental carpets and large, heavy, dark, late Victorian decor – serious furniture – were the only ones that received any special attention. They were the only ones seen by visitors, after all.

J.W.'s stinginess was enhanced by Gladys's Methodist habits of denial. After 1925, when segments of the Methodist, Congregationalist, and Presbyterian churches merged to form the new United Church of Canada. J.W. used his fortune like every other pious capitalist of the 1920s and 1930s – which is to say, he didn't use it. He saw himself as the steward of his wealth: one did one's job, provided for those for whom one was responsible, and was thankful. Privately, J.W. would lend money to his staff or friends to start businesses, or anonymously support charities in the city, but publicly he was a skinflint. Harold Evans, one of J.W.'s closest friends, maintained that Gladys should have been a poor man's wife. She turned the collars on her husband's shirts and hemstitched his handkerchiefs. Evans and his wife Florence eventually stopped taking their winter holidays with the Billeses: J.W. would keep the heat in a ski lodge so low that everyone froze. When J.W. died in 1956, Gladys found a list of chores in his pocket, including a reminder to replace the finish on the hardwood floor near the kitchen door. He was worth six million dollars at the time, but he still planned to paint his own stoop.

Gladys was no more comfortable with their money. She never sliced a loaf of bread at a party until someone actually arrived. She wore cloth coats rather than her mink. This was in part because J.W. and Gladys believed they might some day be poor again, and in part because they hailed from a generation for whom money had never been a plentiful commodity. Florence Evans found their lack of imagination astonishing. "They just didn't know how to use the money," she recalled. J.W. bought homes for his brothers and sisters and gave his family a comfortable life, but those were his responsibilities. He had no right to celebrate his fortune. He never took a formal holiday.

The pleasures he did indulge were middle-class dreams available to any customer of Canadian Tire. J.W. Billes didn't collect art or build architectural monuments to his ego, as Sir Henry Pellatt had in Casa Loma. Instead, he chose to *enhance his leisure time*. The family skied every weekend at Summit, and they spent their summers on Lake Simcoe. J.W.'s one genuine extravagance, beyond a bright yellow 1933 Cadillac that he bought second-hand, was his boats. He and A.J. had owned a boat together in the 1920s, but A.J. only used it twice: his wife Muriel disapproved. J.W. sold the boat, and in 1932, when he grabbed an unexpected $30,000 on the stock market, bought a thirty-two-foot cruiser. He called it the *Jogwendi* after Jo(hn), Gwen and Di(ck), his children. It became a metaphor for the freedom he had relinquished at eighteen.

At work, or at the company's staff parties, which he seldom attended, J.W. was severe and a little stiff. On the boat he was a different man. At seven o'clock after supper at home on a summer evening, J.W. would return to the store at Yonge and Davenport, and, slapping his papers against his leg in his shy way, would ask a few of the boys if they could rig up some contraption for his boat. The boys knew the contraption was an excuse – the old man could never be direct with other people – but they assembled it anyway, knowing what was to follow.

At ten o'clock, after the store had closed, J.W. and A.J. and half a dozen of the lads would head down to the National Yacht Club behind the Toronto baseball diamond and attempt to install whatever they'd devised for J.W.'s boat. Then J.W. would suggest in his faintly chirping voice, as if some superego were choking off his merriment, that maybe they ought to take her out for a spin. Whereupon the lads and A.J. and the founder himself would cruise over to Centre Island, off the city's shoreline, and there – are you ready for this? – everyone would have a swing on the island's maypole. Even Mr. Reserved, Mr. Canadian Tire, thirty-six-year-old Big

Daddy Billes, would have a whirl. When the maypole closed at midnight, J.W. and the lads would hop aboard the *Jogwendi* again and cruise through the western gap of the city's harbor, out into the middle of Lake Ontario. There they would sit, the moon glimmering down of a summer night, until three and four o'clock in the morning. To the four or five employees in their late teens and early twenties, it was as if the Father Almighty had reached down and scooped them up to Heaven for a night. Out on the water, away from his wife, J.W. would break her abstemious spell and flirt with eternal perdition by drinking whisky and smoking a pack of cigarettes. "He was two people," Dick Billes would later remember. "When he was at the lake, he was a different person than when he was with my mother."

Whenever he could, on Sundays, after church, J.W. would take his family out on the water and sail down to St. Catharines or up to Kingston, returning by dark – because, of course, he didn't want to lose the daylight. *Save everything, use it twice.* By 1938, he had traded in the *Jogwendi I* for the *Jogwendi II*, a fifty-two-foot gleaming mahogany Ditchburn (one of the last ones built) that J.W. bought from an American for $9,000.[2] It was the biggest boat on Lake Simcoe, and, to J.W.'s son John, "the only association I ever had with wealth."

J.W. could never bring himself to buy a summer cottage; summer homes were immobile, and he needed to keep moving. In the twenty years J.W. summered at Lake Simcoe, he preferred to install his family in bunks over his boathouse at Dawson's Harbour, near Keswick.

The weekends on Lake Simcoe were often the only time Gladys and the children saw him. After his all-night jaunts on Lake Ontario he would be in to work as usual at ten – he had trouble getting to work any earlier – and would disappear

[2]He kept it until 1948, when he entered one of his periodic depressions, got fed up, and sold it. Later, he bought another thirty-six-foot boat he christened the *Jogwendi III.*

into his office. Occasionally after work, he found time to play
the violin or the piano, sometimes while Gladys and Gwen
took turns singing. The sound of the piano at ten in the
evening was one of the few memories the children had of
their father at home.

Respect, yes: the children had enormous respect for the tall
man they called Father. He was a stern dictator who brooked
no back talk, who kept a tight rein over his company, his
family, his emotions. It was as if an elastic band had been
wrapped around his neck. Their few memories of paternal
warmth stood out like great historical events: the walks on
Sunday through Kilgour Park with the maid's dog (the
children never had one of their own), ski trips to Summit,
and – of course – life on the boat.

Sometimes his absence took some explaining. Throughout
their childhood, whenever their father was late to return
home, Dick and Gwen and John heard the same excuse from
their mother: "Your father will be late," she would say. "He
has A.J. on the carpet again for one of his harebrained
schemes." Years later when they remembered their late
mother, they all remembered *that* scene, *those* words: "A.J."
and "on the carpet" and "harebrained schemes." To J.W.'s
children, as depicted by their mother, A.J., the younger
brother, was a loose cannon on the deck of the great ship
Canadian Tire.

I figure that if someone wanted to trace the bad feeling in
the Billes family back to its source, they'd end up in the
living-room on St. Leonard's, listening to Gladys blame A.J. for
her husband's absence. She turned her children against their
uncle, and helped divide a house against itself. The consequences weren't to manifest themselves for almost fifty years,
but the seed was planted there all the same. The odd thing
was, no one at the company, least of all A.J., remembered J.W.
and A.J. arguing much. Gladys intensified their differences to
explain her husband's absence, while her husband was . . .
well, that's where it all got interesting.

5

THE GREAT WHITE FATHER

THERE IS NO female equivalent of "cuckold," but if there were, Gladys Billes would have qualified for it many times over. J.W.'s girlfriends were the greatest contradiction of his life. The tightly-wound, tight-spending father figure and founder of Canadian Tire was a philanderer of the first order. He had several women on the side, and entertained them throughout his marriage at an apartment he maintained on Davenport Road just west of the main store.

At Canadian Tire – and most of the lads knew about J.W.'s girls – J.W.'s philandering was excused as the habit of a man who desperately needed a release from the great responsibilities he shouldered. For his part, J.W. often treated his girlfriends callously, as if they engaged a part of himself for which he did not feel responsible, that existed outside conventional morality. The boys at the store who knew him were sometimes shocked by how abruptly he dropped his current favorites; they compared J.W.'s affections to a transistor battery: one minute the power was there, and then it simply wasn't.

Others looked upon this behavior, however, as no more than a shopkeeper's version of *le droit de seigneur*. After all, infidelity was usually a habit of kings and princes and dukes; in the little city of Toronto, with its low ceiling and its yearning materialism and its strict, Protestant, middle-class

53

mores, successful merchants, however modest, were the next best thing to kings.

Businessmen have always been characterized (since Dickens's Dombey, in fact) as restrained, but in fact restraint is antithetical to the careening personality of the entrepreneur, for whom the moment is always now. Certainly, marital infidelity was at least as common in the 1930s among Canadian businessmen as it is now. J.W.'s affairs were not particularly difficult to hide, at any rate, thanks to the apartment – the roads were bad, especially in the winter, and sometimes it was too slippery to get home to Gladys and the piano and the kids and . . . and of course Gladys had an excuse for the children, if she needed one, because there was always "A.J." and the "harebrained schemes" on which to pin their father's absence. On the carpet, indeed.

Sex, in fact, was an important part of Canadian Tire's culture, of the entire corporate Family scene, which, in an automotive company, was predominantly male in flavor. The company that worked together often tried to sleep together. The entire place was a beehive of shenanigans that brought the Family closer. If one of J.W.'s closest friends was the man in charge of handing out dealerships, which he then provided for members of his own family, well, that was one of the perquisites of being a part of the Family, and not much different from obtaining a forgivable loan from the founder, or hiding his affairs. The communal steam at Canadian Tire escaped with a loud hiss.

Tiremen drank after work at Willie Morrissey's hotel north of Bloor Street (where Morrissey himself was always entertaining one or another of an endless chain of babes: Tire old-timers maintained with glee that Morrissey would eventually "fuck himself to death"). Afterwards they held chariot races up and down Yonge Street in the wheeled garbage cans used to collect horse droppings after a parade. In between all that,

Tiremen held staff wiener roasts at which they kept book on which of the girls in the office would end up with whom by what hour. J.W. was occasionally included in the betting.

Thirty-five and fifty years later, in the 1970s and 1980s, their rambunctiousness had calmed down a bit, although dating and marriage within the ranks of the staff were still so common that they could have qualified as standard corporate procedure.

Gladys knew of her husband's dalliances. They discouraged her. But like most women of her day, she had little choice in the matter. Hers was the old story: she lacked the education and the independent income that would have given her some independence from her husband. In 1928, after all, magazines were still debating if it was appropriate to have women in the jury box. So Gladys bit her tongue, hid her pride, and tended to her flowers. Her masterpiece was a thick bower of white roses trained around a lovers' swing in the privacy of her back garden.

Only once did she confront him. She had found a cheap ring on J.W.'s bureau, and hid it. When he inquired after it, telling her it was a Christmas present, she snapped that he could have picked it up at any five-and-dime store. That was the extent of her complaining. The Billeses were never a family of communicators.

By the mid-thirties, as a result, Gladys and J.W. were alienated from one another. In the words of Florence Evans, "they weren't pals." After the Second World War J.W. began to settle down and spend more time with his wife and family, but the rift never healed. To their friends, whom they invited over for dinner in the formal dining-room, with its Art Deco crystal wall sconces over each wall lamp and the Bird of Paradise china and the high, unadorned plaster ceiling, beneath the glorious green vitriolite designer bathroom upstairs – to these guests, Gladys and J.W. Billes presented the united front of a couple separated only by the demands of a thriving business. But happy? "Maybe at the last they were,"

Florence Evans said. "But I don't think so. They were very dignified. But I think he lived his life, and she lived hers."

BY the early 1940s, J.W.'s absence, not to mention his reticence, had made him a virtual stranger to his children. Gwen, his eldest, a thin, shy girl with a passion for the piano, adored her father, but she was the wrong sex: women in management had no place in J.W.'s vision of the future at Tire. She had been well-schooled at St. Clement's School, a modest private school in Toronto's north end, but her father forbade her to work.

Even the sons of the founder were not to be favored unless they earned their father's respect and proved themselves as producers. Dick had first worked in the store at the age of seven, counting batteries. He saw Canadian Tire as his father's business – not as Alf's *and* J.W.'s, and not as one whose leadership would ever be shared. His understanding was reinforced by his mother's stories of A.J.'s incompetence. Dick wanted to be an engineer, but by 1950 had decided against going on to university, in part because his father wanted him in the company. At the age of twenty-two, Dick Billes was employed full-time in Canadian Tire's accounts payable department. He was later to regret his decision, but at the time. . . . at the time, the family business had a compelling attraction for Dick, a magnetism he could not ignore. He had always liked the store, loved the smell of the tires and its bustling excitement. Every Saturday he would chase his father – "chase" was Dick's word – down to the magic land of tires. That was understandable. At home J.W. was unapproach-
able, but work was a different story: Canadian Tire, the family business, represented a common language Dick and his father could speak, like the language of boats, albeit in terms of captain and crewman. Finally, they could communicate.

Just as Dick was always willing to take on the unending work the boat required, so he was willing to do what his father required where the company was concerned; he was more conservative, more conforming than his older brother John, a self-described "rebel" who had attended a technical school and preferred motorcycles and girls and parties to revarnishing. John had gone to work in the store's receiving department after high school, before obtaining his high-school diploma. If Dick's goal was to run Canadian Tire, John was content to be a dealer. John was good with his hands, but he played down his mental capabilities – perhaps because his father never played them up. John had no taste for autocracy, either. J.W. pulled no punches, but his prods to motivate his son were exactly the wrong sort of stimulus: John would be silent in his company, and wild later with his girlfriends. One morning during the war J.W. was interrupted at his desk by Mayne Plowman, the manager of the parts department, who had John in tow. Mayne was having difficulty with the boy: he didn't seem to want to work, at least not with the blind dedication that had characterized Plowman's career. "Have I not been a good father to you?" the boy's father asked, with Plowman standing in the room. John nodded that he had. Privately, however, John Billes told anyone who would listen that Canadian Tire had ruined his mother's life. The old man's incessant drive, his complete sublimation of every energy into company matters, had made Canadian Tire an institution but shattered his family life. John's sullenness seemed to mask his secret resentment.

That left Dick as J.W.'s chosen son. J.W. made Dick the executor of his estate, trained him as his chosen successor. That, at least, was the way Dick saw things. As a teenager, he counted share certificates with his friends – albeit in the privacy of his bedroom. In fact, J.W. never *openly* discussed succession or his will with his sons. To do so would have been too personal.

It came as no surprise, then, that after his father's death in 1956, John drifted away from Tire. By the early 1960s, he had fallen foul of his uncle A.J., and left the company, never to work again. He would live on his inheritance, small as it was. Two decades later, with the Billes legacy in Tire in danger of becoming extinct, A.J. would justify firing John Billes on the grounds that John lacked "the intimacy" to run a dealership. It was an offhand but profound remark, for if anything lay at the heart of the J.W. Billes family's eventual failure to seize lasting control of Canadian Tire, it was that fear of intimacy, an inability to speak the common language of the heart that ultimately holds any enterprise together.

J.W. Billes's children had been born to wealth and privilege, but like so many children of dynasties – like Timothy Eaton's son John, and his son David, to name two – their inheritance had not included a solid sense of self. Having never been championed by his father, John could never champion his father's ways at Canadian Tire the way Dick had.

By the time Fred and Martha Billes decided to sell their shares in Canadian Tire in 1986, John had been out of the company for twenty years. By then he was living in a vast reconstructed Victorian farmhouse in Markham, Ontario, in the quasi-country north of Toronto. His sister Gwen lived half an hour away, in a similarly reclusive subdivision. Until a few years before, neither Gwen's nor John's neighbors had known that either of them were members of the family that owned Canadian Tire. That was the way John and Gwen preferred it. John disdained money, privilege, wealth, and the pursuit of all three. He despised the trappings of money as pretension. "I wasn't close to my father," John was willing to tell the rare person who cared to drive out to Markham to ask. "None of us were, really." It was a nice life, at any rate, out there in Markham, clipping coupons and avoiding the fray in a reproduction manor decorated in full Victorian-farmhouse style by his wife Betty, with whom John had first necked over a case of beer on the *Jogwendi*, trying not to wake his father in the next stateroom. John and Betty's house had a belvedere and a bell tower and a turquoise living-room. Among themselves, the neighbors in Markham referred to John Billes's house as Disneyland.

TEN minutes west of St. Leonard's Avenue, A.J. Billes and his wife had raised their own three children in a very different atmosphere. A.J. had always thought of his brother as "half-married," or, at the best, profoundly ambivalent. Not so A.J.: Muriel was the great love of his life.

By A.J.'s working-class standards, Muriel Moore was a girl with "class." Her father, Delford Moore, was a printer turned land developer, a "hard-boiled man," as A.J. described him. A.J. figured his own daughter Martha took after Delford Moore.

A.J. had met Muriel at a dance class his sister had dragged him to and, in his own words, "fell like a load of bricks." After a brief courtship, they were married December 13, 1928, at the Yorkminster Baptist Church. They took a honeymoon to Bermuda, and their names were listed on the ship's manifest, which their daughter Martha still has.

In the early days, living in an apartment at Farnham and Avenue Road, a quarter of an hour away from the store, A.J. and his family thought of J.W. and his family as occupying a separate social class. "They seemed to live in a different crowd," Martha would later say. "They were part of Lawrence Park." The wives of the founders were as different as chalk and cheese. Muriel came from money; Gladys had none. Muriel was outgoing, dominant, vigorous, busty, fashionable, a born performer, sometimes profane, with a figure that in later years reminded the lads at the store of the Queen Mother. Gladys was reserved, passive, sickly, religious, modest, flat-chested, even frumpy. Muriel liked clothes; Gladys preferred gardening.

More importantly, Muriel liked power. Unlike Gladys, she made a distinct effort to go among the troops at Canadian Tire. J.W. had built a wall between his own family and the Family of Canadian Tire, but A.J. had drawn his into the life of the store. Gladys seldom visited the store, and did so less and less often

as the years went by. When she did, she made a beeline for
J.W.'s office, did her business, and left again. She was never
haughty, but she was not a joiner.

Muriel, on the other hand, could often be found in the body
shop inquiring as to how, exactly, the lads vulcanized a tire,
or sitting in the parts department, reading a newspaper while
her son Freddy – "my Freddy," she called him, just as she
referred to "my Alf" – played on the counter. Muriel was A.J.'s
confidante in the business: it was Muriel who thought up the
name Motomaster for the company's private-brand automotive
products, and Muriel who suggested to A.J. that he create a
Gas War Savings Coupon when the company reentered the
gasoline business after J.W. died.

She also recognized that if her side of the Billes family was
to have a lasting presence in the company, her children had to
become entwined with its ownership. Unlike J.W.'s son
Dick, Fred was encouraged from the start to think of himself
as the crown prince of Canadian Tire. He looked the part.
As a tow-headed boy of three, decked out in a muskrat coat
and a beret – he was a flamboyant dresser early on – Fred's
solid, unapologetic bulk had an immovable presence. He
seemed to know the big store at Yonge and Davenport was,
well, *his*. Everyone at the store seemed to accept it, too.

In 1941, when Fred was six, Mayne Plowman had mounted
the store's best-selling car horns on one of the counters so
customers could test them. The air-electrics could flatten a
dog at twenty feet. One morning a customer was testing the
horns in little Freddy's presence. "Hey," Fred said, "don't
do that."

The customer looked at the sturdy little boy – he was big
even then – and turned back to test a Klaxon.

"Hey," Fred repeated. "Don't do that. Do you know who I
am? My old man owns this place."

By 1951, when Fred turned sixteen, his father had already
begun to transfer his shares to his children. Fred had shed his

heft – the only period of his life when he was to do so – and had affected a mustache and a sheikish look that was part Clark Gable, part Elvis, and part Eddie Haskell. By then Fred had a sense of purpose in life, and had confided as much to Mayne Plowman. "There's a saying," Fred told him one afternoon in the 1950s, "that a family goes from blue-collar to blue-collar in three generations. I'm going to try to stop that from happening."

In the late 1950s, at Muriel's urging, A.J. began to set up a voting trust for his children. Its purpose was to keep his shares in his family's hands. But Fred, Martha, and David didn't see the trust as something they were handed on a plate. "Tire was a gutsy, roll-up-your-sleeves-and-get-your-hands-dirty-business," Martha recalled. "And we didn't have any idea there was any money or any prestige to it. I knew my father had a business that was as good as any other, but I wasn't about to go out and flaunt it. It wasn't a matter of being one of the Billeses."

If Fred was imbued early on, at least in his own mind, with a sense of his own importance to the family and the firm, his younger brother David and his little sister Martha seemed untouched by it all. They were quite unlike their older brother. For one thing, they were thin. They were also quieter and more successful at school. Martha and David had worked their way through the Forest Hill public-school system. David, three years Fred's junior, then studied engineering at the University of Toronto. He worked briefly in the quality-control department at Tire and later designed the company's first automatic car wash, but soon tired of it, and began to design racing engines in his own firm. He had never been much interested in Canadian Tire, and when confronted by his father, tended to keep his objections to himself. A.J. was known to be critical of Fred, even in public, and even about his son's weight. Fred would swear, and take off in a huff, but he was always back the next day. David never confronted his father; Fred did battle for the two of them.

The youngest in the family, born in 1942,[1] Martha too wanted to be an engineer. "I had always wanted to go into civil engineering. And my parents wouldn't allow it. So, failing that, I decided I would go into a technical profession." The "technical profession" – and she hated to admit it, even years later – was home economics. True, she graduated summa cum laude from the University of Toronto, but – Home Ec.? It drove her wild. She felt she had always been too passive about asserting her own wishes.

Fred, on the other hand, could never have been described as an academic strongman. Fred had enrolled in the Forest Hill school system, but then transferred to Appleby College, a private boys' school in Oakville; he then transferred again to De La Salle College Oaklands, a private Catholic school in downtown Toronto. After that he managed to go on to the University of Western Ontario for a year, where he studied business, and then on to Brown University in Providence for two years. But Fred didn't seem to need school.

Years later in the midst of her battle with Fred, Martha realized their schooling had made her different from Fred. Fred's Catholic friends at De La Salle tended to be heirs to construction fortunes, whereas Martha and David had grown up among Jewish children who, Martha asserts, worked harder: "The kids I went to school with, you did your damnedest. . . . I guess we all wanted to prove ourselves, not just to our father, but to the world. Freddy is the Catholic influence, I am the Jewish influence. And I don't know about David. We all came out trying to prove ourselves to the world. But Fred is not the nouveau riche push-and-climb of the Jewish community, this work ethic, this push the children. Freddy had this more relaxed approach, less hardworking, but showier."[2]

---

[1]Even as a middle-aged woman, Martha refused to divulge the date of her birth. She seems to have been born in either 1940 or 1942.

[2]Vague as Martha's theory seemed, it was not an uncommon one among the children of the wealthy. Several months after speaking with Martha, I

There was one part of Fred's show Martha could certainly have done without: his (and to a lesser extent, David's) tendency to discount her opinion because she was a woman. Martha was at least as smart as either of her brothers. As children they had often played in the store, and one of Martha's specialties had been getting the boys into trouble while escaping it herself. Fond memories of things to come! The boys retaliated by nicknaming her Auntie Mae, after their aunt Mae Tuckman, a flint-edged battle-ax who oversaw the commissions of the store's salesmen. It was a backhanded tribute, but a tribute nonetheless.

Later on, it was also Martha who first perceived that Fred's pretensions as heir apparent were not necessarily shared by their father, A.J. In her words, "Fred was the number-one son, but he was not number-one son to be running Canadian Tire." The truth was that the real pet of A.J.'s family was none of his three natural children, but what Martha called his "first" child – Canadian Tire itself.

Muriel, their mother, encouraged her children, and especially Fred, to think of Tire as their own. Unlike Gladys Billes, Muriel was publicly thrilled by the perks of ownership, and made no bones about it – even if Gladys, rather than Muriel herself, was the president's wife. It was A.J.'s side of the company's ownership that Muriel supported. She was utterly loyal to her husband, to his flamboyant, original ideas, his sense of noblesse oblige. If her loyalty gradually evolved into antagonism toward J.W. Billes, the *president*, and his wispy wife, that was predictable enough.

The first public fissure between the families occurred not over A.J.'s role in the company but over a boat. J.W. and A.J.

encountered a woman who, like Martha Billes, had grown up as a WASP among the Jews of Westmount, Quebec. She claimed to understand Martha's point perfectly.

"Well," I said. "How are the Jews different? Are they smarter? More aggressive?"

"No," the woman replied. She hesitated for a moment. Then her face lit up. "Paranoid."

had bought their first boat together in the 1920s, when the two couples were still friends, and travelled together. J.W. was by far the more eager sailor; A.J. preferred to ride, and at one point owned two horses. When the brothers did sail, they had a good time – too good a time for Muriel's liking. "The problem between the two wives," Martha would later admit, "and I know where some of it came from, though I don't know why – was that the brothers worked together and they played together." Muriel was by no means the teetotaller Gladys was, but she was a strict Protestant, and she did object to the "hanky-panky" – the drinking, the flirting – that seemed to be de rigueur on any boat ride. She was also afraid of water. Her natural antagonism to A.J.'s boat trips – an antagonism she made quite plain to A.J., for she was clearly the dominant one in their relationship – was later compounded when J.W. sold the boat and bought the first *Jogwendi*, without reimbursing his brother for his share. Muriel seemed to take it personally. For years afterward, A.J. refused to talk about the entire matter, referring to it all as a "no-no question." For his part, J.W. returned the favor by finding little time for his brother's wife.

In 1937, the rift between the families suddenly widened. That year, A.J. began to build Muriel a summer home on Shanty Bay on the western shore of Lake Simcoe, ninety miles north of Toronto. It was a two-story behemoth built from British Columbian fir on thirty-two acres of wooded shore. Inside it resembled nothing so much as a baronial castle; outside it wouldn't have been out of place in Forest Hill, nestled up on the hip of Upper Canada College. J.W. had a fifty-two-foot Ditchburn, the biggest boat on the lake? Fine. Muriel had one of the biggest houses on Lake Simcoe. Gladys had gardens that would have done any woman proud? Fine. Muriel commissioned a handyman's cottage.

Gradually Muriel's one-upmanship took hold. In the early days, camping and boating and skiing and skating and enjoying Canadian Tire-style leisure life with their respective husbands, Gladys and Muriel Billes had been friends. By 1938, as Dick Billes turned ten, whenever J.W. and the children motored the *Jogwendi* across Kempenfeldt Bay to visit A.J., Gladys stayed on the boat, pleading a headache. By 1940, the two families saw each other no more than twice a year.

Whatever hope there was of bridging the gap between the women, however, was demolished when Muriel engineered her move to Forest Hill proper in 1949.

For eighteen years she and "her Alf" had lived in a modest $9,200 house on a big double lot at Chaplin Crescent and Warren Road. It was a small home, brick, fussy, and no match for Gladys's neo-English tulip of grandeur at 177 St. Leonard's Avenue. Like Gladys's, Muriel's house had a rock garden, but it was a small and ineffective one. Muriel's house had a concrete surround framing her door as well, but, alas, it was too elaborate for the door itself, and made the Chaplin Crescent house seem pretentious. Nothing to make the hoity-toity "Lawrence Park crowd" sit up and take notice.

Then A.J. found the mansion at 24 Old Forest Hill Road. He had been looking for a new home for his wife for some time. It was, as A.J. told Mayne Plowman, "a house that Muriel would like." It had been built by John Northway, the founder of the now-defunct Northway chain of department stores, in 1931, and it was a beauty: four stories of limestone and granite and feldspar and copper, with leaded windows (like Gladys's) and a sunroom (like Gladys's) and, unlike Gladys's, all the room a woman could want. It was exactly the sort of house that had made Forest Hill an enviable neighborhood – a huge hunk of solid, permanent stone, dripping in Anglophilic, establish-mentarian permanence. And A.J. had picked it up for $65,000. With the purchase of the house on Old Forest Hill Road, as Martha was later to explain, "we had now become at least equal" to the Forest Hill crowd.

Muriel loved her new abode. She set to work immediately to make it a house befitting the co-owner of Canada's largest

automotive-goods store. Never mind that A.J. cared little for
such trappings, or that he drove an unobtrusive family car, or
that he preached economy and parsimony at work.

At home A.J. and Muriel lived like film stars. It was such an
unlikely thing for a Billes to do, however, that for years
afterward Dick Billes was convinced A.J. had bought the house
after his father had died: "He wouldn't have dared move into
Forest Hill while my Dad was alive," Dick would say, but he
was wrong. Muriel Billes had a statement to make, and she
intended to make it. For his part, A.J. was oblivious to the envy
the house was creating. "I'm afraid that house caused trouble," he would later recall, "but I didn't know it at the time. I
was too busy with business. But women and houses. . . . "

To some monied observers of the Toronto scene, Muriel was
simply climbing the great ziggurat of Society. "They tried to
play the part," a Forest Hill socialite who knew the house
intimately explained later, "but they never really played the
part well." Muriel didn't care. She lavished two-ton Victorian
antique armoires and armchairs on the house's insides, and
filled it with the bright colors she loved: turquoise green and
sky-blue tile floors. And of course there were the bathrooms,
that strange Billes obsession. Every bedroom had its own en
suite bathroom. All the green vitriolite in the world, never
mind the smattering at 177 St. Leonard's, couldn't compare
with an *en suite bathroom for every bedroom*. True, there
was some question as to Muriel's taste in interior decoration:
behind the rich silk damask stage-curtains strangled back from
the wall with pelmets, for instance – pelmets! Just like Versailles! In Canada ! Now, *this* was the big time, true
class! – Muriel had installed light green venetian blinds. The
sun, after all, could fade the carpets.

Needless to say, J.W. and his ultra-reserved family saw
Muriel as a social-climbing insect. It was accepted cant in the
J.W. Billes family that Muriel, and by default A.J., were simply
Pretenders to the Throne Room. "You hear about people who

want to be in the Social Register, but they never make it?"
Betty, John's wife, would say. "They're always on the outside,
and they always want to be on the inside? Muriel always
wanted to be the prima donna but Mother was the president's
wife." Dick's second wife, Norma, agreed wholeheartedly.
"Muriel hated Gladys, [but not] as someone *hates* someone.
She hated her because she wanted to be queen. And she
eventually did."

By 1953, as the company celebrated its' fortieth anniversary
at the Park Plaza, the antagonism between the Billes wives sat
out in the open, for all to see. Muriel was convinced A.J. was
the real brain behind Tire. She felt he deserved more than a
vice-presidency, and she let the world know it.

Behind the mutual antagonism of the Billes women, of
course, was something far more important than a mere status
war. Muriel was orchestrating a critical change in the culture
of the Canadian Tire family. Unlike J.W. and Gladys, whose
conception of duty and wealth had been forged before the
First World War, before affluence had reached the masses,
Muriel was progressive and modern. She understood the
importance of money and success in postwar Canada.

The Canadian Tire Corporation had always been the work-
ing-man's company, an organization dedicated to improving
the life and leisure of the working middle class and those who
helped themselves. But the dreams of the working middle
class had changed radically in the hustling years following the
Second World War. The important words in Canadian life
were no longer "survival" and "self-sacrifice" and "gratitude;" the words now were "success" and "achieve" and
"me too." The war had changed everything. Whatever respect
God and Duty had once commanded was now redirected
toward money and possessions and leisure and the good life.

Muriel's house would be the epitome of that instinct, the
bright shining empyrean embodiment of material betterment,
a gleaming, beckoning model of a middle-class desire toward

which all the Canadian Tire Family's efforts were aimed. The gargantuan house at 24 Old Forest Hill Road wasn't just a mansion; it was a showpiece for a new age and a new corporation, for their insistence that the rich need be no different from you and me.

6

DEALERLAND

GOLF. NOW THERE was a sport that spoke to Canadian Tire dealers. The history of golf in North America was a perfect example of the way the pursuits once exclusive to the upper classes had been overtaken by North America's yearning middle classes. By the middle of the twentieth century, golf courses were springing up everywhere, packed with little men of modest means, bent on proving that they too could whack a small white ball across the pastures as well as any crusty nobleman. The dealers loved it for that very reason: it made them respectable.

If Muriel Billes hoped to use her husband's new-found wealth to establish her middle-class sensibilities in respectable society, her dream found its most telling expression in the lives of Canadian Tire's dealers. By 1953, Dealerland – that was what the dealers called their little domain – was already a land of plenty for the men who ran Canadian Tire's associated stores. They provided for the working man, and the working man rewarded them. By 1986, when the struggle for control of Canadian Tire became public knowledge, Dealerland was arguably *the* Canadian success story of the common man, the holy story of the small-town boy made millionaire. In the intervening years, Dealerland had become as significant a player in the Canadian Tire drama as the Billes family.

So, dear reader, let us delve now into the depths of Dealerland, to see how it grew and prospered, and into the lives of the people who embodied the ethos of its extraordinary success – people like Reg Quinn.

A golf addict who has been known to shoot his last round at the Bayview Golf & Country Club (where Fred Billes was once a member) as late as the third of November, Reg Quinn approaches golf the same way his fellow dealers approach the business of retailing – as a religion. Quinn often arrives at his store at Steeles and Yonge, up there on the edge of the city in solid suburbia, clad in his powder-blue golf clothes – powder blue is Quinn's signature color – with his golf clubs in the trunk of his cherry-red Mercedes 560 SEL ("a beautiful red," as Quinn describes it) planning to take off mid-morning for the links.

Quinn is one of Canadian Tire's top dealers. A short, dapper man with a full set of dark hair that seems to emanate energy in short waves backward from his skull, he never just walks through his store: he hums through it, checking layouts, picking up trash on the floor, taking phone calls, approving displays, answering customers' queries, and generally giving the erroneous impression that he has an attention span of under four seconds. Retail is detail, he likes to say. Quinn's store does nearly $25 million worth of business a year. *Twenty-five million.* A dealer's personal take, after expenses and salaries and profit-sharing and his own salary, averages between two and eight percent of his gross, depending on how much equity and debt the dealer has in his company. Quinn is turning over his store's inventory – that is, selling it out and replenishing it – an astonishing nine times a year, while the rest of the corporation averages between five and six times annually. That means Quinn is pulling down at least five percent of his gross, and therefore making as personal profit at least a million and a quarter a year! For being a shopkeeper! It's a wonderful thing, and the main reason Quinn and his fellow dealers, many of whom come from nothing, are the committed Canadian Tire men they are.

Unlikely as it sounds, the most successful retailing operation
in the country has operated for fifty years as a family, a
brotherhood, a mutually rewarding endeavor based on mutual
trust between the company, the dealers, and their customers – the three points of the famous Canadian Tire triangle.
(So the theory went at head office, at any rate.) The passion
with which the dealers defend Dealerland is what makes it
such a different planet. Dealerland has always been an empire
of service based on a democracy of dollars that gives people,
and especially poor, defenceless middle-class people, what
they *need*. All over Canada, in malls such as the one Quinn's
store anchors, Canadian Tire dealers had been enthusiastic
celebrants of postwar materialism, selling incessantly to the
strains of Muzak that starts up at 8:23 a.m. and wafts about the
malls, around the Famous Players Towne and Countrye cine-
mas, beneath the donut-hole-moderne mall roofs, over the
pod umbrellas and kon-nek-tor tables for ambling, resting
shoppers, amid the Orange Juliuses and Chicken'n Choices
and Hair Cares and Radio Shacks, the electronic stereos, radios
and computers throbbing and humming in the background,
across wheelchair-access ramps and under twenty-foot-high
fountains, just large drinking fountains really, but enough to
get one of the central ideas of North American postwar,
late-twentieth-century culture across: the idea of leisure and
plenty for all at an affordable price. And all this under one
roof.

Quinn's Canadian Tire store anchors the end of the mall
itself, behind glass doors and omnipresent Canadian Tire
"signage" (red for the automotive department, green for
sporting and seasonal goods, yellow for housewares, blue for
hardware, and gray for Sight and Sound), packed wall to wall
with hockey sticks and oil filters and snowshoes and lightbulbs and pastry boards on special and 40 different styles of
extension cord, 25 different choices of toilet seats, Weed'n
Feed lawn fertilizer, Wagner Power Rollers (an electric paint-
roller), Mastercraft this and Motomaster that, Dustbusters

and Spillbusters, deluxe VCR systems, Big Chill ice cream/ frozen delight makers, auto-shut-off digital Mr. Coffees, home spas, Big Pops, multi-purpose electric egg cookers, Bread Brain toasters, kneeboards, $150 water-skis, crossbows (crossbows?!), replica Uzis for "recreational target practice," aqua loungers, barbecues, cool breeze-through complete water-repellency Textilaire lounge chairs, two-line thirty-two-number memory three-way conference telephones, golf shoes, taps, dies, tapered reamers, nut splitters, levels, mallets, wrecking bars, offset screwdrivers – thirty thousand to fifty thousand products, all capitalized and all plural. It is pure poetry, the poetry of Canadian Tire, the gleaming land of home and auto improvement, for which its owners and customers feel the same passion that others feel for poetry, art, and music. As one of their famous company slogans says, the right choice has never been so clear.

Quinn became a dealer in 1969, at the age of twenty-six. He had worked as a calculator salesman after graduating from high school in Welland, Ontario. "It was probably the most exciting day of my life," he remembers of his first morning in his very own Canadian Tire store. Quinn was making $29,000 a year before he joined Canadian Tire. He sold his fridge, stove, and cars to raise the $18,000 he needed for the franchise, and worked his way up from a small store in Delhi, Ontario, to the monster he oversees now at Steeles and Yonge.

After twenty years as a dealer, Quinn, by his own estimate, pulls down anywhere from $1 million to $2 million a year in profit, and has a personal net worth of $4 million. From the son of a steelworker to an independent businessman worth $4 million! That is an accomplishment. He's a member of the Bayview Club and of the Sharif Khan Racquet Club at Highway 7 and Highway 404 (a club located not by history, or by its membership, like those downtown lignite mausoleums such as the Toronto Club or the York, but by an intersection), and has owned a junior hockey team. He is a member in good standing in his community.

So Reg Quinn isn't about to apologize for Dealerland and its curious, eager citizens "I think this business is made up of ninety-five percent extroverts," Quinn says. "And extroverts, as you know, are competitors. And we're all trying to do better than our neighbors. No question about that." But there are limits. "My philosophy in life," he affirms – a successful man, a self-made man especially, had a right to his own philosophy, after all – "is this: we have our jobs, we have our family, and we have our recreation. And if any one of those gets out of proportion, it hurts the others. So I'm trying to keep everything in perspective. So I love my golf and I love my family and I love my business."

Quinn's credo is pure middle-classism. If this brand of bourgeois culture in Canada lacks the scope of the Great Civilizations – the intellectual breadth of ancient Greece, the power of the Roman Empire, the brilliant beauty of Renaissance Italy, and instead concerns itself with time and golf and money and family – well, that is because middle-class Canada has never pretended to care for much more. Its strength has always been its energy, its very freedom from history, the democratic pluralism of its affluence. It is not a culture of snobs. "I know what *down there* is like," Reg Quinn asserts, having been there. "To tell you the truth, I like it more. . . . I can't snob. I can't go out to these big dinners. I can't politic. I can't stand that stuff." Having become his own man, Reg Quinn has no desire to be someone else's.

REMARKABLY, Dealerland has been a secret in the Canadian business world for more than forty years. Canadian Tire dealers are modest about their success, in keeping with the aspirations of the customers they serve. They seldom think to brag publicly about their success as retailers. They don't want to give away any trade secrets. But in fact Dealerland has its own unique history.

Pressed to expand in 1934, J.W. Billes and his brother A.J. decided against branch stores in favor of dealer-owned and operated ones. As legend has it, they believed in the power of independent businessmen. In fact their decision was based on their unfortunate experiences with two branch stores they had opened and closed in Toronto in the late 1920s. But it was the legend that prevailed. The legend was simple. Make a man a branch manager, and he will do only what he has to do to keep his job and his salary. Make him an owner, however, one whose fortunes are tied to his own commitment and effort, and his energy will know no bounds. In return for that and the promise that he will not sell above a set highest price, Canadian Tire provides a dealer with merchandise, handles his advertising, designs his store – does everything to take care of him, that is, except move the goods out of the store. You play the game, you reap the rewards. And of course you are willing to play the game if you can't afford not to – which was why, when he looked for dealers, J.W. chose men who didn't have any money.

J.W.'s plan worked brilliantly. Between 1934, when Walker Anderson opened the first Canadian Tire Associate store in Hamilton, Ontario, (the second opened soon thereafter in Ottawa) and the end of the Second World War, 110 Canadian Tire dealers were brought into the fold throughout Ontario and the Maritimes. Quebec opened up in the early 1950s. The pioneers of Dealerland were an energetic bunch. If anyone epitomized them, it was Walter Muncaster, the great-uncle of Canadian Tire.

Walter Muncaster was born in 1911 and raised on a farm with six brothers in Walford, Ontario, in the gray land between Sudbury and Sault Ste. Marie. The Muncasters were a close family. In 1929, when Walter's younger brother Clarence moved to Sudbury to work, where two of his brothers already lived, his parents decided to move there too, to run a boarding house for the boys to live in. The Depression was on, and Walter had taken a job in a local hardware store that catered to the miners of Inco (International Nickel Company of Canada Ltd.) and Falconbridge (Nickel Mines Ltd.). He'd left school in eighth grade. "I enjoyed the hardware store," Walter Muncaster remembered a little while ago. "Because you met people from all walks of life, and you never knew who your next customer was going to be."

Canadian Tire's profile in the Muncasters' new town was determinedly blue-collar. The competition spread the word among the miners at Inco and Falconbridge that Canadian Tire sold lousy parts, but Tire had better prices that appealed to the working-class population. "Canadian Tire was the little guy," Walter said. "When we started in Sudbury, we never had all the lawyers and doctors you see today. If you saw one or two a year that was something."

Nonetheless, a Canadian Tire dealership was an attractive proposition to a man with some mechanical sense. The corporation made only two stipulations: a dealer had to find his own premises, and his first order had to be for $1,000 worth of goods. Canadian Tire also promised "day after tomorrow service," thanks to Canadian National Railways' overnight freight service from Toronto. Goods were paid for, in cash, every Friday. Other than that, the managers were on their own.

Four of Muncaster's brothers had become Canadian Tire dealers by 1938, all in Northern Ontario. The following year Walter decided to follow suit, and applied to be manager of the only local Tire outlet in Sudbury, which had done $49,000 worth of business the previous year. Walter drove down to Toronto to ask J.W. Billes for a store of his own. To his surprise, J.W. said yes. J.W. told twenty-eight-year-old Walter he could have the Sudbury dealership, provided he could raise $13,000 to buy the inventory from its previous owner.

Back in the car in front of company headquarters at 837 Yonge Street, where his young wife Bea was waiting with their three children, Walter figured he was in big trouble. He was

making $35 a week as manager of the store, and couldn't save.
But he cashed his life insurance, and borrowed from his
uncle, friends, and sister. When he next approached J.W.,
Walter had $7,000 in his pocket. J.W. loaned him the balance.
Walter never had to sign a note for the loan: that was the way
things were done in the Canadian Tire family. As late as the
1950s, a dealer could arrange a $5,000 loan from head office
by a single phone call. The dealers paid their bills by sending
the Corporation four blank checks each month.

But J.W. still called the shots, and a prospective dealer had
to be willing to heed them. The early route to obtaining a
Canadian Tire store and becoming that great unsung hero of
Canadian business, the small-town millionaire with a big
house on the hill, was best travelled by men who were fuelled
by a strong desire to please. William Dawson, who later
became vice-president of marketing at Canadian Tire's head
office, was working in the industrial-sales division of Imperial
Oil in Belleville, Ontario, in 1951 when the Canadian Tire
dealer in town told him a new dealership was available. The
next day, April 15, 1951, at eight o'clock in the morning,
Dawson met Joe Haggas, Canadian Tire's dealer-relations man.
Haggas showed Dawson a broken-down feed mill in Campbellford, Ontario, and told him the company wanted to open a
new store there. The rent was $25 a month, and the feed mill
was a wreck. This was Monday; Haggas wanted the store open
by Thursday. Dawson said he had a job to quit. Haggas said
fine, Friday latest: did Dawson want it or not? Yes.

Two days later, on Wednesday, Dawson sold his house for
$9,000 (the amount of money he needed to invest in
inventory), bought an old panel truck, and started hauling
shelves, bins, an adding machine, and merchandise into the
feed mill.

On Thursday the home-office men installed a neon triangle
outside the door, which Dawson found "very pretty."

Friday, having risen at 6 a.m. to drive the thirty miles to
Campbellford from Belleville, Dawson opened for business

with a Canadian Tire catalogue tucked in his back pocket. In one week his life had been changed forever. His first customer walked in that morning and bought a quarter-horsepower motor for $16; "I coulda kissed him I was so happy." Dawson had to go next door to the grocery store to change a twenty-dollar bill. He made $36 his first day, a figure he would remember for the rest of his life. By 1964, he managed three-quarters of a million dollars' worth of business a year, owned a cottage and a home, and was worth $100,000.

The first year was no breeze for any dealer, but the new converts were obsessed by their work. Up in Sudbury, working with only his kid brother and his wife, his mother-in-law and children as part-time helpers in the store, Walter Muncaster had paid off his $6,000 loan to J.W. Billes within two years. Four years later, in 1945, Muncaster's store did a few dollars shy of $74,000 worth of business. By the late 1940s he had expanded three times, and Canadian Tire Associate Store number 105 commanded 100 feet of frontage on Sudbury's main street. In 1953 he added a six-bay garage and revamped the store once again, and opened what was then the biggest store in the chain, at 12,000 square feet. By then, the corporation insisted on owning its own real estate, on which Muncaster paid four percent of his gross sales as rent. The new expenses didn't stop Muncaster, however. In 1956 he did a million dollars' worth of business for the first time. By 1959, he had doubled the store again and was running the first self-service store in the chain. (The rest were still over-the-counter operations, some of which survived until the late 1960s.)

Even so, being a Canadian Tire dealer in northern Ontario was more than just a material dream come true. Up in the remote north, with pines trees for company, Dealerland was already a fact of life. By the fall of 1952, Walter Muncaster was good friends with Sandy MacDonald, the dealer in North Bay, eighty miles away. MacDonald and Muncaster would often get together to chew over company matters. It was around Walter

Muncaster's dining-room table that the Northern Dealers' Association was thus formed in the fall of 1952. By the following year the meetings had been expanded to include Ed Leroy from Ottawa. The lads would crack a few beers and yak about Head Office: why wasn't merchandise coming through fast enough? Why didn't they improve margins? "We used to go down [to Head Office] to talk about things individually," Walter Muncaster explained, "but you weren't getting any-where alone." Head Office in Toronto still set dealer prices, margins, and forbade sales. Banded together, however, the dealers found there was strength in numbers, and J.W., who knew a captive market when he saw it, was more than willing to listen to their suggestions.

By the early 1960s, the dealers had formed a national association, spawning the confrontational but mutually bene-ficial system that Bill Dawson and every other dealer referred to as "a big family," the Canadian Tire family. Dawson, in fact, later renamed the Corporation in Toronto "Home Office." *Home Office!* The great white mother, run by the great white father, for the great white children. No one ever said Canadian Tire wasn't paternalistic. But paternalism worked well in a huge new country with a sparse population. "We trusted each other," Muncaster said. "Simple as that. There's just never been anything like it."

By the time Walter Muncaster retired in 1965, Dealerland had become a cult. Muncaster himself was finally beginning to enjoy the good life – at least as much as a child of the Depression Dealerland could enjoy it. He owned a mobile home – not a condo, not a house; a modest mobile home – in Florida and refurbished classic cars as a hobby. His son Dean had become president of Canadian Tire. Canadian Tire was a family obsession.[1] Bea Muncaster and Sandy MacDonald's wife forbade the men to talk about business when they holidayed

---

[1] When Carol Muncaster, Walter's daughter, went away to college, she developed a trick to overcome homesickness: she walked into a Canadian Tire store and smelled the tires. Her homesickness evaporated instantly.

together in Florida. But the obsession was a prosperous one, an obsession that gave the families a sense of control over their lives, and one that reflected the growing prosperity of the country. For Muncaster's generation of dealers, Canadian Tire had been the route not just to riches, but to self-improvement – at a time when education, today's authorized route to respectability, was financially impossible for the majority of Canadians. It was little wonder they gravitated to the Tire family.

Twenty years later, talking about the brotherhood within the corporation as Dealerland threatened to fall apart before him, Walter Muncaster expressed a genuine sadness. "There's 420 independent businessmen who have one of the greatest connections with head office that you could ever wish for. And the same thing goes for the employees of head office. They're a great bunch of people. They would do anything for you. And do it quickly. We just had it so good that it was almost unbelievable. Here was a little guy off the farm with grade-eight education that gets into a business like that with only two of us to start out and ends up with 105 employees, with – what did we have? – with thousands of square feet, with the garage and so on and so forth, of floor space, you know. Just an opportunity of a *lifetime*, to be a Canadian Tire dealer."

Muriel Billes understood the power within her husband's company: the power to make a rich life affordable to ordinary men and women, and to provide its employees with a material ideal toward which they could strive. Muriel's goal was to join the ranks of the privileged classes, and the dealers embraced it. Materialism, and the unrepentant capitalism that made it possible, were unquestionably Good Things.

BY the early 1980s, Tire's dealers were still entrepreneurs who believed in the modest but achievable dream of materialism. But, as the ranks of Canadian management became better educated and, as modesty had it, more professional, so had the company's franchisees. Peter Lige was one of a growing army of International Business Machine executives who bailed out of Big Blue to become Tire dealers when he applied for a dealership in 1975. (He was made Canadian Tire's vice-president of dealer relations in 1985.) "Canadian Tire had an attractiveness for IBM guys looking for their own businesses," Lige said recently, "because it offered an effective program that let you be your own boss ninety-nine percent of the time. But it still had the security of being part of a franchise system." There was also the lure of lucre: Lige went from $60,000 at IBM to between $200,000 and $300,000 a year as a Canadian Tire dealer.

The procedure by which a prospective dealer gained entrance to Dealerland had also become more sophisticated. In 1966, Richard Hobbs, a former dealer and a graduate of the University of Western Ontario, joined his fraternity brother Dean Muncaster, the first non-Billes to be president of Canadian Tire, to help him modernize the corporation. Hobbs – and he was a story unto himself – had been a victim of the old, arbitrary dealer-selection system dominated by A.J. Billes. In the past A.J. had occasionally allowed stores to be handed out to dealers' widows and siblings. Muncaster and Hobbs, who wanted to make a distinctive break from A.J.'s regime, would have none of that. From Hobbs' day on, prospective dealers (the company advertised for them in its catalogues) had to make formal application to the corporation. An initial interview gave way to battery of aptitude, IQ, and selection tests. "They give the corporation some idea of whether you are suitable to work as an independent businessman," Lige said. The corporation looked for men – women were urged to apply, but none had been willing to relocate – who didn't need constant supervision.

Survivors were then subjected to eight personal interviews with various executives over the course of two days. The prospective dealers invariably donned their best blue suits. Then came the financial arrangements: a dealer had to be able to raise the amount needed to invest in inventory and fixtures, of which at least ten percent had to be his own cash. (By 1987, a new dealer needed roughly $400,000 to invest in inventory.) The rest was often financed by a bank, because the loans were backed by Canadian Tire, the company that never lost money. (The corporation itself no longer financed dealers, except as a temporary last resort.) The money a dealer put up for his store was still an important goad to make him work hard. "We didn't care how much money you had," Rich Hobbs explained. "We wanted it *all*."

Having survived this gauntlet of tests and interviews, and having laid his financial life on the line, a fledgling dealer then trained for six months at a small, a medium, and a large store in turn. For this he earned enough to cover a few living expenses, or roughly $325 a month. That was it: $325 a month! Life was hard, but by now the new dealer was standing before the very gates of Dealerland. When he finished, he was prepared to enter Paradise – generally through the smallest store available, where $1.5 million in annual sales might with luck yield an income of $50,000. As many as ten percent of the small stores lost money, as they do to this day.

From such humble beginnings, dealers traditionally moved up by improving their sales and relocating to a larger store. The largest stores in the chain, such as Reg Quinn's, ran up sales of $25 million to $35 million a year: an established dealer in a large store could easily take home over a million dollars, and earnings of anywhere from $100,000 to $500,000 a year were common. Relocations created turmoil in a dealer's family, but what was a relocation next to the chance to do better for oneself, to improve, to have *more*? It was an uncanny thing. "The business grew by taking a guy and putting him in a store," Hobbs said. "And the business grew. And then you'd put him into a bigger store, and replace him with a new guy, and then the store would grow again. It worked nine times out of ten."

Between the late 1950s and the late 1970s, the number of

dealerships in the chain doubled as the corporation eagerly built new outlets. Wherever Hobbs could find 25,000 potential customers not already served by an existing Canadian Tire store, he built a new one. He had an uncanny knack for knowing where to find new markets, sometimes within old ones. Three stores could exist within a few miles of one another, as they do in Oshawa to the east of Toronto, and not encroach on one another's territory, because their markets were urban, suburban, and rural, respectively. Rural stores were a particular boon, because farmers were the last great do-it-yourselfers alive, and also owned several vehicles. Downtown stores, which catered to greater numbers of apartment dwellers, did a smaller volume of sales, but were less vulnerable to seasonal highs and lows. Different locales suited different dealers. Every time a new store opened up near an old one, the existing dealer hollered blue murder. And every time, within two years, business at both stores was up fifteen percent. Sometimes it seemed that the god of retailing was paying special attention to Canadian Tire.

By 1965, a Canadian Tire dealership was a much coveted thing. To this day, 1,200 people apply to be dealers every year; the company selects ten or twelve of them. The current failure rate is less than one percent. And while the average age of a new dealer had risen over the years, from the early twenties to thirty-five by the mid-1980s, once a dealer became a dealer, he stayed one. In 1987, the average age of a Canadian Tire dealer was 48.5 years.

Other merchandising operations, like Eaton's or Sears, consisted of a head office buying merchandise for company stores which were managed by branch managers. The balance of power between head office and the field was an important component of the corporate culture in any retailing empire, and tended to shift back and forth, sometimes with startling results. At Eaton's in the 1960s, for instance, the manager of the Montreal store was the son of R.Y. Eaton, a nephew of Timothy, who had run the company for Lady Eaton in the

1920s after the death of her husband, Sir John, until his son
John David was old enough to assume control. R.Y.'s son
resented the "real" Eatons at head office, and cost the
company $10 million by undermining the power of Eaton's
head office in Toronto. By contrast, Edward Telling, the
chairman of Sears, revitalized the huge American retailer in
the early 1980s by restoring control to head office from the
once dominant field, in which he had been a main player. The
history of both organizations revolved to a great extent around
the balance of power between two camps.

At Canadian Tire, the tension between Home Office and
Dealerland had never been questioned: it was encouraged.
Home Office bought the merchandise, set margins, organized
advertising, and shipped product out to the stores. The
dealers put it into the hands of the eager public. Profits were,
as a general rule, split sixty percent to the dealer, forty
percent to the corporation. Home Office needed Dealerland,
and Dealerland needed Home Office. A keen symbiosis prevailed: each camp served the other, and each watched the
other keenly to protect its own interest. Greed and mutual
self-interest made everyone behave reasonably. No one felt
any need to apologize.

UNTIL the mid-1960s, the Canadian economy grew in lockstep with Canada's expanding population. Canadian Tire
couldn't grow fast enough, and the company's head office had
only to operate as a glorified purchasing-department for
Dealerland. But in 1965, the company's first outside president arrived on the scene in the person of Dean Muncaster.
Muncaster transformed Home Office into a "marketing"
organization. He subsequently "grew" the company, as the
current phrase has it at business schools, from one doing
$100 million worth of business a year in 1965 into a
behemoth with annual sales in 1985 of $2 billion – a two
thousand percent increase in twenty years.

Muncaster achieved such results by emphasizing something

called "marketing." Marketing wasn't just sales: it was a whole strategic mindset. His system remains in place to this day, although there are old-timers in the company who maintain that Muncaster simply refined J.W.'s techniques.

"Marketing" begins with the company's seventy buyers. Each buyer is responsible for at least one of the company's 70-odd product classes, which themselves subsume some 50,000 separate items. There is, for instance, a single person in charge of buying all the company's automobile floor mats. A thrilling job. The product classes are further broken down into "fine line categories" – different colors of floor mats, front seat/back seat, summer/winter. A buyer might be responsible for anywhere from 500 to 600 distinctions, or "stock-keeping units" (SKUs). The buyer's goal is to buy floor mats of the same quality as the leading national brands, but in such quantity, and at prices low enough that savings can be passed on to value-conscious consumers and still make a thirty percent profit.

Every month, buyers compare Tire's prices on 600 national brands in eleven cities against all competitive stores. This is called "shopping the competition." Buyers attend conventions, keep track of new products, monitor new packaging, watch sales trends, keep an eye on fads, and read the trade press. When they have finally selected a supplier, they buy. For this a Canadian Tire buyer earns anywhere from $35,000 to $50,000 a year.

It's a tough job. Anybody who doubts that has only to talk to Dave Antcliffe. Antcliffe, a tall, balding smoker and hockey enthusiast in his mid-thirties, is responsible for buying everything in Product Category 63, plumbing supplies. By the fall of 1986 Antcliffe had been Tire's main plumbing-supply man for more than ten years. Canadian Tire has been in the retail plumbing business since the early 1950s; Antcliffe and his assistant are responsible for fourteen pages' worth of merchandise in the catalogue. There are seven plumbing buyers at Sears – but then, Sears sells home furnishings, whereas

Canadian Tire specializes in the smaller home-repair market. One of Antcliffe's special responsibilities, and one of which he is very proud, is the fine-line category of toilet seats. Canadian Tire sells more than a quarter of the toilet seats purchased every year in Canada. A quarter of all the toilet seats in Canada! Think of it! Antcliffe studies toilet seats in plumbing-supply magazines the way a monk studies incunabula in a dark cell in a monastery. "It's only six, seven years that you would've seen a cushion seat in any sort of quantity," Antcliffe will tell most anyone who asks – and ask they do, at the office and at parties. He buys hundreds of thousands of toilet seats a year from two suppliers. One of the companies, Centoco Manufacturing of Windsor, happens to make steering wheels for Chrysler cars as well.

Time was, toilet seats were sold in a closed box. Antcliffe figured people would buy more toilet seats from Canadian Tire stores if they could touch and squeeze the things. So he designed an open-box package for toilet seats. Then, in conjunction with Home Office's retail planning department, which designs everything inside a store, from signs to merchandise bins to wall displays, he created a wall rack for them. Sales in 1987 shot up 50 percent, from the low-end $5.99 plastic job to the high-end cushioned wood composition flip-up number with an embroidered butterfly, for $25.99.

To further improve the profit margin on toilet seats, Antcliffe has insisted his suppliers manufacture all the chain's toilet seats under Canadian Tire's own "private label" – hence Mastercraft toilet seats. Because he orders a massive volume of toilet seats, Antcliffe can tell his suppliers how he wants his seats packaged.

Antcliffe's ingenuity reflects the legacy of Muncaster's marketing philosophy. So does the Canadian Tire approach to advertising. Muncaster expanded the use of flyers – some seven million a week, inserted into newspapers across the country – backed up by television advertisements. Tire's customers believed these flyers came from the individual dealers, but in fact they were another service provided by the folks at Home Office. The only advertising a dealer did, really, was local advertising – and even there Home Office helped prepare the ads and picked up half the cost. This is still the case today.

Home Office also decided which items to feature in which season, using the buyers as the source for such decisions. For example: if Antcliffe wanted to put seats on special in the spring, when people traditionally do home repairs, Home Office arranged it. All the dealer had to do was order the stock.

All this information, including order sheets, newsletters, and bulletins, made up some six pounds of paper distributed to each dealer every day. Home Office (this time in the person of Richard Hobbs) also built the stores, designed their "fixtur-ing" – lights and signs and cashiers – and even provided dealers with planograms, or computerized mockups, of what a shelf of merchandise ought to look like for any given product, in small-, medium- and large-sized displays. Signs, posters, window cards, and other advertising paraphernalia were also created and provided by Home Office. Whenever the dealers ordered mer-chandise (via computer), the corporation stocked it in three warehouses until it was time to ship the goods out by the company's fleet of 400 tractor-trailers. Even the "pickers" in the warehouse – the workers who fetched goods off the shelves in the warehouse with the help of computerized retrieval devices – did so on commission.

All of which led to a very interesting consideration: with Home Office doing all this baby-sitting, what was left for the dealer to do to justify his salary? Good question! The dealer was responsible for his staff (a big store might hire 350 employees), for buying his inventory, for running a tight, clean ship, and for trouble-shooting at the store level. He was also responsible for selling the goods. But Canadian Tire stores were by now self-serve emporiums, so even the selling function was more or less automatic.

Home Office's refinements in store placement, merchandis-
ing, buying, and advertising had, by the mid-1980s, made
Canadian Tire the most profitable retailing organization in
Canada, bar none. (The company's net earnings in 1986, after
taxes, were more than $89 million.) Eighty percent of
Canadians lived within fifteen minutes' drive of a Canadian
Tire store, and eighty percent of them shopped at a Canadian
Tire store at least once every six weeks. Only food stores were
visited more frequently. Customers spent an average of $17 to
$18 a visit. By one measure, Canadian Tire's sales per square
foot of retail space – a big secret – were more than $500, and
could run as high as $700, as opposed to $200 to $300 for
other retailing chains.

More than a third of Tire's sales derived from its most
profitable products, the high-margin automotive items. Most
of these provided a dealer with a margin of profit of more than
thirty percent of the item's price. (If a car battery cost $30 in
the store and had a profit margin of 33 percent – and some
automotive products had profit margins of 50 percent – $10
was profit.) Just under half of the corporation's sales was in
slightly less profitable home products – hardware, plumbing
goods (toilet seats!), and appliances. The remaining seventeen percent derived from sporting goods.

With more than 300 stores across Canada by the early
1970s, Tire was able to buy huge volumes of goods from its
suppliers at pronounced discounts.[2] These discounts in turn
meant low prices in the stores, which attracted even greater
numbers of customers. This pattern – known to business-
school students in the 1980s as "order of magnitude buying,"
or simply "cornering the market" – resulted in Tire dominat-
ing the national market for scores of products by the 1980s. In
1986, for instance, more than half the Armor All – a car
upholstery cleaner and protector – purchased in Canada was

[2]Despite its enormous buying power, only one employee in Canadian
Tire's history has been charged with being on the take from suppliers. And
he was arrested. Stealing just wasn't acceptable to A.J. Billes.

sold through Canadian Tire. The company controlled thirty percent of the national hockey equipment market, nearly half the fishing and hunting gear, and had at least twenty percent of the market in bikes, camping equipment, marine products, barbecues, coolers, and even golf equipment, to name just a few.

Canadian Tire might be beaten on the price of specific items – on appliances by Consumers Distributing, for instance, by Zellers on housewares or toys, by Home Hardware in rural locations – but no store or chain offered Canadian Tire's unique "auto and home improvement mix" in one store. There simply was no competition.

Instead, the dealers competed with Home Office for the right to claim responsibility for Canadian Tire's success, to see, as the phrase had it, who "drove the corporation." By the fall of 1986, that competition was more than occasionally tinged with resentment. When the company was expanding at breakneck speed in the 1960s, Home Office employees stood a good chance of being made dealers. As fewer stores came into being in the mid-1980s, such promotions were rare. Home Office employees therefore worked ever harder to get ahead at Home Office. New ideas streamed out of the woodwork, along with new products – such as Hallowe'en candy – that many Canadian Tire dealers considered inappropriate, part of the "Zellerization" of Canadian Tire. Any complaints the dealers had, like their concern over the corporation's waning price competitiveness in the fall of 1986, were aired at monthly meetings of the joint Dealer-Home Office Marketing Advisory Council, whose minutes were subsequently published, albeit in edited form.

The dealers knew how much power lay in Home Office's hands, and they weren't about to take it lying down. This was particularly true after the so-called Revolution of 1977. In the fall of that year, a feeble economy and hepped-up competition from Consumers Distributing had resulted in nearly a third of the dealers losing money. The dealers rebelled. They extracted a series of concessions from the corporation, including financial aid packages and a promise that Home Office's annual bonus to dealers – a reward J.W. Billes had created in the 1930s as both a prize for performance and a way of keeping them in line – would never be retracted. Having asserted their presence once, the dealers never looked back.

The average Canadian Tire store in 1987 did $6 million of business a year, and earned its dealer an average net profit of $300,000. That is not a bad living. Yet, even then, skirmishes between Home Office and Dealerland were breaking out more frequently. One point of contention was low-margin items, which the dealers disliked for obvious reasons. Video-cassette recorders were a case in point: Home Office introduced them to the dealerships at a four percent gross profit margin. The dealers raised hell, but fortunately (for them) the VCRs sold. At other times dealers might respond by refusing to carry a low-margin item, but then the advertising department would feature it in a weekly flyer – thereby forcing the dealers, by law, to carry the hated product.

But the dealers didn't give up easily. By way of retaliation, they practised "forward buying." Whenever the company reduced the price of an item for a promotion, and therefore its cost to the dealer, the dealer would overbuy the item, sometimes by as much as forty percent of his regular order. Thus when the price returned to normal, the dealer's margin was that much greater. By 1987, forward buying was so pervasive that the company was trying to devise ways to curb it, but with little success. Dealerland was now a power in its own right. Steve Groch, the dealers' representative on Tire's board of directors – a concession the dealers had wangled in the 1950s – put it very clearly. "If you're part of the manage-ment Home Office team," Groch said, "you would like to be more in control of your destiny, and you would like to convince the dealers as to how you see life. [But] the dealers are more independent. So both groups want to have more control."

BY the fall of 1986, however, it was clear that Home Office was beginning to dominate in the war over what the dealers sold, and how they sold it, thanks to the company's hugely sophisticated computers.

The company's "systems," as they were known, were another innovation introduced in the mid-1960s by the new president, Dean Muncaster, and his crowd of professional managers. The systems were so complex, so pervasive, and so phenomenally articulate that by the fall of 1986 the debate as to whether the dealers or the corporation "drove" Canadian Tire was largely irrelevant: what actually drove Canadian Tire was a forty-eight channel, 128-megabyte Amdahl 5890 Model 300E IBM-plot-compatible computer capable of performing 23 million instructions per second.* Up on the sixteenth floor of the company's head office at 2180 Yonge Street where the systems hummed quietly away, one could find the real organization chart of the company – one depicting central processors and data sentries and the other arcana of computerized life.

A computer-controlled inventory system made it easy to see retailing patterns in concrete form. It also enabled dealers not just to work harder, as Home Office wisdom had it, but to "work smarter." And the company's systems didn't stop there.

By the fall of 1987, Home Office had also developed elaborate research techniques no marketing executive anywhere had ever seen. Findings from focus groups (in which groups of customers were interviewed behind a one-way

---

*Since updated to a 196 – megabyte Amdahl 5890 – 600E capable of performing 88 million instructions per second.

mirror), surveys, and most recently, "barrier studies" (in which a researcher asked a customer to draw a picture of "the experience of shopping at Canadian Tire") had resulted in a multitude of changes. These included modifications in sign design (one bright color per department against a neutral wall, supplemented by end-of-aisle signs), aisle layout (to direct customers into more remote zones of the store), and even "racetrack" patterns (specially colored tiles in the floor, or baffles hanging from the ceiling) to guide a buyer, unconsciously, past as many departments as possible. The studies had also provided Canadian Tire's buyers with a peculiarly intimate knowledge of their customers' preferences. Buyers suddenly knew that Newfoundlanders, unlike other Canadians, bought a lot of kerosene, or that women in the west bought wide-mouthed mason jars, except during the herring catch, while easterners preferred narrow-mouthed jars.

And then there was Project Oracle. That was what they called it: Oracle, after the ancient Greeks. Terrific! It was a simple idea with fabulous power, that of marrying computerized records of credit-card sales to demographic information from Statistics Canada. The link was the postal code on each credit card, which StatsCan used to sort data for geographical areas as small as one side of half a city block.

The Management Information Systems (MIS) department, led by Henning Mikkelsen and his next-in-command, analyst Arny Augustin, would pump the StatsCan data into the Amdahl and produce portraits of the living and buying habits of the entire country by postal code. Then they fed lists of Tire's credit card holders, sorted by postal code, into the Amdahl. Output included detailed three-dimensional maps in full color of the primary and secondary market area of any Canadian Tire store, its customer base, and its sales potential. The results were remarkably sophisticated. It was possible, for example, to advise a dealer in Victoria on the usefulness of stocking ice skates in early November, to give a dealer in North Bay a breakdown of the car ownership in his neighbourhood, by make, year, engine size, and wear-out factor, so that he would know what parts to keep in stock.

As well, Oracle could track overall marketing trends. Home Office made some discoveries. More than thirty percent of Tire's customers were women; and a store's primary market area did not necessarily lie in its immediate vicinity, as had been thought for decades, but depended more on the route the store's customers drove to and from work.

But Oracle's crowning achievement had been the discovery of a huge blob of Calgarians isolated by the Bow River and the city's subway in the north of the city who weren't shopping at Canadian Tire. Soon a Canadian Tire was up and running among the infidels. Ten years earlier, then-president Dean Muncaster had declared that Canadian Tire had no room to grow domestically. By the late eighties, thanks to Oracle, management realized that there still might be plenty of opportunities to expand.

The system! It was a marvellous thing, an entity of sublime achievement, and it was there for the dealers to access at will, one more lobe in the vast octopoidal binary Canadian Tire brain dedicated to one single, pure end: to make it ever easier for people to buy things. And with telemarketing, which the company was already looking into, anything was possible. Mr. and Mrs. Canadian would be able to sit down at their television, punch their Canadian Tire credit-card number into a remote-control box, and the Amdahl would tell *them* what they needed, or that the muffler on the Omni was about to fall off, or that those pipe reamers they ordered were on their way over right now. All Mr. and Mrs. would have to do was consume! No muss, no fuss, no lineups, no decisions.

The MIS department had even developed an emergency plan that enabled them to relocate to a secret location in Chicago if the system went down, and, within forty-eight hours, *have goods being delivered from the warehouse again*. If there were a fire, an earthquake, a flood, a chemical disaster, even a nuclear wipeout presumably, despite famine and pestilence and anything else the gods could dream up, Canadian Tire would get the goods through. It just wouldn't do, after all, to lose a sales opportunity. Never mind that there might not be anyone left to buy a single tin of Easy Flow House Paint. That wasn't the point. Home Office would hold up its end of the bargain, its point of the holy triangle, and guarantee that Canadians got what they needed when they needed it at a price they could afford. If anything captured the spirit of Canadian Tire, the ferocious dedication of its employees to maximizing the company's profitability, it was the disaster plan.

ALL of which is only to say that, by the mid-1980s, Home Office had made it very easy for anyone in Dealerland to make a great deal of money with a minimum of effort. Many dealers had the time, as a result, to branch out into other businesses. Such diversification always frightened Home Office, which made a point of reprimanding absentee dealers. But Dealer-land ran itself: dealers were fond of saying that a successful dealer automatically worked himself out of a job.

Suddenly, in the mid-1980s, dealers were no longer store-keepers, but big-time businessmen. Real estate was one of their favorite options, but there were also Canadian Tire dealers involved – often in partnership with one another – in enterprises as diverse as paper-box manufacturing, software, transmission repair, charter fishing in the Caribbean, wire-hanger brokering, and apartment buildings. Successes far outnumbered failures. Arch Brown was living proof of that.

Brown had created a virtual empire out of his profits from his Canadian Tire dealership in Barrie, Ontario, north of Toronto. A tall, mountainous man whose white, curly hair gave him a distinct resemblance to a Charolais bull, Brown had been the youngest district manager in the General Motors organization in Canada when he was hired by Dick Billes in December of 1958, at the age of thirty, as a dealer supervisor at Canadian Tire. Brown and Dick had gone to school together. One of Brown's conditions for taking the job was that he be given a dealership within five years. He had taken a salary cut, his boss at General Motors had told him Canadian Tire would never amount to anything, and his mother had cried.

He was a big success anyway. As the dealer representative at Home Office between 1958 and 1963, Brown had been instrumental in transforming the ranks of Canadian Tire's dealers from a group of relatively uneducated, passive store-keepers, "the majority [of whom] did not have any specialized sales experience" (and who were almost subserviently grateful for the largesse of the Great White Father, J.W. Billes) into a more aggressive, independent crowd who, while they still lacked formal business education (the MBA-armed IBM crowd were still at IBM), nevertheless had specific business and sales experience for the first time in Tire's history. Brown took on his own store in 1963 in part because he knew he lacked the education necessary to survive in the new computer-conscious head office regime of Dean Muncaster. By the fall of 1986 he had transformed a 20,000-square-foot store in Barrie doing $40,000 worth of business in 1963 into a colossus with 50,000 square feet of retail space and annual sales of $18 million. Brown's take was at least $500,000 a year – "a nice living," as he described it. Even his store manager was worth $150,000 in Canadian Tire stock.

But Brown had been equally successful outside Dealerland. He worked incessantly. When he couldn't sleep at night, he was in the habit of getting up at 3 a.m. to read the day's *Globe and Mail*. He had founded CHAY radio, was a shareholder in an industrial real-estate consortium, a partner in the Horse-shoe Valley ski resort and condominium complex north of Barrie ("the Granite Club of Simcoe County"), a partner in a $12-million hotel on 880 acres of prime land, a governor of the local community college, a Rotarian, a director of the Barrie Chamber of Commerce, a director of Junior

Achievement, and the proud inventor of Kempenfeldt Kelly, Lake Simcoe's version of the Loch Ness Monster.

Brown's store, like the stores of many other dealers, had afforded him a fat life. By 1986, he was taking three-week trips around the world. He owned classic cars, and a forty-two-foot Carver cruiser (the *CHAY Aboard*) that he never had time to use. He was a member of the Granite Club. He had bought and sold a De Lorean and a Zimmer. Brown considered his acquisitions the fruit of "the silly stage," as he called it, through which all the dealers seemed to go in lockstep. It was an amazing phenomenon. It took only one dealer to buy a classic car, or build a tennis court, or purchase a condominium in Pompano Beach, and suddenly all 346 of them had one.

Even their offices, located over the store floor, were similar. These were furnished in a hybrid style that was a cross between a Ramada Inn lobby and the nave of a New Church of Christ chapel in Elk City, Texas – a total look known as Rec Room Plus. The color scheme was vegetable-stew brown. The ceilings were asbestos tile. On the walls, every dealer had his special presentation prints of the company's first three stores, plus two or three color photographs of a classic car (even if he didn't own one) as well as at least one "painting" from the Bruise-on-the-Wall School. A forest of pen-stands, a cupboard or two or three of local hockey trophies, a sofa, two armchairs, a framed copy of the Canadian Tire Dealers' Code of Ethics, $1 million in shredded deminted U.S. currency in a huge Plexiglas dollar sign, and (of course) the de rigueur fifty-cent Canadian Tire coupon, also in Plexiglas: it was all part of the Dealerland mindset. To hell with taste, it said: this is the land of the middle-class everyman, and we're proud of it. The few dealers who had broken away from the Rec Room Plus style – like Des Keon in the west end of Ottawa, who had upholstered his entire office in matching blue and silver chintz and silk, complete with matching valances and

matching pelmets and matching swags, matching everything – well, dealers like Des were legends.

Nor did the Matching Look of Dealerland stop there. It
extended even to personal effects, to matching jewelry and
color-coordinated jacket-and-slacks combos.[3] Dealerland
seemed to have a jewelry Flavor of the Month. In October of
1986, for instance, the flavor was diamond rings and solid-
gold Rolexes – Rolexes so yellow and heavy it was amazing
that the dealers could lift their forearms. If the watches and
the diamond pinky rings didn't give a group of dealers away,
their hair did. Collectively, their hair was astonishing, a living
monument to the look-sharp-feel-sharp-file-your-head-to-a-
point school of salesmanship. No matter how much a dealer
had or didn't have on top, his hair was invariably combed,
coiffed, puffed, oiled, lacquered, rope-thrown, and blow-
dried to seamless perfection, every damn strand bolted down
in place. God knows how they did it.

A dealer's success, however, was often won at considerable
personal cost. The signs were everywhere. Reg Quinn's first
wife had died as they made their way together up the ladder of
Dealerland, but a portrait of her hung in his office well into
his second marriage – as if he had never had enough time to
know her when she was alive. Other dealers lamented the
time they had devoted to their businesses, only to discover
their children were grown and gone. The saddest case of all,
the cautionary tale all the dealers related when discussing
their sacrifices, was that of Bill Dawson.

Dawson had wanted the Peterborough store after making a
huge success of his Campbellford dealership, where he was
already doing the highest per capita sales in any Canadian Tire
trading area. But he was given Walter Muncaster's store in
Sudbury instead. "My wife would never move," Dawson
said, "but I had to go. I just *had* to go. So I left her in

[3]Has anyone else noticed that color-coordination seems to be a peculiarly
Canadian habit?

Campbellford. And my beautiful kids." A year later, living alone in an apartment in Sudbury and notching up sales increases of nothing less than fifty percent a year, Dawson finally convinced his wife to join him. Several years later she committed suicide.

Divorce, too, was like a plague in Dealerland. Once a dealer started to make money and live a fast, extended life, Reg Quinn knew, things changed. "Now his wife he had is no longer good enough for him. She's a small-town girl. Now he needs a big flashy girl. Now they've got more money than their mentalities can handle. Their families fall apart. Their home lives fall apart."

Middle-class capitalism is demanding enough, but the glorious cause of Dealerland seems to exact special sacrifices.

▼

PART II

A MEAN SET OF WHEELS

7

FUN WITH DICK AND A.J.

THE BILLES BROTHERS ran Canadian Tire with one voice and one vision – usually that of J.W., the older brother, the acknowledged leader of the firm. Fussy and "womanish," as his employees called him, J.W. operated the company as a small business, even after the company went public for $100,000 in 1944. Annual meetings were conducted in J.W.'s office. The board of directors, such as it was, consisted of J.W.; A.J.; their sister, Mae Tuckman, who acted as secretary; and (by the late 1950s) a representative from the dealers and the staff. There were no real company records until 1945, even though the firm did nearly $3 million worth of business that year. In his files, J.W. kept three sheets of annual sales figures, a few pages of gross margin notes, copies of his persistent letters to his suppliers and customers, and a ream of information about his great passion, motor boats. The rest he stored between his ears.

But at night, after the store had closed at ten o'clock, A.J. and J.W. had their "conversations." The conversations always took place in the same room – the Throne Room, as J.W.'s office was called, with A.J. standing and J.W. sitting behind his desk – and almost invariably involved the same issue. It wasn't money. Though J.W. owned fractionally more shares than A.J., both men drew salaries of $10,000 a year from their stock dividends.[1] The issue of contention between them was how quickly the company ought to expand.

A.J., the would-be missionary, envisioned what was already the largest automotive discount store in Canada as a national institution. J.W. was more concerned with consolidating his existing business. He was cautious of growth. "Learn to crawl before you walk," he was fond of telling his brother and anyone on his staff who would listen. Night after night, A.J. would implore his brother to spend the company's profits, and night after night J.W. would listen, and then dismiss the notion.

A.J. liked real estate, which made it a persistent sore point. J.W. was a merchant: he felt the company's profits were best reinvested in merchandise. Having purchased a former super-market at 837-847 Yonge Street for $200,000 to house the store and the office, and the building across the street, and having built a five-story mail-order outlet behind it, by 1950 J.W. felt he owned enough bricks and land and mortar. But A.J., who ran the mail-order shipping department, was a month behind in his orders for lack of space. He wanted more room. In the end – and it was one of his few victories – A.J. got the room he wanted.

The disputes didn't end there. A.J. wanted to extend credit to the store's customers; J.W. wouldn't hear of it. (And so no changes occurred until J.W. died.) A.J. wanted to print the catalogue in French and expand into Quebec; J.W. nixed the idea. A.J. in particular wanted to sell gasoline, but J.W., who had closed the company's gas pumps in 1929, considered the fuel business too unpredictable and competitive to guarantee the high profit margins he liked. J.W. was also more con-cerned about the power of the petroleum companies, and wanted Canadian Tire to grow silently, so as not to attract their attention. A.J. was more flamboyant, a born retailer

---

[1]A.J. continued to pay himself no more than $10,000 a year until the early 1970s.

who always had a new scheme. J.W. was a rationalist who cherished predictability and was wary of change, and was therefore the dealers' ally.

Whatever their differences, the brothers generally agreed in the end. And they always presented a united front. Their loyalty to Canadian Tire was absolute – at least in A.J.'s mind. What A.J. and the dealers didn't know was that J.W. occasionally entertained the idea of selling Canadian Tire. There was something seething in the man. J.W.'s workaholic habits, his straight and narrow ways, his profound conformism, were bricks in a bulwark erected to keep his rebelliousness in check. There was always a part of J.W. Billes that, like his halting, fly-sprung voice, seemed about to flip beyond control by force of the very pressure of control. All his life, J.W. suffered from periodic depression – a "family tradition" A.J. described as "the whimwhams." When the whimwhams washed over J.W., he sold a boat, or considered selling the company. He oftened complained to Mayne Plowman that Canadian Tire had become a headache, that he wished he owned a little sporting goods store on Yonge Street.

The war seemed to make things worse. On two separate occasions thereafter, in 1946 and 1954, J.W. Billes seriously considered divesting himself of Canadian Tire – once to Gamble Stores Inc. of Minneapolis, and again, as part of a merger, to the Western Auto chain. Gamble came closest, but its owners offered $25 a share; J.W. wanted $30. "He was a merchant," Dick Billes, J.W.'s son, would later say of the proposed sell-out. "Everything was for sale." Dick was the only one who knew about his father's plans: it was one of the secrets Dick kept to himself, as last guardian of the Billes tradition, just as it was he, unbeknownst to the rest of the company, who finally put the Western Auto offer to bed in 1958, after his father died. Dick could appreciate his old man's desire to escape it all; "I understand my father a lot better now than I did even ten years ago," he later explained.

"You get into these businesses, and sometimes they just weigh upon you. During the war years, the hours he put into the business, I don't know how he took it. I was very, very much aware of it. And you could sympathize with him."

HAD J.W. trusted his younger brother more, delegated responsibility to him, he might have found time to stop and smell the roses he loved to tend in his garden. But for all their midnight conversations, there was a gap between the brothers – one of age and temperament, and trust. There had always been . . . a frisson of reserve. Nothing serious, mind you, nothing that prevented A.J. from calling his brother "a fantastic man" in years to come. Just a frisson. . . .

For one thing, there was the matter of the shares. In 1944, when Canadian Tire became a public company, more than 87 percent of the company's 100,000 shares were held by four people – the two brothers and their direct family. (The only other sizeable block, some 10,000 shares, was held by 183 employees and the like, no one of whom held more than 100 shares.) But the brothers' shares were not split evenly. A.J. had put up most of the money to buy Hamilton Tire & Garage, but he owned fewer Tire shares than his brother. J.W. was the older brother, the boss; and someone had to have control . . . to call the shots.

"J.W. wasn't about to give anybody anything," A.J. told me one evening in his condominium in north Toronto in the winter of 1988. He was eighty-six by then, and had one plastic hip. But he still moved spryly, slightly bent, a human parenthesis, always smiling, always patting backs, always and forever the salesman on the salesfloor. His taste in clothes ran to thoughtless plaids . . . that was probably why all the old Tiremen wore those goddamn sportscoats to the conventions . . . and his mind could wander. But when A.J. talked about Tire, he remembered every detail, every screw, every name . . . except, of course, the ones he didn't want you to know

about. Even in his eighties, A.J. went to the office every
morning, though by then he represented little more than a
memory to which Canadian Tire's older employees still
clung. People were hard pressed to explain what A.J. still did
every day at the corporation. He went in every day anyway. He
couldn't stop. A.J. liked to get on the subway by half-past six
in the morning, to beat the crowds, and he never left the
office until six. He had been talking with journalists more
frequently about the fall of the house of Billes, but few of
them ever asked him about J.W., the old man who taught him
everything he knew.

A.J. was always complimentary when he spoke of J.W., but
he remembered the less fantastic side of his brother, too.
There had been temptations. "I nearly broke away once," he
recalled. "We had an offer, from Dunlop Tire, another chap
and I. It sounded like a good deal. They were probably
offering better than twenty-five percent, which was what I
was getting from Fred – I mean, J.W. So the laws of supply and
demand sometimes came into effect." A.J. never used the
threat of moving to Dunlop to extract more shares from his
brother – at least, he claimed, "not directly. That wouldn't
have been brotherly love, would it?"

Nevertheless, A.J. felt the discrepancy deeply. He was
denied his due authority. In 1944, Julia Billes, the brothers'
mother, bequeathed her shares of the company in her will to
A.J.'s three children, Fred, Martha, and David, the oldest of
whom, Fred, was nine years old at the time. Her will,
however, named J.W. – not A.J. – as the executor and trustee
of the estate. Nor did it contain any provision for the transfer of
those shares to A.J. as the trustee of his own children. Clearly,
J.W.'s family considered him the boss. When Julia died in
1951, J.W. became the executor of his mother's estate and the
trustee of his niece's and nephews' shares. By the end of that
year J.W. had agreed to transfer the shares to A.J., as trustee for
his own children – provided A.J. indemnified his older brother against all claims arising from those shares and Julia's

estate. As A.J. noted, J.W. never gave anything away for free – even that which was not his in the first place. But J.W. accommodated his brother to the extent he had to: "I think J.W. felt more secure with me around," A.J. said. "I'm sure I was better off with him. Because the commercial tire business is a dog-eat-dog business."

Not that J.W. actually asked A.J. to stay on as his partner. "He didn't operate that way," A.J. said. It seems remarkable that, faced with his own brother's possible defection, J.W. would still be incapable of telling his brother he needed him. But perhaps his reaction was predictable. Perhaps his reticence was merely a cultural signpost, a habit shared by other well-to-do WASP families, who regarded direct expressions of love and affection as taboo, rude, and unnecessary. For them, and for J.W., declarations of need and love had been replaced by a substitute language – the Esperanto of business and hard cash.

But love is not money, and money is not the stuff of love, as another generation of Billeses was later to discover.

WHEN J.W. Billes died on November 16, 1956, his estate was worth $6,208,760.32. That was a nice J.W. touch, the thirty-two cents. The size of his fortune shocked his children: having never lived like the children of a millionaire, they never imagined he was one.

His death had come suddenly. He had decided to spray the lawn a last time. In October, no less. His arms came up in welts, and later his breathing became laboured. On the way to the hospital, in the ambulance, J.W. had repeated one phrase over and over to Gladys: "There's something wrong with my will," he said. "There's something wrong with my will." Three days later he was dead of complications from pernicious anemia brought on, it was said, by drugs prescribed for an earlier bout of pneumonia. But it was never completely clear how he had died – a final obscurity, a last secret from a man whose life had been filled with private thoughts.

The next day, Dick moved into his father's cluttered office, known throughout the corporation as the Throne Room. He intended to carry out the job for which his father had been training him – to be the president of Canadian Tire. Meanwhile, A.J. had been reading his brother's will. A.J. knew the battle for control of Canadian Tire that was to ensue would not be resolved in an office but in a boardroom, with votes and shares and real power.

What A.J. found in his brother's will horrified him almost as much as it horrified his brother's family. If the family were surprised how wealthy J.W. had become – and $6 million was not a huge fortune, even for the mid-1950s, except by Billes standards – they were especially surprised that he had left nearly all his shares to charity. A.J. got nothing. Control of Canadian Tire still eluded A.J.

Instead, J.W.'s will was divided into 93 parcels of Canadian Tire shares. Ten parcels were designated for scholarships for theology and divinity students at various University of Toronto colleges; another ten went to students in other fields of study. Seven parcels of shares were marked for the Department of Medical Research at the Banting Institute. The other 66 packets were divided among a host of charities, and held in safekeeping by National Trust: the dividends from the shares provided the charities with an annual income, while the shares themselves were to be voted, within the corporation, by the three trustees of J.W.'s estate – J.W.'s son Dick, his wife Gladys, and National Trust. Many of the charities were organizations Gladys had championed: the Canadian Mothercraft Society, for whom Gladys had worked unstintingly, the Community Chest of Greater Toronto, the Hospital for Sick Children, the Canadian Red Cross Society, the Salvation Army, the Toronto Humane Society, and, last but not least, the Boy Scouts. J.W. had ignored and cheated on his wife for much of their married life, but she had her say in his will, in his legacy, and ultimately in the final destiny of the company, for the shares left in trust would later complicate the Billes family's life beyond measure. That was a lesson for the future: *never underestimate the Billes women.*

J.W. had set aside a remaining $750,000 worth of Canadian Tire shares for Gladys and his children. The shares were to yield Gladys an annual income of $25,000, and the children a yearly gift of $15,000 each. Fifteen thousand dollars was substantial for the time, but it was also nothing. Unfortunately, the federal government's inheritance laws had stymied J.W. He loathed the prospect of paying succession taxes: his affection for the government was minimal. And of course there was the question of making his children earn their own way in the world. The irony was that by dissipating his fortune, giving his shares to charity, and making his children earn their living, he set Canadian Tire on a fractious course that would, in time, split the family asunder in a bitter battle for control, and eventually result in the company almost passing out of the Billes family's hands. Forty years of fraternal conflict fanned by a family rivalry and the invisible force of two warring wives was about to make its first public appearance.

THE Canadian Tire J.W. Billes left behind was set to embark upon a new period of unrivalled growth. In its early days, the store's main attraction to customers had been its low prices. But by the 1950s, it was clear that the charm of Canadian Tire lay in more than value. The catalogue had featured do-it-yourself equipment from the beginning, but as the 1950s ushered in the second decade of the postwar era, the do-it-yourself movement was coming into its own. Canadian Tire beckoned to a hitherto unrecognized but distinctly Canadian state of mind: that of the self-improver, the self-sufficient man, an ideal that thrives to this day.

Self-sufficiency was touted as the revenge of the working middle class, the great leveller of education and wealth and accomplishment, and hardware was the epitome of its new do-it-yourself *gestalt*. How many men in the 1950s who couldn't tell a Phillips from a blade screwdriver went leafing through the Canadian Tire catalogue and bought the fully equipped basement workshop anyway, complete with drill press and lathe and motorized table saw and three hammers and a plunge-cut router and an angle grinder and maybe even a mitre saw? And how many ever used the goddamn things? Don't ask.

In the 1950s, fueled by the home renovation craze, the shame of not being handy was a secret plague. Soon the disgrace of the unhandy was known throughout suburbia. Grown men, accomplished men, men who read and skied and made money, would meet the girl of their dreams, marry, live in bliss, until . . . one day, the Mistress of the House would be sitting at the breakfast table, and would remark upon the leaking kitchen faucet, and the awful filthy truth would leak out too: the Man of the House – as if he deserved the name – didn't know how to repair it! He wasn't handy! Suddenly he was branded with a scarlet letter. It was a U, for Useless. And then the happy couple would be discussing the woman's last beau, the unlucky bastard who'd missed his chance, who was a drunk, or perhaps a mass murderer, or a molester of swans, but who, nonetheless, give him his credit, was *handy*. At least *he* could fix a dripping tap.

Whereupon the shameful mate would head on down to the Canadian Tire store, and buy eighteen gallons of green and yellow paint, and go home and paint the entire house. Which was approved of by Her Majesty, but which was – well, it was nice, thank you, but it was only *painting*. It wasn't genuine Handiness. And so Mr. Useless would head *back* to Canadian Tire, lured by the catalogue's promise of a sense of accomplishment for even the most hopeless klutz, to buy a complete work bench with which he could then lay a few floors or build an extension onto the kitchen. After all, as the catalogue beckoned, "Good Tools Soon Pay for Themselves."

Being Handy was the working middle class's consolation for not having any real money, the real life suburban version of Marlon Brando's working class appeal. Of course, Brando the actor didn't knock them dead playing Mr. Fix-It, the popular TV idol of the unhandy in those days. Still, with the right tools, Mr. Useless could feel like a man again. As the years went by, he became a specialist. Now he wouldn't take on a home repair job until he had *exactly the right tool*! There was something almost sexual about it. Almost? It was priapic. You could always tell a man who was handy: he was the real man, the strong, silent one at the cocktail party, the one in the cardigan, with most of his hair left, who rocked back on his heels and examined the moulding. *Nice work . . . hmmm . . . three-eighths, eh? I'd have used half inch myself . . . balls? You bet. Made 'em myself on the lathe.*

Canadian Tire had not singlehandedly created the do-it-yourself mentality, to be sure, but it capitalized on the phenomenon. J.W. had seen it all. Canadian Tire's unofficial motto, whether selling car parts or hacksaws, was Be Prepared. Nowhere else in the world did such an organization exist, for in no other country but Canada, Land of Survival, was everyday life lived to exalt the motto of the Boy Scout movement.

THOUGH his father had died the previous evening, Dick Billes was sufficiently collected the morning of October 17, 1956, to arrive at Canadian Tire's headquarters at 837-847 Yonge Street in good time to move into the old man's office before his uncle Alf had the chance. The Throne Room, as J.W.'s cluttered headquarters was called, was to Dick the locus of power at Canadian Tire, and his rightful place. It was true Dick was only twenty-eight, and as yet unripe to run a corporation doing $9 million worth of business a year. But Dick had toiled at Tire ever since his father convinced him to abandon university at the age of twenty-two. He had served as secretary of the company's board of directors for four years. By the time his father died in the fall of 1956, Dick's life was falling into place quite nicely. A becoming future lay stretched out before him. That August, Dick had married Norma Cole, a thin, pretty teenage friend from Lake Simcoe – thereby putting to rest J.W.'s dismay over Dick's divorce from his first wife, Beverley, several months earlier. Within months Dick and Norma had purchased a rambling, $63,000 ravine-backed ranch-style home on the fringe of Toronto's wealthy Bridle Path district. The house befitted an up-and-coming corporate leader. E.P. Taylor lived half a mile away. As Dick Billes saw it, his father had been grooming him to take over Tire. A.J., "a vice-president in name" only, as Dick thought of him, would fill in as president until Dick worked off a little of his inexperience, as if it were a few unnecessary pounds.

Unfortunately for Dick, life wasn't to work out that way. A.J. was fifty-four years old. Having endured his older brother's domineering rule for more than thirty years, A.J. had no intention of forfeiting the power he had waited so long to wield. "There was no question," a dealer close to the action later recalled, "that A.J. wanted the top when J.W. died." With the approval of the board, and by dint of his experience A.J. immediately had himself proclaimed president of Canadian Tire. Over the next ten years, in the course of establishing a spot in the Retailing Hall of Fame at least as prominent as his brother's, A.J. Billes turned Canadian Tire into the country's best-loved emporium of consumerism. If, to do so, he had to set mutinous Dick Billes adrift from the great ship Tire – well, the loss of a nephew was easier to withstand than the loss of an empire.

As for Dick's preemptive bid on the Throne Room, A.J. seemed not to notice. Within weeks, though, the sound of hammering filled the warrens of Canadian Tire's corporate offices. A.J. was having them rebuilt at the other end of the building. Dick could have the Throne Room. A.J. wanted control.

A.J. wasted no time refashioning Canadian Tire in his own younger-brother image. His style of management had an aura all its own. If his brother had watched over Tire with rational, Apollonian detachment, A.J. had an instinctive, Dionysian love of day-to-day detail, the rough-and-tumble of store life. "What they call seat-of-the-pants management," one of his employees remembered. "That was his strong suit."

The omniabsence with which J.W. dominated Tire was now replaced by a tall, energetic man with a mustache and a face that resembled the unsuccessful lawyer in a Billy Wilder movie. A.J. couldn't keep his finger out of any pie. He maintained his broomcloset office on the main floor of the store where, a complete workaholic, he often toiled until 2 a.m., only to be back at the office the next morning at seven, having taken the subway to work.

The subway was one of A.J.'s favorite pretensions. He may have lived in a mansion the size of a small county, but at work he was the eternal scraper, handling his nickels as if they were manhole covers. Even a request for a raise subjected an employee to a bout of A.J.'s "figuring." He never replied with a simple yes or no; he tried to reason you out of it. "What are you spending your money on?" he would ask. "How much was that suit you're wearing? Fifty dollars? Go see my friend Sammy. He'll give you twenty-five dollars off. So we've already saved twenty-five dollars." A.J. could do anything with a pencil. "It was patriarchal to the nth degree," one of his former managers observed.

If he wasn't saving money, he was pushing the work ethic. Peter Montgomery, who left Woolworth's to manage Tire's main store after A.J. became president, recalled driving through the country one day with A.J. when they spotted a foursome of golfers. "Those poor guys," A.J. said, looking out the window.

Montgomery was driving. He glanced out the window. Golfers. "Why are they poor?" he said.

"Well, look, they're playing golf. Not working. Those poor guys," A.J. repeated.

A week later Montgomery told his father the president of Canadian Tire was "a few bricks short of a load." It was years before he could play golf again without feeling guilty. A.J. knew how to get to a man.

IN the spring of 1957, less than six months after his brother's death, A.J. instructed Robert (Robin) Law, a young lawyer at Blackwell Law, the company's waspish Bay Street law firm (its founding partner, Leslie Blackwell, had been attorney general of Ontario), to create Canadian Tire's first profit-sharing plan. J.W. had paid annual bonuses since the 1930s, but adamantly resisted the notion that his employees might want to own shares in their company. J.W. thought of his employees as his children, unfit, and perhaps unwilling, to take on the responsibilities and risks of ownership.

A.J. saw things differently. In 1946, after many arguments, A.J. had finally convinced his older brother to let their employees defer their bonuses, which the company would then invest for its own expansion and pay back, with interest, ten years later. This was a solid savings plan for the employees; and it created capital to pay for a few of A.J.'s schemes. With these deferred payments coming due in the spring of 1957, and J.W. out of the way, it was easy for A.J. to suggest that each employee deflect some or all of his bonus payments into Canadian Tire common shares – thereby rolling the money over, once again, and plowing it back into the corporation.

A.J. – who as a boy had wanted to be a missionary – touted profit-sharing with religious zeal, and Canadian Tire's revolutionary plan, one of the first three in Canada, quickly became a canon of Family Tire's philosophy. The idea of owning a share of the rock of Canadian Tire combined in a chemical way with the Depression-bred conservatism and dependency of the company's longtime employees, and A.J. knew it. He wrote letters to the staff – Papal encomiums come to mind – that were legendary, conflations of religious revivalism, capitalism, vaudeville, and sheer entrepreneurial enthusiasm, all of which seemed to be one and the same thing in A.J.'s mind. "Christ, while upon this earth," he wrote in his Christmas letter to the staff on December 23, 1958, "said, 'The poor ye shall have with you always.' This passage does not say that the poor need remain poor. . . ." That led him to the need for hard work and reward, and thence to profit-sharing, the plan in which "THE EMPLOYEES WILL BE THE COMPANY! To some this may sound a bit like communism. In a way it is a perfect combination of both capitalism and communism. . . ." Amen. "When the guy made a speech," an employee of the time recalled, "he was better than Billy Graham at the best. When he was on a roll, he was pure emotion."

What A.J. didn't say – he was devious – was that profit-sharing was also distinctly in the Billes family's interests. A.J. had always been terrified of the devils of socialism: like the Eatons and every other retailer in Canada, he was convinced unionized labor would demolish Tire's profit margins. Profit-sharing was his main line of defence against them. But profit-sharing was also good for the corporation. Employee contributions toward shares were new capital pouring into the company; the company in turn claimed them as expenses to reduce its own taxes. Most importantly, as one manager later pointed out, "what A.J. was trying to do was buy employee loyalty at no cost to the company."

Furthermore, the profit-sharing plan had the less visible effect of creating a substantial block of shareholders who would arguably be loyal to A.J. If A.J. couldn't control the company through his direct holdings, perhaps he could control it indirectly, through loyalty to his cause. This would in fact turn out to be the case.

As A.J. was aware, by the early 1960s, the ownership of the company broke down roughly as follows:

SHAREHOLDER	COMMON VOTING SHARES	
	NUMBER	% OF TOTAL
J.W. Billes Estate	70,000	30
A.J. Billes family	66,331	29
Employees' profit- sharing plans	29,000	13
Others	64,669	28 (small blocks)
TOTAL	230,000	100

Profit-sharing was only one of A.J.'s schemes, however. By the late 1950s he had jumped back into the gasoline business. As stated earlier, J.W. found the gas business too competitive and worried about attracting the ire of the large oil companies, with whom he had no desire to compete. But A.J. saw it as one more way to establish and assert himself as a Canadian Tire founder in his own right.

In November of 1958 *The Financial Post* carried news of Canadian Tire – the "giant" 165-store automotive service chain – and its plan to invade the service station business. Tire's first gas bar, located on Yonge Street next to the main store, featured a "revolutionary" eighteen-yard, twelve-foot-a-minute overhead car conveyor: while grease monkeys underneath lubed a car, mechanics above ground ministered to its upper parts. The conveyor had A.J. Billes written all over it. He adored complexity. Whether designing a profit-sharing plan or constructing a merchandise retrieval system such as the Rube Goldberg-style device that tangled the innards of the main store, A.J. always wanted his schemes to do more than one thing at the same time. The new 200,000 square-foot warehouse at Sheppard Avenue – another of A.J.'s baubles, for which he had turned the sod shortly after J.W.'s death – sported a tire retrieval system so complex it took subsequent executives *ten years* to dismantle it. The new warehouse and the new gas stations represented the Future, the land where A.J. intended to stake his claim to greatness in Canadian Tire history.

But Dick? Dick Billes hated the service stations: his best line of attack against A.J. lay in keeping his father's cautious ways alive. His father had no desire to own gas stations; therefore Dick hadn't either. "The station is strictly an experiment," vice-president Dick Billes soberly informed the *Post*, adding that the company had no plans to open others in the future.

But Dick Billes was wrong, not to mention outperformed and outvoted. By 1960, the company's second gas bar, on O'Connor Drive in Toronto, had sold 3,000,000 gallons of gas. By December of that year, A.J. had plans for twenty-three new gas bars in Ontario. The following spring he added eight more. At first the gas bars met serious resistance from the dealers, who had wanted to own them outright. A.J., who often doubted the intentions of the dealers – a holdover from the old days, when he ran the main store as his own empire, and left Dealerland to his older brother – wouldn't hear of it. Fortunately the gas bars drew hordes of customers to dealers' stores, and they forgave him. No small part of this was due to A.J.'s insistence that Canadian Tire gas stations would offer the ultimate in service to their customers. "We used to say they'd wipe everything but your ass," Bill Dawson, the Sudbury dealer at the time, recalled. "They would, too." Within two years, Canadian Tire was the biggest independent gas retailer in Toronto.

Tire's invasion of the city's petrol business was all the more remarkable because Canada's major oil companies, from whom A.J. bought most of his gas, had until then enjoyed a taut monopoly on the retail fuel trade. A.J. had first persuaded the majors to supply him with gas at competitive prices by employing his patented Little Hick From the Country act. Dressed in a $50 suit and a tie that might have been dreamed

up by a drug-crazed linoleum designer, A.J. would no sooner
be through the door of Imperial Oil's offices when he would
go into Deep Awe over everything in the office – the thickness
of the carpet, the paintings on the wall, the generous terms of
the contract, oohs and ahhs escaping from every opening on
his face. Thus disarmed, the majors thought little of selling
gas to this brick from a second-rate auto supply store. A.J.
called the technique "closing the trap."

Before long, however, with the O'Connor Drive store
selling more gas than any other retail outlet in the world, the
majors had realized their mistake, and Canadian Tire was
engaged in one of the country's first serious gas wars. History
may not remember Esso's Tiger in Your Tank campaign,
which featured acrylic tiger tails one attached to the aerial of
one's father's car, or trading gas receipts for a complete set of
glass tumblers, a barbecue, a wading pool, for beach balls,
flash cameras, teepees, straw hats, and every other curlicue of
suburban leisure life, but the people who avidly amassed
these gewgaws certainly do. They were the offspring of the
major oil companies' battle with Canadian Tire.

To steal business from other service stations, A.J. sold his
gas at a four percent discount. The oil companies did a huge
volume of business, however, that enabled them to out-
last any gas war declared by a competitor. Against their staying
power, A.J. pitted his devious ingenuity. "The oil companies
sold gas at a fantastic margin of profit," A.J. later explained. "I
couldn't resist it, but I didn't dare cut prices. So I realized the
only way you could [compete] was through cross-merchandis-
ing. But no one had ever done that."

It was Muriel, A.J.'s wife, who came up with the gimmick
that made retailing history. Fresh from a trip to Europe, and
inspired by Italian money and War Bonds, Muriel suggested
Canadian Tire issue a Gas War Bond. Anyone who bought gas
at Canadian Tire received a coupon that was good for a fifteen
percent discount on future purchases of gas – but only once

the gas war ended. It was the first time anyone had ever tried such a thing.[2]

The coupons worked so well that, by 1962, A.J. handed out discount coupons to customers buying merchandise in the stores as well. The coupons could then be used against subsequent purchases, like gift certificates. A.J.'s master stroke was to hire the British American Bank Note Company, which printed Canada's currency, to print the coupons on the paper used for legal tender, so that they looked and felt like real money – one more step in the creation of a self-contained Canadian Tire universe of Consumerism. The notes, which came in regular denominations from one cent to a dollar, were engraved with a picture of that old frugal Scotsman, Sandy McTire. (A.J. originally wanted an engraving of the goddess Diana, semi-nude, pursued by three dogs, because he thought that would appeal more to Canadian Tire's male clientele, but Muriel nixed the idea.) Canadian Tire money was born – the greatest single innovation in the history of Canadian retailing since Timothy Eaton's revolutionary satisfaction-or-your-money-back guarantee. Within three years, Canadian Tire money was already the stuff of legends: one criminal managed to spend his way across the Caribbean with the bogus bills before he was apprehended.

Canadian Tire money, as well as being the product of thoroughly bizarre genius, had enormous publicity value for the company. It was an advertisement for Canadian Tire in everyone's wallet, and it couldn't be spent elsewhere. It also enabled A.J. to paint Canadian Tire once again as the savior of the working man taking on the big bad uglies of Canadian capitalism.

Meanwhile the gas bars were an astounding success. At the

---

[2]J.W. Billes had in fact given his preferred "shareholders" cash discount coupons for a short time in the 1920s. Years later, when anyone celebrated Muriel and A.J.'s invention, Dick Billes always reminded them his father had thought of it first.

height of the gas wars, one of Tire's gas bars could lose $25,000 a week; most of the time, however, they slurped in such a fortune that Simpson-Sears and Eaton's took up Tire's example and tried to sell gas. Not to be outdone, Esso and Shell began to sell household goods. When, by way of retaliation, the majors cut off Tire's supply of gas in June of 1960, A.J. made headlines when he bought 60 million gallons of gas from the Soviet Union. The "cold war gas" cost him 15 cents a gallon; taxes added 6 cents more to the cost. Even at the height of the gas wars, however, A.J. never sold the stuff for less than 35 cents a gallon.

THE desire to prove himself to history that made A.J. an unsurpassed salesman also made him a nightmare as a manager. The company J.W. Billes lifted off the ground was small enough to be run by one man: A.J. inherited an institution. A national corporation whose fortunes depend on the cooperation of more than two hundred small-town entrepreneurs is not the sort of business that can be run on the force of one man's personality. A.J., the younger brother who always wanted to be liked, could never understand that. Years later, looking back on his remarkable life, he simply blocked the thought from consciousness.

His problem lay in Dealerland. Canadian Tire's dealers, an inherently conservative gaggle of penny-conscious shopkeepers, had always mistrusted A.J. In J.W.'s day, A.J.'s power lay with his employees at head office, in the company's shipping department and the main store. It was J.W., the Great White Father of Dealerland, who took the dealers' side in any dispute with the shipping department at home office, which meant a dispute with A.J. Within months of Big Daddy's demise, dealers were referring to their "bitter competition" with the new president.

The predictable anxiety the dealers felt upon J.W.'s death

was magnified when A.J., his presidential chair barely warm, began to scheme. It wasn't his schemes that troubled the dealers as much as A.J.'s habit of changing them once they were underway. No sooner would one project be tottering down the road, than A.J. would have the road itself under construction. He was, after all, formally uneducated: he needed concrete results before his ideas could evolve.

A.J.'s first blunder, shortly after J.W.'s death, had been to suggest the creation of an entirely separate chain of discount outlets to be known as the Joe Blow Stores. The name was only the first problem. A.J. believed Joe Blow stores could service a retail market even more value-conscious than Canadian Tire's, while providing Canadian Tire dealers with what A.J. considered some much-needed disciplinary competition. This was akin to suggesting to a hot-dog vendor that another hot-dog vendor parked right beside him, boasting lower prices, will help the first hot-dog vendor sell more hot dogs. "A.J. always thought that tension and conflict was a way you got more out of people," one of A.J.'s associates from that time has observed. That, at least, was A.J.'s rationale. His motives were more transparent: he wanted to be seen, once again, as a founder in his own right, and not just as a lucky little brother who happened to climb on board at the right time – which happens to be his reputation to this day in certain parts of Dealerland. The Joe Blow proposal was eventually shelved, but not before A.J. had thoroughly undermined the dealers' confidence in head office. "He just about demolished the corporation over that," Dick Billes said years later, in one of his characteristic snipes at his uncle.

Invariably, A.J. wanted the store of tomorrow installed yesterday. The first automatic car wash designed for the company – and for the country, thanks in large part to plans designed by A.J.'s second son, David – was rushed into service before its designers had been able to cure it of ripping off car bumpers. But the automatic car wash was the Future, the shape of things to come. . . .[3]

A.J. adored technology and schemes. Inasmuch as they eliminated that old scoundrel, human error, they produced a *system*, another environment he could *control*. One of the company's first (and ultimately disastrous) computer punch-card order systems was installed at the corporation's O'Connor Drive store in what was then suburban Toronto. J.W. had built the O'Connor store with enormous trepidation: it was too large, and it was in the suburbs, and neither element was part of Tire's winning formula. But to A.J., the O'Connor Drive store was *the* Shining Future, A.J.'s home away from home where he would triumph, the forward-looking brother. The dealers thought he was nuts. "A.J. was okay until he thought he had a better idea than you had," Walter Muncaster would note. "But on the other hand, you never knew if he was kidding."

A.J. never kidded. Not where the future of Tire was concerned. He was a Cuisinart of new ideas. "If I have ten ideas," A.J. was fond of telling anyone who would listen, "and six of them work, that's okay with me." Unfortunately it wasn't so okay with Mr. Status Quo, the Canadian Tire dealer. Dealers saw A.J. as a loose cannon on the deck of the Great Ship Tire. The Canadian Tire money scheme in particular

---

[3]Yet another example of A.J.'s obsession with "systems" and complexity was the computerized inventory-control system he installed at several dealers' stores, much against their wishes, in the late 1950s. Throughout the retail business, over-the-counter hardware stores were converting to self-serve systems first introduced in the grocery business in the United States in the 1920s. A.J. hated the idea of self-service: he figured customers would shoplift his profits. When IBM introduced a computer that could process punch cards, A.J. installed one. A customer marked his selections on a punch card after surveying a store's wares in a series of Plexiglas cases, handed his card to a counterman, and picked up his parcel from a conveyor. The system cut back on theft, to be sure, but in towns like Sudbury, where a good proportion of the rapidly growing population of European immigrants could hardly speak English, never mind read it, the system was a disaster. Still, A.J. hung on to it as long as he could.

threw them into apoplexy. As they saw it, or as A.J. explained it, not without his requisite dose of complication and contradictory memos and sub-memos – *what, another one? What is the Insane Genius up to now?* – coupons meant a five percent cut in a dealer's profits. Never mind that A.J. sidestepped this problem by simply raising the price of 40,000 items by five percent (he made Dick do it, too – by hand): the dealers saw the entire scheme as complicated, untried, and dumb.[4]

Toward the end of the 1950s, Canada's first wave of professionally trained managers, soon to be known as Master of Business Administration graduates, were beginning to transform the once free-form act of being a businessman into "the science of management." At Canadian Tire, it was more like weird science. The company's management, if one chose to use the word, was a one-man show – the A.J. Billes Variety Hour. Sales in 1961 were $9.3 million, and dropping. Directors' meetings were informal at the best of times, and never more frequent than quarterly, and there was no executive committee. A.J. spent as much time designing lunchrooms for his employees as he did thinking about expansion into the suburbs or Quebec, where he now superstitiously hesitated to invest any of the company's money. He still signed all the company's checks, by hand. "A.J. was not a very good delegator," Arch Brown, the field man-turned-dealer, explained. "He wanted to have his hand in everything. We really did not have at that point the advantage of the business schools."

Other executives, who did have business degrees, were appalled by A.J.'s capacity for creating mayhem. "There were no systems in place," one of A.J.'s managers remembered. "It was almost as if everyone did his own thing. There was no

---

[4]It was a testament to Canadian Tire's reputation for delivering "low-cost value" to the working man that no one noticed the price increase – with the predictable exception of Gordon Sinclair, the Toronto-based radio broadcaster.

common focus, no common objectives. A.J. was not a good manager, not a good leader. He considered himself a Messiah, I guess. But on a day-to-day basis he didn't so much lead as react." The company's organization chart, which A.J.'s personnel manager published, was shaped like a star – with A.J. at the center. In 1959, Dick Billes, ever the subversive, projected Tire's earnings out, and predicted the company would be broke by 1969.

But A.J.'s staff, thanks largely to profit-sharing, felt absolutely committed to a common purpose. A.J.'s men often referred to having "triangles all over our asses." They didn't mean it as a joke. Their kamikaze loyalty to Canadian Tire was often the reason the company was cited as an ideal of entrepreneurial capitalism. In fact it was just as often a model of Machiavellian management. A.J., as Captain Cuttle said of old Solomon Gills in Dickens's *Dombey and Son*, was "wicked devious." One had only to look at the company's sole level of senior management, the department managers in charge of parts, accessories, sporting goods, and the like. They never bore formal titles. Later, during the company's trials in Texas, this fact became a point of pride among Tiremen of A.J.'s era, evidence (at least in their own minds) that they concerned themselves with business rather than status. But the lack of obvious distinctions between management and non-management served A.J.'s invisible ends: this way, he could push one executive into another's path if necessary.

"A.J. always recognized personal weaknesses or holes," Arch Malcolm, A.J.'s manager of the petroleum division, later recalled. "And I think that became one of his greatest strengths." Malcolm had dragged himself up from managing a restaurant to handling parts and accessories at Tire's Sheppard Avenue warehouse when, to his surprise, A.J. put him in charge of Tire's fledgling petroleum division. But A.J. never told anybody in the petroleum division that Malcolm was their new boss, and Malcolm found himself running a department that everyone (especially the dealers) resented, and with no clear mandate to do so. Malcolm's only defence was to guard his territory jealously, with the result that the petroleum division became even more isolated from the rest of the corporation. That suited A.J. just fine: he wanted to keep it as his own inviolate domain. But the same could not be said of Malcolm. "A.J. created a personality in me as a result of all this," he later realized. "I became the most defensive guy."

The difficulties of A.J.'s tenure as president were intimately tied to A.J.'s invisible psychological agenda. For all his genius as a promoter, for all his evangelical fervor as a motivator, for all his daring confidence and new ideas, there was a profoundly unconfident side to A.J. Billes – the side that needed desperately both to carve out his own territory, and to prove himself to his brother. It was as if old Lurch were watching from the grave.

If he was, the old man couldn't have liked what he saw. A.J.'s success had been achieved by ignoring many of J.W.'s conservative tenets and the wishes of his favorites, the dealers. By March of 1960, in one of the first newspaper profiles written about the company since J.W.'s death, A.J. had rewritten history. "[J.W.]'s brother, Alfred J., who was with him from the start, heads the company today," the *Toronto Daily Star* enthused. Finally, with J.W. out of the way, A.J. could be a co-founder whenever he wanted.

BY then, A.J. was devoting more and more time to a problem of another order: the question of who would take over the helm of Canadian Tire when he stepped down.

Twenty-five years later, by the mid-1980s, succession matters and family businesses would be subjects of intense study in business schools all over North America. In 1988, some 700,000 firms – seventy-five percent of all the businesses in Canada (and ninety percent in the United States) – were family-owned or family-controlled. Twenty percent of the *Financial Post 500* corporations are family-controlled, accounting for roughly a third of the economy, a quarter of the country's public companies, and more than half the privately owned ones. Today, family feuds – those of the Billeses and the Steinbergs are just two – litter the pages of the newspapers. The explosions have occurred all at once because dynasties (many of which were born in the 1920s) require at least two generations to fall apart. As family businesses have been studied more carefully, distinct rules concerning their operation have emerged. The Canadian Association of Family Enterprises (CAFE), an organization formed in 1983 to promote family businesses, has codified the rules necessary to preserve dynasties. Plan succession ten years ahead of time; choose one successor, and buy the other children off, or sell the company; make sure everyone talks to one another; watch out for wives and in-laws, the tarantulas and gorillas, as family business theorists have dubbed them. With forethought and discipline, the experts claim, dynasties can be preserved.[5] The goal, according to William Tilden, a member of CAFE who with his brother inherited his father's rental car business, is to leave one's offspring "enough to do anything, but not enough to do nothing."

None of this latter-day wisdom, however, was available to A.J. in 1959, when succession problems plagued Canadian business. Inheritance taxes were so strict only half of Canada's family businesses made it to a second generation; the

---

[5]Some of the disputes that have surfaced as second- and third-generation family dynasties came of age in the 1970s and 1980s would make great B movies. Perhaps the most remarkable involved Seabrook Farms, the New Jersey frozen vegetable concern. Seabrook, Senior, the founder, was getting on in years, and was turning into a bit of a vegetable himself, in the opinion of his son Jack. But he was reluctant to leave the family firm. Jack Seabrook had his father committed to a mental institution and then took over the company. The mental institution didn't have bars on the second-floor windows, however. The elder Seabrook escaped, took a taxi downtown to his lawyer, had his son disinherited, and re-established himself as head of the company. His son was left with no choice but to set out on his own, and eventually ended up as president and chief executive officer of International Utilities.

subsequent buyouts of family firms were one of the main reasons Americans controlled more than sixty percent of the Canadian economy in the 1970s.

A.J. had already passed his common shares in Canadian Tire to his three children in an attempt to avoid succession duties and inheritance taxes. An infamous voting trust of the late 1950s and early 1960s, set up at the urging of his wife Muriel, engineered a truce between Alfred, Martha, and David on the one hand, and Dick Billes, J.W.'s son, on the other. The pact ensured that no Billes child could sell his shares without first offering them to his cousins or siblings. Another condition of the pact – again at Muriel Billes's insistence – was that her children be allowed, over time, to purchase enough common shares on the open market to bring their holdings equal to those of J.W. Billes's estate, which was controlled by Dick Billes. (It was 1969 before this condition was met.) But while owning the company was one issue, the question of power, of who would *run* it, was another matter altogether.

A.J.'s most pressing concern here was Dick Billes. Dick had not abandoned his desire to be president of Canadian Tire, but his plans had undergone serious revision almost from the moment his father died. Under the terms of his father's will, Dick's access to power at Tire was indirect at best, as one of three trustees who voted his father's shares, along with his mother and National Trust, who represented the charities named in J.W.'s will.

J.W. Billes was barely cold in his grave when National Trust began, in January of 1957, to pressure Dick and his mother to sell J.W.'s shares. The trust company was being squeezed by a number of charities named in J.W.'s will, notably the Toronto Humane Society, to sell its Canadian Tire shares for cash, which the charities wanted to invest in a company that paid a dividend of more than twenty cents a share. The ingratitude of the charities burned Dick up. Had he been able to afford to buy the shares, he might have; but the measly stipend his father left him was insufficient for that purpose, and Dick was still too young and inexperienced to convince a bank to back him.

Nevertheless, Dick and his mother controlled a majority (two out of three) of the trustees' votes, which gave Dick effective voting control of the shares J.W. had passed down to his family and the charities. Using that block of shares, Dick did everything in his power to thwart A.J.

Relations between the two men had become so acrimonious that they barely spoke to one another from one quarterly board meeting to the next. A.J.'s schemes – harebrained and otherwise – drove Dick crazy. Invariably, he took what he imagined to be his father's side on every issue. He had unsuccessfully opposed A.J.'s decision to move into the gas business; he had successfully opposed the Joe Blow stores; he had reservations about credit cards and discount coupons. As much as he could, he operated his own empire from his position as vice-president of purchasing. Dick's opposition to A.J. went beyond Dick's innately more conservative nature; beyond reason, even. It travelled back into the past.

A.J.'s main tactic where Dick was concerned was to ignore him, which only drove the young man crazier. "Dick never forgave me," A.J. would say, "because when his father died, he thought he should be president. . . . I never intended Dick to be president. I intended him to earn his place. In a lot of ways Dick was very capable. But as president? No. Dick wasn't old enough. And I think he was a little too conservative." That was a common view: Dick's obsession with details, his caution with inventory, his mistrust of the new, led several dealers to think of him as "an old woman." At other times, A.J. would say "I think in the end what worried Dick was not me, but [my son] Fred. He saw Fred as a competitor. Because Fred was a lot more outgoing, he had a lot more oomph than Dick. I think that was as much trouble as anything."

In fact, Dick thought Fred was an idiot. He had no respect for his experience as a retailer – Fred had none, beyond having grown up within Family Tire – and no taste for his foul tongue and temper. All in all, it was a bad situation. Already, at the age of thirty-two, Dick would arrive home at the end of the day in pieces. "He just couldn't cope with A.J., because A.J. was too irrational," Norma, Dick's wife, explained. "They never gave Dick the time of day after J.W. died. I can only surmise that they wanted to erase the J.W. Billes family off the face of the earth." Dick offered an alternative explanation. "My father drove A.J. nuts because he wouldn't let him run Canadian Tire," Dick said. "I represented the continuation of what my father was doing. And A.J. didn't like it. Because I'm pretty strong. And if I saw him doing something wrong, I'd say so."

The unpleasantries between uncle and nephew came to a head shortly before Christmas in 1959. "The final nail in the coffin," as Dick called it, was so insignificant, so puny, that a casual observer, had he not understood the intensity of the animosity between the two men, or the weight of the history between them, might have wondered what all the fuss was about.

The issue was whether or not the company's Toronto stores ought to open Boxing Day. A.J. thought so. Shortly before he left for a three-week cruise in the Caribbean, A.J. informed Peter Montgomery, the manager of the company's main store at Yonge and Davenport, that he wanted all Toronto dealers to open for business on Boxing Day. Montgomery knew the dealers would object. "The dealers as a group," he said, "are very reactionary." Running a store did that to you: you wanted regular hours, dependable events, predictable routines, and no surprises for your customers. Dick was no exception, and after canvassing Toronto's dealers, he countermanded A.J.'s order while the old man was on holiday. "Dick was sort of a dealer's guy," Montgomery remembered. "Because he was sort of straight ahead."

Montgomery knew, however, that A.J. would erupt when he returned, so he asked Dick for a letter authorizing the closing. Dick sent him one. That was when A.J. showed up three days early, having caught wind in the Caribbean of what he immediately interpreted as a coup d'etat on Dick's part, and that was when Dick walked out of Canadian Tire's head office. Recalling the incident, A.J. remembered "I simply said, Dick, don't ever do that sort of thing again. And I just walked away. And he quit.'' But it wasn't a clean break – far from it. Three months later, at the company's spring board meeting in the offices above the main store, Dick made his play. He asked the board to depose A.J., and make him the new president in the old man's place. The board voted Dick down, and Dick Billes said goodbye to his dreams.

Technically, of course, Dick might have brought the weight of the shares he voted in the estate to bear on the board's decision. But he had no guarantee that the profit-sharing plans would not vote with their savior, A.J. And, anyway, Dick wasn't the type to act as a dictator. His father had made him a steward of power, not its owner; and Dick was obedient to his father, even to the grave. To complicate matters, Dick's own ambivalence toward Canadian Tire, or at least toward running it – an ambivalence even his father had demonstrated on occasion – had a strong influence on him. His quixotic demand that A.J. be fired, and his passive acceptance of the board's refusal, were evidence of that feeling. Dick could have challenged the board, and A.J., using the weight of the estate's shares to push his views; but there was a part of Dick that wasn't willing to risk it, because – in the vernacular of the company – he didn't want it enough. So he left.

For years afterward Tiremen debated the split, and the ultimate consequences a different outcome might have had for the course of the company. Many dealers regretted Dick's departure – he was an effective counterweight to A.J.'s wildness – but it didn't do to stand in A.J.'s way. Arch Brown, who was Dick's high-school friend and protégé at Tire, believed that Dick's departure was inevitable. ''I do not think Dick had the education or the drive to be an effective president,'' Brown said. ''He could have, had he accepted it, been a very effective vice-president. But I just don't think he had the forwardness of his uncle.'' The consensus on Dick Billes was that he had lived in awe of his father, with whom he tried so hard to form a bond even after the old man's death, and that had left him living in the past.

But Dick Billes wasn't quite finished with A.J. He was more resilient than he sometimes seemed, even in exile. Free of his responsibilities at Tire, Dick went to work as a consultant for Shell Oil. He made no secret of it, either. Executives at Shell, irritated by A.J.'s incursions into the petroleum business, had been considering their own string of automotive and home repair outlets, to be named Handy Andy stores. Shell welcomed the advice of Dick Billes, who knew Tire so well, and Dick Billes welcomed the chance to deliver a death blow to his uncle. If Dick couldn't run Canadian Tire, he would destroy it. Before long, rumors of an impending takeover of Canadian Tire – perhaps by Shell, perhaps by Imperial Oil? – were circulating.

The rumors were never more than that. But they troubled A.J., sensitive as he was to the question of ownership and control. Ever since J.W.'s death, the stand-off had prevailed between J.W.'s estate (in the person of Dick) and A.J.'s family: the estate's fractionally larger holding of common shares (70,000 shares, or thirty percent of the company) made it difficult for A.J. and his family (66,331 shares, or twenty-nine percent of the company) to control Canadian Tire outright. True, A.J. could perhaps convince the profit-sharing plans to vote on his side of an issue, but the stand-off between the families had never been to A.J.'s liking. He was president of Canadian Tire, a bona fide marketing genius, a co-founder in name, if not in fact – but his hold on the company was insecure. As the years went by, A.J. became obsessed with the issue of control.

A.J.'s insecurity, in fact, was one reason Tire began to issue non-voting shares. Prior to 1960, Canadian Tire shares came in one variety, and one variety only: good old common shares, each with one vote in company affairs decided at annual meetings. The constant threat that the charities might unload their common shares to an unknown outsider, however, made A.J. nervous. So did the company's profit-sharing plan, which had grown so quickly that by 1960 Canadian Tire employees owned twelve percent of the company. Every time the company issued new common shares, A.J.'s control slipped a little farther away.

Non-voting shares were a way around A.J.'s dilemma. The beauty of non-voting shares was that, while they sold on the stock exchange and brought capital into the company, they didn't dilute the family's control of the company. A non-voting shareholder earned dividends, but he didn't have a say in how the company was run, or who would be president, or whether or not the company ought to accept a takeover bid. It was for this reason – because non-voting shares are not democratic – that older, more established stock markets such as the New York Stock Exchange had long since prohibited the use of non-voting shares. Toronto, however, was a young, rash market. It couldn't afford the luxury of New York's principles. Alex Barron, Tire's chairman, had in fact been one of the pioneers of non-voting shares on Bay Street in the 1940s, when he called them "participating preferreds."

The upshot was that in March of 1960, with A.J.'s blessing, Canadian Tire split each of its existing common shares five ways, into three non-voting shares ("A shares") and two common shares. Non-voting shares, A.J. explained to the *Globe and Mail* at the time, would "permit employees to become partners in the enterprise. We think an employee's extra effort should be interpolated into long-range financial reward to give workmen stature. If we don't accomplish this, Russia will show us the way to get the co-operation of the workers. . . ." Or, as one of A.J.'s confidants put it later, "they didn't want to keep issuing common shares because eventually the employees would control the company." Participating as a miniature capitalist in Family Tire's great enterprise was one thing; gaining power over A.J. was another.

Thus, in 1963, when rumors began to waft through Canadian Tire's hallways that Imperial Oil or Shell were thinking of making a run for Tire, A.J. wildly fanned the unsubstantiated gossip. As a result, he convinced Canadian Tire's ever-paranoid dealers in March of that year to buy 20,000 common shares of Canadian Tire at $50 a share. He even offered to lend them a million dollars. To sway them, A.J. enlisted the help of a man who twenty-five years later would spearhead the dealers' own efforts to buy Canadian Tire: Lawrence A. Warren (as he was known at the time), a flamboyant Canadian Tire dealer whose desire to ascend the ladder of management was so intense he had talked himself into a head office job as the dealers' representative. "Canadian Tire Corporation dealers have a very high regard for present management," Warren told the *Financial Post* when news of the dealers' purchase came to light. "The possibility of someone else getting control of the company had to be avoided at all costs." The *Post* headline on its story was "CTC's 'Happy Family' Keeps Control at Home." Irony is a fine thing. Never mind that Alex Barron resigned as chairman of Tire for three years after A.J. accused him of being behind the takeover. Never mind that the rumors never matured into even the shred of a possibility of a reality, or that neither Shell nor Imperial nor even Dick Billes knew anything about a takeover bid. With the dealers' ten percent of the company virtually in his pocket, A.J. had pulled off his own coup. There would be no further challenges to his authority.

As a result of his maneuverings, the share structure of the company by the spring of 1963 was as follows:

SHAREHOLDER	COMMON VOTING SHARES		CLASS A NON-VOTING	
	NUMBER	% OF TOTAL	NUMBER	% OF TOTAL
J.W. Billes Estate	70,000	30		
A.J. Billes family	66,331	29	131,000	34
Dealers' Association	20,000	9		
Employees' profit-sharing plans	29,000	13		
Buying public	44,669	19	253,677	66
TOTAL	230,000	100	384,677	100

As it stood, with Dick gone, there remained but one reminder of J.W. Billes in the company: his eldest son, John. A tall, strikingly handsome man with looks not unlike Charlton Heston's, John had been shattered by Dick's departure. His own career at Tire had been less than brilliant by his own admission, and his resentment of his father's obsessive dedication to his job left him cold where Canadian Tire was concerned as he struggled to move from home office to the field. Dick, his younger brother, had been his protector. With Dick out of the way, the odds of John succeeding to a dealership were slim. A.J. thought John lacked enthusiasm. "You don't give somebody something they don't want," A.J. said of John. "And they have to know why they want it. He couldn't have handled the *intimacy* of running a business."

By 1962, John Billes had retired from the company as well, never to work again, to join the gallery of gargoyles of Canadian family capitalism known as The Lost Relatives. John could rationalize the loss: the trappings of wealth, so he said, were unimportant to him. For years he and Betty had lived near the Bridle Path on property that backed onto E.P. Taylor's home, but John hated standing in the Taylors' box at the racetrack, or at countless cocktail parties they attended. John and Betty would often escape the parties early, regretting, at least publicly, that they had other obligations.

The visible presence of money made John question what he had, or, more to the point, hadn't done with his life. Even years later, when Betty watched *Lifestyles of the Rich and Famous*, John found it "disgusting."

8

THE SILVER SEVEN

WITH DICK BILLES finally out of his hair, A.J.'s search for a successor became both easier and more intense. Easier, because Dick was off the roster. More intense, because Muriel, A.J.'s wife, was pushing her husband to make Fred, their elder son, now thirty years old, the next president of Canadian Tire. Muriel may have been the only person in the universe who thought Freddy was the best man for the job.

For most Tiremen, Fred didn't figure as the next president of the corporation. It wasn't just his lack of experience, his youth, or his patchwork education: those were common qualities in the ranks of Canadian Tire's dealers. Fred had a more serious drawback: he was perceived to be difficult to approach, was famous for his foul mouth, and demonstrated a lack of patience. A few people saw these qualities as part of a "down-to-earth" and straightforward attitude. They understood his bluster as part of the man's basic shyness. The majority, however, were afraid of Fred: three hundred-odd pounds at his lightest, he was what people referred to as "a big man." He was also said to be unpredictable and apparently made enemies easily. The odds of his working as president of Tire with Dick Billes, who was still a trustee of the estate, were microscopic. "Freddy would not work with Dick at all," Fred's sister Martha claimed. "Fred considered Dick an enemy." The tension between the two sons was so thick it was visible. "There's got to be massive rivalry there," a family

133

insider explained. "Because they were both their fathers' sons, and they both thought they were going to be head of the corporation, even before they went on the board."

A.J. was aware of Fred's defects and tried to nudge him in a more appropriate direction. There was, for example, the question of Fred's weight. A.J. had been known to suggest, in front of his employees, that Fred, then in his twenties, play a little handball. Handball! Fred! An interesting idea! A.J. would suggest such a thing, and Fred would jump up from where he was sitting, cry "Jesus Christ!", and flee. But the next day he'd be back, calm as a turtle, as if nothing had happened.

Beneath A.J.'s criticism, however, lay a desperate desire to see his sons succeed. Privately, A.J. had confided in at least three of his closest associates about Fred and David. "There's a fortune waiting for anyone who can make a success out of my sons," he told them. He always used the same words: *a fortune to be made . . . make a success out of my sons.* None of them ever figured out that this cryptic injunction was tantamount to an admission by A.J. that he couldn't do it himself, and that his workaholic ways and his single-minded pursuit of his own purpose in the world had left him out of touch with his children and their aspirations.

Fred may have thought of himself as the logical next president of Canadian Tire – he had been made an officer of the company shortly after J.W. died – but A.J. had no confidence in him. Fred was too brash, too outspoken, too impetuous. He was his father's son without his father's brilliant marketing ideas.

There was always the possibility that in time, and with experience, Fred might mature to the point that he could take over the company. A.J. never dismissed that possibility, though he kept it to himself. But that was the future. "I felt that Fred wasn't the appropriate person at that particular time," A.J. said years later. "And there was also the problem with Dick: that would really have brought the wrath of Dick down on my head."

But if Fred was not to be president, what would happen to him? Here A.J. was on clearer ground: in 1960, he handed Fred the main store, the crown jewel of Tire's empire, perched like a ten-carat diamond in the middle of Toronto at Yonge Street and Davenport Road. (Peter Montgomery, the store's previous manager, was given his own dealership.) A dealership – and that dealership in particular – would placate Fred and provide him with the practical experience he might later transform into the stuff of presidencies. A.J.'s decision, which many Tiremen found difficult to fathom, particularly incensed Dick Billes, who claimed, "that would never have happened if my father had been alive."

Bestowing the main store on Fred solved A.J.'s problem at home. It also left him free to find the best possible replacement for himself. Muriel and A.J. had one overwhelming priority: the new president had to get along with the family. To fill the job A.J. turned, with Muriel's reluctant approval, and to everyone's astonishment, outside the family. He found his replacement in a young man from Sudbury named Joseph Dean Muncaster.

Dean Muncaster was perfect. He was the son of Walter Muncaster, the well-known and much-beloved Sudbury dealer, and so enjoyed the trust of Dealerland. He was a graduate of not one but two business schools, and brought a much needed discipline and objectivity to the family-run company. He was also thirty-two years old, young enough to be a loyal and obedient adopted son. If A.J. saw Muncaster's presidency merely as an interregnum until his offspring were ready to take over the controls of the company, A.J. kept those plans to himself.

For the moment, everyone admired A.J. for overriding his own deepest instincts, for following his reason rather than his heart. "One of the things that should really be recognized," an executive of the time was to say much later, "was his recognition that his son wasn't capable of managing the business. And one of his great negatives was that he was then never prepared to leave it alone.''

THE appealing thing about retailing is that it offers a man so many ways to keep score. A retailer can measure sales and profits and return on investment, as bankers and stockbrokers and mining men do, but for a retailer these are merely the preliminaries of the game. Retailers sell actual objects to actual people, and the minutiae of the entire transaction, from warehouse to checkout counter, can be translated into more scales of performance than a dog has hairs on its back. A good retailer can, and does, measure sales per square foot, inventory turns, weeknight versus weekend shopping habits, gross margin return on inventory invested, seasonal and promotional differentials, purchasing habits by neighborhood and sex and income and profession, stock-keeping unit movement, market areas, traffic patterns, and much else – by day, by month, and by year, and compared to the same day and month and year one, two, five, and ten years ago. . . .

Retailing is definitely a game for the competitive. Ask a banker why he likes banking and he is likely to embark on an explanation of the four pillars of economic strength, the role of capital in the development of a sound economic system . . . zzzzzzzzzzzz . . . Ask a retail man to explain the attraction of selling things, on the other hand, and he will almost always say something simply profound, such as ''It's fun.'' The retail business is a video arcade for adults. Retailing isn't a complicated business compared to, say, the oil and gas industry, and it has never enjoyed the professional status of Canada's oldest monopolies (banking, agriculture, and transportation). But retailing's rude charm, its high profile and the opportunities it presents to measure performance – look how well I've done! – more than compensate for its lower status.

Retailing is capitalism, supply-and-demand-and-conquer, in its raw form. A retail man needs very little capital to launch himself, and his satisfactions are instantaneous. Canada's best retailers – the likes of Timothy Eaton, Don McGiverin at the Hudson's Bay Company, Joe Segal at Zellers, not to mention J.W. Billes and his brother A.J. – have always been impatient poor boys who fought their way off working-class streets into the hearts and minds of the buying public. They brag of their lowly roots as the source of their ability to know the tastes of the common man. Not surprisingly, they are usually short, often outsiders, always intensely competitive, and invariably ego-driven.

JOSEPH DEAN MUNCASTER was no exception to this model, although he played down the egomania. He certainly qualified as an outsider. Muncaster had grown up in Sudbury, a nickel-rich company town (Inco Ltd.) two hundred and fifty miles and several psychological time zones north of Toronto, where his father, Walter Muncaster, was the country's leading Canadian Tire dealer for more than twenty years. Walter was a peace-loving man. His habits were well-respected in Dealerland: fellow dealers liked to say Walter had never taken an unplanned step in his life. Dean was twelve years old when he went to work behind his father's counter and began to learn the importance of caution and order. The Muncaster children considered Canadian Tire an extension of their own family. One of Walter's sons became the company's president; the other became a dealer.

Muncaster had wanted to be an architect before he enrolled instead as a business student at the University of Western Ontario, Canada's first serious school of management. The Second World War had gouged a hole in the country's management talent, and businessmen graduating in the 1950s were beginning to emerge as Canada's new heroes. Dean Muncaster was better suited for capitalism anyway. He had a computer-like memory for numbers, and the only surprise when he graduated second in his class at Western after penning a thesis on the operations of Canadian Tire was that he hadn't graduated first. Muncaster had yet to emerge from

Northwestern University with a Master of Business Administration degree when A.J. Billes read his thesis and offered him a job. Dean Muncaster was the first Canadian Tire executive to be recruited directly out of business school. He was twenty-four years old.

Within two years, Dean Muncaster found himself touted in the press by A.J. as one of Tire's brightest lights. Muncaster was not an imposing physical specimen: short and stocky, he wore his hair in a severe crewcut that, sitting atop his close-set features, gave him a distinct resemblance to a chipmunk. But he was articulate, precise, tactful, even-tempered, and refused to gossip. If A.J. saw in Dean Muncaster someone who might become a loyal and obedient adopted son, well, that was understandable too.

Muncaster's prospects at Tire had improved mightily when Dick left the company. Dick Billes was Dean's friend, but Dean had never envisaged a secondary role for himself. Though he might feel sorry for Dick, Dean was too sensible to regret the course of fate. Instead he moved to Toronto and bought a house across the street from Dick Billes's on Brian Cliff Drive near The Bridle Path. Norma, Dick's wife, was incensed: she was certain that Muncaster had moved there to spy on Dick. She needn't have worried: as the company's new vice-president of purchasing, systems, and development, Muncaster had no time for espionage. Nor was he the type. He insisted everyone at head office call him Dean, and at Christmas shook everyone's hand. If the rest of the time Muncaster seemed to prefer results and numbers to confrontation and intimate dealings with people, it was considered a small failing.

But there was more in store for Dean Muncaster than a role as a pawn in A.J.'s end run around Dick Billes. By 1965, A.J. had been instructed by his doctors to slow down; he had a heart condition. Since the late 1950s, Robin Law, the company's lawyer, had been stitching together a voting trust between A.J.'s children and Dick to ensure that the Billes family's common shares could not be sold without first being offered to Fred, Martha, and David. By 1966 the pact was in place: at the company's annual meeting that spring, A.J. announced that Dean Muncaster, now thirty-two years old, was the new president of Canadian Tire. A.J. was stepping down – "graduating" as he put it – to his old job in the tire department, down where his roots were. Dean Muncaster was to preside over one of the more spectacular runs in the history of Canadian retailing. He would also demonstrate, not incidentally, that there is precious little difference between playing corporate politics and wrestling an anaconda, except that the former could make you rich and powerful.

In the newspapers the day after the annual meeting, Muncaster expressed surprise at A.J.'s timing. It would have been bad form to seem eager. In fact Muncaster had known for six months that he was to become president, and had already gone to lengths to immobilize A.J. and his family. The shareholders gathered at Tire's annual meeting that spring day in 1966 elected Fred and David Billes to Tire's board of directors to fill A.J.'s spot. As an antidote to their presence, Muncaster and Law engineered the reinstatement of Alex Barron and Dick Billes to the board as well. Barron had resigned briefly as chairman three years earlier after his disagreement with A.J. With him and Dick Billes on the 1966 board of directors were David Billes, Fred Billes, Dean Muncaster, Robin Law, A.L. Sherring (National Trust), and two dealers, Ed Leroy and D.J. Wilkins.

That Dick and A.J. had made up their differences, and that Dick was now a dealer in Scarborough, might have seemed surprising, but such mercurial reversals were typical of A.J. If A.J. and his sons had objections to Dick's presence, they kept them to themselves. Besides, there were good reasons, complex reasons, for bringing Dick back into the fold. Dick was, after all, the son of the founder, and he commanded considerable loyalty among J.W.'s cronies in Dealerland. He was still the main trustee of the shares voted by J.W.'s estate; sitting on the board, where A.J. and his sons could keep an eye on him, he was less likely to get up to mischief. And Muncaster wanted Dick on the board – publicly, to give the company a unified appearance, and privately, to balance the presence of Fred and David. There was even a faction amongst the dealers who felt that A.J.'s brush with mortality – the heart disease his doctor had apparently diagnosed – had made him a more forgiving man. Whatever the reasons, A.J. agreed to Dick's presence. The balance of power between the two sides of the family was restored; professional management was in place; profits were up thirty percent. The future beckoned. Life looked good in Consumerland.

To celebrate his ascension to the presidency, Muncaster immediately took two days off with his wife Grace, his friend Arch Brown, Tire's dealer in Barrie, and Brown's wife Helen. The foursome passed a pleasant weekend at Talisman, a small resort north of Toronto. Grace and Helen were best friends; the Browns often babysat the Muncaster children when Dean and Grace travelled out of town. It was to Arch Brown, in fact, that Dean Muncaster had some months earlier made a startling confession. "I would never belong to a company," Dean had said, "that I couldn't eventually be head of."

THE Canadian Tire boardroom was a little room on the second floor of Tire's main store on Yonge Street. Muncaster's office was an even smaller nook at the back of the store. Muncaster affected few airs. He was too busy contemplating his Vision of Canadian Tire. Muncaster saw Canadian Tire as "a big, workable organization," that spanned the globe's second largest country. Muncaster didn't drive the machine: he would tell others how to drive it, where to drive it, how fast to go. To use another of the metaphors popular in the office at the time, Muncaster often conceived of himself as the Great Quarterback.

Perhaps because the Great Quarterback's vision never

flickered, Muncaster emanated an aura of immense confidence to the men and women who knew him. Or it seemed like confidence: the truth was, Muncaster was a cipher. He emanated calm – the fruit of his faith in the Rational Mind – and seldom showed any emotion. Rationalism had been the special of the day at Western, the young business school's claim to respect in the corporate world. The greatest compliment Muncaster could pay a man was to say that he was "rational." Even in conversation Muncaster's voice was as flat as an overcast day on the prairies, its high points consisting of a stable of technical phrases known as Muncasterisms. "Seasonally adjusted" was a Muncasterism. Every time Muncaster hauled a number or a performance measure out of his brain, it was "seasonally adjusted," as if to say, "These aren't just any old numbers you're getting. These are the Truth."

The only signs Muncaster gave that he was ever uncomfortable were when he fidgeted, or when he rolled his tongue lengthwise. A tricky subject would come up, and Muncaster's tongue would dart out and form a tube from back to front like a little flesh cannoli. Then it would zip inside his thin mouth again. Otherwise, everything was always under control. Muncaster was the sort of man who could describe his wife's job as an interior decorator as "one of her two main functions."

TIRE was anything but rational, however. By 1966, in the middle of one of the grand economic booms in history, Tire was banging into itself in eastern Canada, where it had already begun to saturate its market. The company Muncaster inherited also suffered from A.J.'s inability to let others do anything on their own.

The catalogue was only one problem, but in Muncaster's mind it was a prime example of management à la A.J. Canadian Tire ran two major promotions a year – one at Christmas, and the other in June, to take advantage of the home-repair season and the summer leisure season. Muncaster arrived on the scene and discovered A.J. to be so inefficient that the summer catalogue wasn't being published until July. Furthermore, none of the merchandise advertised was in the stores when the damn thing came out. If Tire were to become the great machine Muncaster envisioned, it had to become more efficient. To become more efficient, it needed new blood. For this transfusion Muncaster turned to Western, the Parthenon of rational capitalism, and to two fellow graduates, Richard Hobbs and John Kron. Peter Edmonson, another former classmate from Western, also became a senior executive at Tire. Other important advisers to Muncaster who had studied at Western included R. John (Jack) Lawrence, later president of Burns Fry, Alex Barron's brokerage house, and John Carroll, later president and chief executive officer of Molson Breweries.

Muncaster had met Hobbs and Kron at Delta Upsilon, the Western fraternity to which all three men had belonged as students. Muncaster and Kron were good friends and housemates as well. Hobbs was the outsider. Born and raised in Riverdale, at that time the closest thing to a slum Toronto had ever known, Hobbs had grown up watching his father get drunk at home, a victim of the Depression.

Tall, energetic, hot-tempered and a considerable ladies' man, Hobbs never hesitated to go out on a limb. He had created a fracas at Delta Upsilon, for instance, when he nominated a black friend as a member of the all-white fraternity. Rich Hobbs considered himself a victim of circumstance, and the belligerent fighter's stance he displayed to the world grew out of his desire to wreak revenge on his past. He never could stop fighting. He fought with Vic Muncaster, Dean's uncle, for whom he went to work in Tire's Thunder Bay store after he graduated with an MBA from Columbia. He fought with the dealer-selection committee. The fights were of the shouting-match variety. By 1965, Hobbs had yelled his way into a dealership in Hamilton and a salary of $100,000 a year. But the fights had taken their toll. That same year,

Muncaster tapped his angry friend as the company's first vice-president of merchandising.

Hobbs was a risk-taker who went about his job noisily. His energy was legendary, his drive directly proportional to the geography he wished to put between himself and Riverdale. He dressed expensively, collected art, spoke in complete sentences, and plowed through the middle of any controversy. Hobbs always let you know he was coming.

John Kron, on the other hand, was the perfect organization man, quiet yet ruthlessly efficient. Kron had grown up as a trucker's son in Kenora, Ontario, in the hard heart of the Canadian Shield east of the Manitoba border, and he, too, carried his past in the air about him.

Kron had wrestled inter-collegiately at Western, and he had a wrestler's compact build. His suit jackets could have been cut by a cardboard box manufacturer. He had toiled for his father's trucking company after he graduated from Western in 1956. He had learned to drive a tractor-trailer at fourteen, before he knew how to steer a car. In 1966, he received a telephone call from his pal Dean Muncaster. There was a good chance Dean was going to be made president of Canadian Tire. Would Kron come and help him run the place – particularly "physical distribution," as buzzword-happy Muncaster referred to Tire's puny trucking operation?

Kron would. In 1966, when he arrived at Canadian Tire, the company owned four trucks. Four. A.J. was afraid of unions, and therefore of the Teamsters, and therefore of trucking. *Irrational*! Within ten years at Tire, Kron commanded 100 tractors and 600 trailers, one of the largest fleets in North America. He plastered red inverted triangles all over them. He was also responsible for overseeing 60 million cubic feet of warehouse space, a vast block of air that included an automated warehouse in Brampton, northwest of Toronto. Tire's mechanical storage plant was several billion conceptual miles from the roller skates A.J. had made his stockboys wear in the 1950s, a maze of man-aboard stacking machines, driverless towcarts, electronic sizers, algorithmic storage optimizers, stocker lines, zone-picking systems, high-rise storage areas, and hooked-into-power built-in diagnostics, all eerily devoid of people. The automated warehouse was John Kron's idea. It cost the company $23 million. Old-timers called it Kron's Folly. But it was five times cheaper to run than a standard warehouse. Dean Muncaster knew John Kron would never let him down.

A man who wants to take over another man's company without going through the formality of paying for it has to proceed daintily. From the beginning, Muncaster planned to make changes in the company invisibly, to protect what the Western set euphemistically referred to as Tire's "delicate corporate culture." Hobbs and Kron had been spirited in without firing anyone; Muncaster had delicately engineered Dick's return to the board. Put another way, Muncaster didn't want A.J. to flip out. He was careful never to challenge the old man's prominence. "A.J.'d get up and everybody would cheer him," John Kron said, describing the company's weekly staff meetings. "And he'd be the spiritual leader of the company, of the Church. And then the political and business leader, Dean, would get up and say 'This is what we're gonna do.' . . . Dean was masterful at not playing down A.J. or his significant role, but of course what happened was that the epicenter shifted."

"Shifted" was an understatement. Muncaster's problem was the existing level of "management," the old-time Tiremen who had toiled at Tire for thirty years. The old guard, in the sentimental opinion of the new boys, had "matured out." Sometimes the Western crowd thought they'd stumbled by mistake into a wax museum. The old-timers operated on the basis of conventional knowledge and experience. Mayne Plowman, who still sat on the dealer-selection committee in 1965, for example, had never wavered in his conviction that men who got along with their fathers made the best dealers.

This was touching, but it didn't fit with the scientific approach Muncaster required if the Great Ship Tire were to become the Great Machine.

Worse, the old-timers still considered A.J. president of the corporation. Muncaster would order a change, and A.J.'s men would then check it out with the patriarch. It was Hobbs, Muncaster's heavy, who finally set off the well-planned skirmish that established Muncaster's authority once and for all. Hobbs had made some appointments in the company's adjusting department, and Ian Davidson, A.J.'s fiercely loyal personnel manager – the same man who published the organization chart of the company shaped like a star, with A.J. at the center – ran to A.J. to object. Hobbs went to Muncaster. Davidson was an important pigeon: "whoever controls the personnel department controls the corporation" was a favorite Muncasterism. Hobbs, not Muncaster, had initiated the dirty work; all Muncaster had to do was back Hobbs up. Davidson was fired – Hobbs refused to grant him a dealership as a consolation prize – and by the closing months of 1966, Muncaster, rather than A.J., was established as the real head of the corporation. The new crowd was in.

ONCE inside the corporation, with the door closed behind them, Muncaster and his team set to making Canadian Tire their company. Their audacity was quite possibly without parallel in the annals of Canadian business. Muncaster's modus operandi was to give his lieutenants free rein: all they had to do was perform. If that technique – which twenty years later would be called "intrapreneurialism" – was suited to an economic boom, it also suited a company of gigantic, well-educated egos where executive mobility was limited by the presence of the Billes family.

The appeal of being an executive at Tire was not Gucci loafers and Dior suits or a palace syndrome: it lay in the fact that half a dozen men in their thirties had each been handed a corporation of their own to run as they saw fit. Never mind that they didn't own it. Steven Bochen, a British Columbia native who had worked at Eaton's, spent his first morning as Ian Davidson's replacement chatting with Muncaster about where the company was headed. After that, Bochen was on his own. He was twenty-nine years old. "The surprising thing [at Canadian Tire]," he later said, "coming from a family-structured situation [like Eaton's], was the amount of autonomy you had."

Every couple of Saturdays, Dean and his management team would meet at The Inn on the Park in north Toronto to discuss "strategy." Strategy was another Very Big Idea at Western. Tire's strategy derived from a five-year plan Muncaster had drawn up. Its thrust was simple: make Tire a billion-dollar corporation with stores from coast to coast. Whenever a new year came along, Muncaster tacked another year and a few hundred million in sales onto the existing scheme. All Muncaster asked was that his executives meet their targets.

The system was perfect for a would-be president like Richard Hobbs. Hobbs had no sooner moved to Tire's head office than he began to build stores like a madman. J.W. Billes had carefully expanded into small towns; A.J. ventured into large eastern Canadian cities. Hobbs moved off Main Street and surged into the suburbs, and into Winnipeg and the west. And what stores they were! Hobbs was building stores of 25,000, 35,000, 40,000 square feet – huge for the time.

"We were testing our outer limits," he explained one day not long ago. From the window of his art-strewn penthouse in Toronto's Don Mills, surrounded by Persian and Asian carvings and tapestries, it was possible to see Riverdale, where he had grown up. "We were taking on stores as big as we possibly thought they could be. One of the things we did, that Dean and the board supported" – that was just like Hobbsy, to make sure credit fell where it was due – "that Dean called my domino theory, was that in small communities we should be prepared to be the biggest store in the area, with the exception of food stores. . . . If you looked at the way the country has grown, you saw that people gave up living in the small towns and moved to the big cities. So my theory was that we'd get them when they still lived in the small town, so we'd own them when they came to the big city."

In the past Canadian Tire dealers had rented their premises. Hobbs now insisted that head office own real estate wherever it could, and then lease the buildings back to the dealers. Real estate quickly became the company's second most valuable asset after its merchandising operations. No sooner had Hobbs bought a store than he would tear it down and rebuild it with standardized decor, color schemes, and fixtures. Two years later he would rebuild it again. Today this practice is familiar to anyone who shops at Loblaws: at the time it was revolutionary, or at least evidence that Hobbs was berserk. "You see, if you're a student of retailing at all," Hobbs would explain, "you realize that the big successes in retailing have always been willing to tear down their stores and rebuild without relocating." Hobbs intended to keep his customers entertained.

Hobbs seldom discussed these changes with Dealerland. The Canadian Tire Family had become the Canadian Tire team: the technocrats at head office now called the shots. Among the dealers, descriptions of Hobbs ranged all the way from "arrogant" to "dictatorial." For his part, Hobbs thought the dealers had it too soft, and he said as much. It was not unusual, in the early shakedown days in the mid-1960s, for Hobbs to fire twenty dealers a year. He always did the dirty work himself, and replaced them with well-trained and highly disciplined refugees from IBM. "The people who didn't like Rich," a dealer once explained, "were the people who didn't like to look into the future." The irony was that, thanks to Hobbs, the dealers made even more money than they had before.

Of course, the more Hobbs standardized procedures, the more power he gathered unto himself. He had never concealed his desire to be president of Canadian Tire. "The

difficulty,'' Hobbs would say, ''was that without a policy – well, I could always make a tough decision, but if I
wasn't there, who would? Because if people have to make a
tough decision, they always take the easy way out.'' There was
no way Richard Hobbs could have known how prophetic his
words would be.

BY 1968, to help him reshape Tire from a chain of hardware
and automotive stores into a national emporium of Leisure
Life – to transform the company from a distribution problem
into a marketing organization, in the lexicon of head
office – Muncaster had hired another key player: William
Dawson, the company's first vice-president of marketing.
Dawson was not a graduate of any business school – he
referred to Muncaster et al. as ''the Western kids'' – but he was
a legendary Tireman. Dawson's years as the Canadian Tire
dealer in Campbellford, Ontario, near Kingston, under the
rough-and-tumble dictatorship of Joe Haggas, the company's
hard-drinking field man in the early 1950s, had made Dawson
a classic dealer of the old school. He could still remember
the first thing he ever sold, that quarter-horsepower motor for
$16 on his first day in his first store. Later, after Walter
Muncaster anointed him heir to Sudbury's valuable dealership, Dawson turned in the best performance in Canada four
years in a row, running up sales increases of fifty percent
a year.
    Dawson was a ''full-wagon man'' – a favorite Dawson max-
im being ''you can't sell from an empty wagon.'' It was
Dawson who standardized the company's advertising and
within two years made Tire the biggest retail advertiser in the
country, including Eaton's; Dawson who ventured into small
appliances, of which the company was the country's largest
supplier within two years; Dawson who introduced monthly
newspaper promotional flyers. It was Dawson, too, who
exiled Sandy McTire from the cover of the catalogue, replacing the old coot and his sons with lawnmowers and tires and

other emblems of the corporation – the new team's corporation, that is. Dawson maintained he wasn't a political animal, but there were many who disagreed. It didn't do to mess with Bill Dawson. He was six-foot-three, for starters, and he had a quick temper.

He also had an ego, a sense of confidence, the width of a two-car garage – but one easily justified by his performance. Hobbs and Dawson were constantly at each other's throats, which in itself was a trick, since they went through bouts of barely speaking to one another. "Those guys never listened," a colleague has noted. "The only reason Bill Dawson had fucking ears was to hold glasses on." Hobbs and Dawson argued incessantly: about shelf height, warehouse space, anything. Their rivalry was part of Muncaster's brilliant management strategy, and part of the way they worked; Dawson and Hobbs spurred one another on while they balanced one another's excesses. Within the corporation, the enmity between the pair was passed off as just another manifestation of Tire's unique taste for healthy intramural competition. The resolution of any battle was less important than the proof that Muncaster's executives were free to fend for themselves. Muncaster stayed out of the fray.

INSTEAD, Muncaster concerned himself with his Grand Plan. If it were to become reality, he realized by the early 1970s, Tire needed a computer to link Tire's warehouse to Dealer-land, and both of them to head office. Information was Truth. "Retailing is all about trying to find some unfair advantage over others," a Canadian Tire executive once explained. "One has to become more sophisticated to make money."

To become more sophisticated Muncaster turned in 1974 to Gary Philbrick, a burly, blond, Tennessee-born management consultant at Management Horizons Ltd. Philbrick appealed to Muncaster: he was a systems-and-numbers man, he was creative, and he was Rational. Philbrick, for his part, experienced a "bonding" with Muncaster, and considered

him one of the brightest men he had ever met. Soon they were
on the phone to each other every day, devising "the system of
the eighties" that in five years would become the inventory-
management network for which Canadian Tire is still
famous.

Philbrick was one of the most important and eccentric
executives ever to work at Canadian Tire. He often read four
books a day. And he knew computers. Better still, he could
explain them. "One of the problems retailers have," he
observed, "is that they love their merchandise. They fall in
love with the stuff." The more they fall in love with it,
Philbrick continued, the more irrational they become. Soon
they are trying to unload stuff they have no business selling.

That was where Philbrick's system for the eighties came in:
the system removed sticky human emotions from the act of
retailing, and replaced them with crisp, clean, machine-made
Reason. The new computer brain Philbrick devised for Tire
was astonishing. (It was also the forefather of Arny Augustin's
Project Oracle, which was developed in the mid-1980s.) The
new system revolved around in-store computers, which were
linked to head office's central processor via a store's cash-
registers. An in-store computer could track every item a dealer
sold; automatically reorder merchandise from the company's
warehouse when the dealer needed it, without requiring his
involvement; schedule shipments; process and deliver paper-
work; forecast sales; track the five-year sales history of any
item; and compare all these "trends" store by store, store
against store, year by year, day by day, hour by hour. . . . A
single purchase at a single store could even trigger an order
from a manufacturer, again without consulting anyone. Entire
new vistas of scorekeeping opened up.

Philbrick called his system "The Moneymaker." The Moneymaker not only ran Tire; it provided a moment-by-moment
electroencephalogram of the company's collective brain.
Modifying beta factors and jog indexes and smoothing con-
stants and velocity codes, and coating the whole load in a

Tennessee accent as thick and slow and friendly as a big bag o' honey an' butterflies, Philbrick convinced Tire's dealers to concentrate on the 20 percent of their merchandise – and it was always the same 20 percent, thanks to the natural laws of retailing – that accounted for 80 percent of their sales. Philbrick called it "cranking the turns out of the top."

The Moneymaker was nothing short of – yes! – *scientific management*. The massive clerical work of checking inventory, reordering, invoicing, sending memos, reviewing the books, shipping, and paying one's bills was eliminated: the computer now did all that automatically. The time required to restock an item in a store was reduced by two weeks. This in turn meant a dealer had two weeks' worth of space in his store that no longer had to be tied up storing unproductive inventory – and space, and how one uses it to sell which product, is the Holy Grail, the center of the earth of all retailing.

What was the most profitable way for a dealer to use this now-free space in his store? Philbrick designed a system and software to figure out that problem, too. He called it GMROI, for gross margin return on inventory. A car battery that took up a square foot of a store's valuable shelf space might "turn over" four times a year – that is, four batteries would be sold from that space in a year. If the profit on a battery was $5, that square foot of space would earn $20 a year in profit for its dealer. A spark plug, on the other hand, might earn only one dollar in profit, and turn over fifteen times a year, for an annual profit of $15 per square foot. But a square foot of shelf space holds many more spark plugs than it does batteries. Therefore, use the extra space to sell spark plugs.

Such analysis was simply common sense, but no dealer had time to do it himself product by product. Besides, he might have fallen in love with batteries and that $5 margin: such things happened. Now, thanks to the Moneymaker and GMROI, the computer, the King of Reason, did a dealer's thinking for him. And not just for his own store, but on a "benchmark basis," which allowed any dealer to compare his results with two other "peer group stores" anywhere in the country.

Then Philbrick would walk into a dealer's store and rearrange paint cans into vertical patterns – "vertical striping," he called it – so that all the most profitable items sat in a customer's "visual strike zone," the area from his knees to his nose. The competitive combinations were endless. Philbrick had broken the game of retailing down into dozens of brand new, infinitely detailed subgames. He had studied two main plays, purchasing and distribution, and invented a game of infinitesimal strategies. Philbrick had transformed football into baseball.

Dawson, an "intuitive" merchant, thought Philbrick's innovations were just one more foolish trick from a "numbers man." But the numbers spoke for themselves. In 1975, when Philbrick showed up, the average Canadian Tire dealer replaced his inventory 4.3 times a year. By the end of 1975, the best dealers were turning over their inventories 8.6 times a year.

In this freewheeling, "zero bureaucracy" environment, of course, Muncaster's real sleight of hand went unnoticed. By handing his dealers the tools with which to make ever more money for themselves – by playing to their middle-class greed, the pure, odorless fuel that drove Dealerland – Muncaster obscured the fact that head office, and not Dealerland, now drove the corporation. (The change in nomenclature was significant: the Home Office of A.J.'s era had been replaced by the more technocratic phrase "head office.") Muncaster's management structure was occasionally criticized by some niggardly stock market analyst for being too flat, for lacking a hierarchy, but *flatness* was what made working at Tire so terrific in the first place. Hobbs could sign checks. Budgets were unheard of. Instead, each executive prepared an annual forecast of his financial needs – and that was that. Muncaster often saw the forecasts only after the fact, as a matter of form.

IN this happy fashion, ten years slid by. Muncaster was surprised: he had intended to stay only seven. But Tire kept changing, and every time it changed, the picture became rosier, and the Quarterback's Vision became more impressive. The number of stores in the Tire chain had grown slowly during Muncaster's reign, from 225 to 295, but the stores and the company were radically different. In 1966, the year he became president, Canadian Tire had sales of $97.8 million. Muncaster had pushed sales up an *average* of twenty percent a year every year thereafter, to $683 million in 1976. Profits exploded from $3.6 million to $25 million in 1975. Working capital? Where the company once spent $4 million a year, Muncaster now breezily disposed of $33 million annually. Canadian Tire was everyone's favorite growth stock, an exercise in capitalistic democracy, and proof of the democracy of capitalism. Dean's team was playing the game as it had never been played before. Around the office, and even on Bay Street, Dean's team was known as The Silver Seven. They were named in their later years for the thick silver hair many of them sported. The club included Muncaster; Kron; Hobbs; Dawson; Peter Edmondson, later vice-president of dealer relations; Fred Sasaki, the company's treasurer and secretary of the board; and Alex Barron, the chairman.

The strange thing was that for all Muncaster's rationality, the pleasure of the enterprise lay in more than just results. Muncaster's boys were friends, part of an emotional team. The thrill of male bonding, of superheated intelligence dedicated to one almighty, unambivalent goal! Therein lay the unmentioned secret of successful business. Of course you didn't call it "bonding": hell, no. That was too . . . weird. It was too hard to describe. But for years afterward, no matter how far afield former Tiremen travelled, no matter how high or low their fortunes veered, no matter what greatness they subsequently achieved, each and every one remembered Muncaster as a pure shining white light, as if they were old Catholic women remembering a single kiss from the Pope himself. "I think what's always kept people here," one of the team later recalled, "is this sense of commitment. You talk about a sense of family. If you didn't make it, you were a dead man. But there was a sense of righteousness, that if you earned your spurs, *you were always a part of it.*" The sentiment was irrational, to be sure, but it was a charming illusion.

9

TROUBLE IN MIND

BOARDS OF DIRECTORS are the platypuses of the corporate world – unlikely animals at best. By law, directors of a public company are responsible to a company's shareholders, whose interests directors must protect. Ideally, a board of directors is a company's superego, an objective, uninvolved, arm's-length referee of last resort as to what is and what isn't wise behavior. Directors of public companies have little to do with the day-to-day operations of their wards. They oversee a company's operations four times a year or, if the board is exceptionally energetic, month by month. They determine a company's overall direction; set executive salaries and bonuses; monitor senior management's performance.

Other than that, directors collect fees and feel important. At Canadian Tire in the late 1980s, in return for eight meetings a year, a directorship was worth a lot of free air travel and $12,800 a year (the low end of the national range), not including fees for committee work, stock options, and bonuses. Thirteen thousand dollars a year is not a fortune, but the fee is largely symbolic: perhaps the most important job a director does is to provide solace and support to the company's chief executive officer. For that reason if no other, chief executives tend to choose as their directors men they like, and who like them in return. Sometimes this becomes a bad habit. Inbred boards were directly responsible for Eaton's wallowing in the toilet of unprofitability in the 1960s, for the

Hudson's Bay Company's disastrous investments and debt-collecting in the late 1970s, and for the turgid performance of both the mining industry and the pulp and paper business throughout much of the same period.

Muncaster's board at Canadian Tire, by fascinating contrast, was run by the same men who operated the company. "I could never understand," a longtime Canadian Tire executive pondered recently, "how you could have members of the board who were also reporting as vice-presidents to Dean Muncaster." The company's superego was also its id and its ego, its fingers and thumbs, its mind and body. Muncaster's job on the board was to act as a buffer between the family and his management team. Among themselves, Muncaster's team referred to the boss's maneuvering on the board as "managing the gap."

Muncaster felt quite at home sitting around a table with men of like mind. This was no surprise: by 1968 he had engineered a board of directors very much to his advantage. The board comprised Alex Barron, Tire's chairman and Muncaster's ally; Muncaster; Robert (Robin) Law, the company's lawyer, who had joined the company at Barron's suggestion contemporaneously with Muncaster, and had become one of Muncaster's most trusted advisers; Dick Billes, who still bore a grudge against A.J.; Hobbs, who was part of Muncaster's management team; two dealers, both of whom had to be approved by the Billes family, but who were also keen supporters of Muncaster's highly profitable innovations; a representative of National Trust, who invariably voted with management; and, as the representatives of A.J.'s family, Fred and David Billes. Fred and David and A.J. still controlled thirty percent of Tire's voting shares, but their power was neutralized by everyone else on the board, who let Dean's team do as it pleased.

Worse still, from Fred's and David's point of view, Muncaster and his colleagues on the board had their own ideas about their fiduciary responsibilities to the company's shareholders.

Muncaster had no patience for the idea that a family with less than ten percent of a public company's equity should determine its destiny, especially as the non-voting and voting shares traded on the stock exchange at roughly the same price.[1] The very notion was undemocratic. It was irrational. In Dean Muncaster's mind, the public owned the company, and he and his management team ran it for the public. Period. Voting control was irrelevant.

But the politics of Tire's boardroom consisted of far more than mathematical formulae. They were a miracle of boardroom legerdemain orchestrated in large part by Alex Ethelred Barron, the chairman of Canadian Tire's board of directors, and Robert Law, the company's secretary.

The son of a dentist in Paris, Ontario, Barron had arrived in Toronto in 1935 at the age of seventeen to work as a stockbroker. Three years later he joined Fry & Company – later Burns Fry Limited – a Bay Street investment firm of which he eventually became president. It was Alex Barron who convinced J.W. Billes to make Canadian Tire a public company in 1944, and it was on Barron that J.W. subsequently bestowed the chairmanship of the company. Barron – later accompanied by Muncaster – was Canadian Tire's front man on Bay Street. Tall, gray, thoughtful, of faintly Roman bearing and impeccably dressed (he had a fondness for three-piece suits with lapelled vests), Barron was the very opposite of the jutting, emotional, slapped-together A.J. Billes. If A.J. felt uncomfortable on his infrequent visits to Bay Street – "There's nothing as artificial to me as Bay Street and the Granite Club," A.J. would say – Barron was *the* professional director. And whereas A.J. used to ask Fred Sasaki, the company's loyal treasurer, to accompany him to board meetings, Barron, as a consumate financier, always had the facts and figures at his fingertips.

[1]By 1975, thanks to constant stock splits, there were 7,652,358 non-voting Tire shares and 3,450,000 voting shares outstanding in the marketplace. A.J. and his children owned 1,021,625, or about nine percent of the total.

No wonder. On his own and through his association with
Colonel Maxwell Meighen, Canadian General Investments
and Bud McDougald, the founder (with E.P. Taylor) of Argus
Corp., Barron was a director of some of the most prominent
companies in Canada, including Canada Trust, Domtar,
Great Canadian Oil Sands (in which A.J. was another early
investor), London Life Insurance, Dominion Stores, and
Standard Broadcasting Corporation.

Barron was also always a gentleman.[2] After his wife died, he
actually asked Dean Muncaster's permission to date Muncaster's secretary Beverley, whom he later married. If Muncaster
was a buffer between the family and management, Barron was
a buffer between the family and Muncaster. He was also
Muncaster's tutor in the boardroom. Around Canadian Tire,
the general opinion was that "Alex brought Dean along."

Because A.J. and his family as owners held sufficient power
to make life difficult for management's radical ideas, Barron
stick-handled them through the boardroom with extreme
caution. If, as happened in 1971, Muncaster wanted for the
first time in the company's history to borrow money to
expand, instead of issuing stock or drawing on profits, Barron
would first canvas all the members of the board privately. He
knew A.J. abhorred debt. If half the directors agreed to the
proposal – not unlikely, given the way Muncaster had structured the board – Barron would raise the issue at a board
meeting, but only for discussion. Behind the scenes, he would
continue his canvassing, his gentle persuasion.

Only when he knew everyone would vote for the new plan
would he let it come to a vote. Within the company's
management offices, the process of canvass-discuss-canvass-

[2]Some would say too much so. In 1978, Bud McDougald, the founder of
Argus Corp., died. To Barron's shock, a brash young man named Conrad
Black appeared on the scene and took control of Argus from McDougald's
wife, Barron, and others. Throughout the fracas, Barron continued to
behave like an Edwardian gentleman caught in a time warp.

vote was known as "Alex's four stages of approval." Robin Law wrote up the minutes that outlined the board's decisions. Law, whose grandfather had been the principal of Knox College and a major-league Presbyterian, who had grown up in the Town of Mount Royal in Montreal, who had studied at McGill and Osgoode, and whose every impulse as a lawyer was to negotiation and settlement, shared Barron's concerns for decorum, and his minutes reflected Barron's desire to show the board as achieving harmonious consensus on the issues before it.

BUT Tire's board meetings were in fact anything but parables of peace and good behavior. Canadian Tire board meetings had a reputation on Bay Street for being the best show in town. The two main attractions were A.J. Billes and his son Fred.

After turning his company over to Muncaster, A.J. had concerned himself for several years with its tire marketing program. Bill Dawson, Muncaster's vice-president of marketing, didn't appreciate the interference, however, and considered A.J. devious to the point of incompetence, and believed he had fired the old man. By 1971, with nothing else to do, A.J. was trying to insinuate himself into the company's affairs: by now, he claimed, he had put sufficient distance between himself and management. He had also discovered that he didn't have a serious heart condition. In the boardroom, he launched a new crusade: having installed profit-sharing at head office, A.J. wanted to see it adopted throughout Dealerland.

Hobbs, for one, and Muncaster, for another, thought this was a dumb idea, at least as A.J. conceived of it – which is to say as a program administered from head office by A.J. A.J. considered that the dealers were being too niggardly with their staff; he wanted to collect a percentage of their profits and redistribute them through Dealerland as he saw fit, either on the basis of store-by-store performance or as a reflection of the corporation's overall profitability.

Muncaster could and did count on Hobbs to make his

objections to this plan known at the boardroom table. Hobbs agreed that the dealers were greedy; but he considered it foolish to lump all the dealers' profits together, or even to take a straight percentage of them store by store, as that would penalize the better operations. As well, Hobbs knew head office had commandeered all but one aspect of a dealer's business: who a dealer hired, and how a dealer paid the staff he hired. Take that away from the dealer, and there was nothing left for the poor guy to do to justify his huge earnings. Nor did Hobbs relish the idea of A.J. fidgeting once again with the company's fortunes – and A.J.'s plan would have plopped A.J. right back in the middle of the company's affairs, something neither Hobbs nor Muncaster wanted. "Profit-sharing for A.J. was almost a religion," Muncaster once remarked. "He has characterized it at times as the only answer to communism." Hobbs was willing to go even further. "I have always maintained," he said, "that A.J. would do *anything* to implement his profit-sharing plan, even if it meant the destruction of the company." Hobbs often said as much at board meetings, in a very loud voice, while he banged his fist on the table. As always, Muncaster let Hobbs fight the battle. In the end, a system of profit-sharing was installed throughout Dealerland, but the amount contributed out of a dealer's profits, above a certain minimum, was left up to individual dealers.

A.J. was a sideshow, however, compared to Fred Billes. By the early 1970s Fred was in his late thirties, but he was no less erratic and temperamental than he had been as a child of six.[3] Like Dick Billes, Fred took the dealers' view on board matters.

---

[3]Fred was the only member of A.J.'s family who was active on the board. David sat on the board and voted his shares with Fred, but otherwise took no part in the company's affairs, beyond insisting his photograph not be published in the company's annual reports. Martha wanted to join the board, but she was still considered the wrong sex. In 1970 she began to accost members of the board – her brothers, father, and Alex Barron among them – about a seat on the board commensurate with her substantial

He was not devoid of good ideas. Fred possessed a dealer's front-line knowledge of what did and did not work in the trenches. Like many dealers, he became impatient with head office's caution, its fondness for analysis and re-analysis. Muncaster's team studied the possibility of television advertising ad nauseam before launching the company's first (and highly successful) electronic advertising campaign in the late 1970s. Fred had insisted it would work from the start.

Nor was he shy about problems in the company's shipping and adjusting departments, whose mistakes Fred experienced firsthand. The trouble was that instead of simply complaining to the adjusting department – which he did anyway, often in language that could curl plywood – Fred would bring up these matters, which Muncaster regarded as picayune, right in the boardroom.

It made for quite a scene. One minute the board is discussing a matter of broad corporate policy, and in the next, Fred is covering the boardroom table with . . . defective toasters. Or cans of paint. He actually lugs them into the boardroom and flings them across the table. Outrage! Such things are not done! Canadian Tire is no longer a hardware store; it is a national institution! Nor is Fred entirely rational in his tirades. Here he is, three hundred and more glowering pounds. Perhaps he is sporting one of his distinctive gray moiré Ultrasuede blazers, and a tie with a knot the size of a peach . . . somehow Fred's clothes always look as if they are about to explode and fly away. Or maybe he is doing his watch thing. Fred has a strange occasional habit of sometimes wearing his wristwatch on the *outside* of the sleeve of his

shareholding. Martha claims their reply was " 'Get lost, babe. We were here first. We're also male. We know about the business world. And you don't.' So I said 'Bye-bye, Tire. Bye-bye, Toronto.' And went to Calgary." There she started Marlore Enterprises Ltd., a successful oil and gas company. She was not to say hello again to Toronto and Canadian Tire until 1980.

turtleneck jersey. This is a very distinctive, snappy thing to do: one doesn't have to pull up one's shirtsleeves. Maybe it is because Fred is a big man, with big arms. Maybe it is because Fred has always had a thing about efficiency, the result of the thwarted engineer's genes that course through the Billes blood. The only thing is, the watch trick is a little disconcerting to those who see it. Disconcerting? It is . . . weird. Here is Fred, shouting on about the toasters or the paint cans or the adjusting department, gesticulating . . . while down at the other end of the table, Muncaster is glaring at him, a silent stone of resentment, the flesh cannoli popping in and out of his thin mouth . . . *Irrational! Brrzzzzzt! Please sit down! . . .*

Years later, Hobbs couldn't recall Fred's boardroom antics without laughing. He certainly didn't have a high opinion of Fred; indeed, it bordered on the vindictive. Fred was, by most reports, one of the most practical, hands-on board members at the company, but somehow he offended Hobbs. "The conversations and the arguments were endless," Hobbs explained. "And in the fifteen years or so I was on the board they never stopped . . . Fred was difficult because he was bad-tempered, volatile, ill-mannered, and not very bright. Alex would come to Fred, and say 'Fred, what do you think about this?' Sometimes it would take as long as three or four minutes for everyone to understand what Fred was talking about. He would wander all around. He might talk for five minutes, insult most members of management, and some of our customers, and then he'd say, 'Well, I don't really have anything to say about this, so I'll shut up.' Half the people in the room were now furious, and he had said nothing." Fred had committed the cardinal sin of having emotions.

Fred's management of his store at Yonge Street and Davenport Road, the crown jewel in the Tire chain, didn't go over well either. Oh, Fred knew how to make money: he was generous with his employees and he could control expenses with the best of them; but, in the opinion of management, he maximized his margins by refusing to stock many low-margin items the great minds at head office wanted dealers to carry to reinforce Canadian Tire's value-conscious image. Fred also irritated the head office boys because he didn't take their rules very seriously: he owned the company, after all. "You fucking office guys don't understand anything," he might tell an employee in the marketing department. "If you didn't stand up to him," one of his targets recalled, "you got nowhere."

But Fred's store *was* an eyesore. The showpiece of Tiredom was old and rundown and as disorganized as a teenager's bedroom, and Fred made little effort to improve it. He didn't care much, outwardly, for appearances . . . except, say, for the odd conference at the University of Western Ontario, where Muncaster would discover that Fred had registered himself as the president of Canadian Tire. Muncaster was openly embarrassed by the store at Yonge and Davenport. His friends on Bay Street would drive by Fred's ramshackle kingdom and wonder what Muncaster was doing with the chain. "It's always been the feeling that the field men would not have permitted the perpetuation of that store if it had been anyone but Fred," a former field man has admitted. Nor was it possible to build a second competitive store in Toronto's downtown core: as Muncaster said, "Fred Billes controlled the core of downtown Toronto," and resisted any competition in his neighborhood.

BUT if life at Canadian Tire on the inside sometimes resembled a scene from a Three Stooges movie, to the outside world the company was a paragon of progressive Canadian management. Muncaster's performance as president had made him both a wealthy man – his shares in Canadian Tire were now worth more than $2 million – and a well-known one. Bay Street analysts love a sure thing, and they touted Tire's stock to the skies. They had long appreciated Muncaster's habit of predicting that the company would grow twenty percent a year – whereupon he made the joint do just that. Muncaster was the only executive at Tire who talked to the investment community and the press, much to the irritation of Hobbs and Dawson. Naturally, it was Muncaster who became the hero.

What this meant was that by the late 1970s Dean Muncaster was not just the president and chief executive officer of Canadian Tire, one of the best growth companies in Canada: he was possibly the most recognized name in Canadian business.[4] Someone should have named a candy bar after him. The praise was well-deserved, but Muncaster had also worked hard to polish his reputation. In 1971 he was appointed chairman of Taskforce Hydro, a provincial commission set up to reorganize Ontario Hydro, the province's huge utility; by the late 1970s, he sat on the boards of half a dozen corporations, and had co-founded the Business Council on National Issues. Muncaster's office at Tire was on the eleventh floor (the lowest of the six that Tire occupied) of the company's headquarters at 2180 Yonge Street, a glass and steel tube south of Eglinton Avenue to which the company moved in 1978, at last leaving behind the rabbit warren above the main store at Yonge and Davenport. He sat next to the personnel and accounting departments, where he spent most of his time, just like an ordinary employee. But by 1978, he was spending less and less time there, and more and more time on his outside pursuits. "Sure I liked being there where things were happening," Muncaster said by way of explanation.

Those were the heady days, the late 1970s. Muncaster was often compared, publicly, to John Turner, a Toronto lawyer widely touted as the country's next prime minister. Turner was the best-known businessman in political life; Muncaster was the best-known capitalist in the corporate world. In the mid-1970s, journalists tapped Muncaster for proclamations

---

[4]When Walter Muncaster, Dean's father, retired to Owen Sound from Sudbury in the late 1960s, the local newspaper thought he was the founder of the company, and dubbed him Mr. Canadian Tire.

on everything from separatism to the Anti-Inflation Board.
"What do you think is wrong with the way Canada is
managed?" a journalist would ask. Sometimes the journalists,
the women, developed crushes on him; he had a power that
way that was unexpected, given his unprepossessing looks.
Dean would gaze back into her eyes and without a moment's
hesitation reply, "I don't think Prime Minister Trudeau has
ever thought of himself as the chief executive officer of this
country. . . ''

Dean Muncaster had travelled a long way from Sudbury, but
Sudbury was never far away in Muncaster's mind. He had a
slight inferiority complex about it. The bright kid from
Sudbury never quite lost his sense of being a hick in the
Toronto big leagues. "I had some of that," Muncaster said one
day not long ago. "I had come out of Sudbury. And being at
Western amongst the Upper Canada College types, you were
pretty conscious of the fact that you had something to prove
to these people." But having by now proven himself, what
was there left to experience? Why, the normal residues of an
accomplished professional life: fame, fortune, and the despair
of emptiness.

As Muncaster became famous, subtle and not-so-subtle
changes began to bend his personal life. By the early 1980s he
had divorced twice. This wasn't unusual in Tireland, of
course: Hobbs, Dawson, Peter Edmonson (the other frat
brother who later served as vice-president of dealer relations), and a raft of dealers were all known for their ability to
go through wives and girlfriends, sometimes one another's. It
was the job, the constant work, the total marriage of man and
corporation that did it. But Muncaster had never been a flashy
man, and his new glimmering life made him the subject of
considerable speculation within the company.

Muncaster referred to his first wife, Grace, a "down-to-earth
girl" he had married in Sudbury, as "my great leveller."
Among some of Muncaster's closest friends, Grace's name
evoked a pained wince. "Grace matched Dean's thinking

ability, so she was good that way," a dealer and friend of Muncaster's later remembered. "But she lacked the social graces of a president's wife." Grace was *too* down-to-earth: she swore like a teenager. Several friends considered her a social liability; many others could see the split coming. Muncaster's second wife was a secretary who later became the manager of a rock band. A rock band! At Canadian Tire! The collective mind boggled. By then Muncaster had moved from the quiet, respectable suburbs of Brian Cliff Drive, where he lived opposite Dick Billes, to an apartment in the ManuLife Centre at Bloor and Bay streets. People began to say the fast life had affected Mr. Rationality.

But if anything suggested Dean Muncaster was developing an awareness of his own image, it was his hair. The evolution of Muncaster's coiffure in the boom years at Tire was one of the uncelebrated semiotic wonders of Canadian capitalism. His hair was incredible. When Muncaster joined Canadian Tire, he wore a brush-cut. It was not a pretty sight. The brush-cut was an inch long, and stood straight up. The cut, his high hairline, his prominent brow, his round, fleshy face and his thick-framed glasses gave Muncaster a distinct resemblance to the president of the high-school rocket club. This look was oddly perfect for the president of Canadian Tire, however: here was a no-nonsense man, unconcerned with appearances and pretension, the anthropomorphization of the company he ran.

In 1970, however, though he still wore his thick, black Nana Mouskouri glasses, Muncaster started to grow his hair – not much, at first, but enough to have it "styled" into a smooth and wavy brush-cut cap. By now, like the rest of North America, Muncaster – still only thirty-seven years old, after all – was wearing suits with coast-to-coast lapels and ties that might have been designed by a numerologist on magic mushrooms. "Being marketers," Robin Law later said, "[management was] always style conscious." A.J. Billes would have laughed the idea out of the room, but. . . . In 1972,

Muncaster's hair was distinctly long, which is to say, about as long as the Beatles' on the Ed Sullivan Show.

There are those, of course, who will claim such signs are irrelevant. Perhaps they are. But among the rank and file at Tire they were hints, confirmations of the rumors that Dean Muncaster was becoming style-conscious, even vain. There were rumors that he was bored. "It's very easy to get stars in your eyes from your own success," Bill Dawson once observed, and maybe there was something to that too.

ALL of which might have been irrelevant had comeuppance not arrived in the form of the dealer revolution of 1977. The year was a difficult one for Canadian Tire. As Tire had grown, it had become more vulnerable to competition. Dean Muncaster and his team weren't content to run Tire as if it were their own; they intended to transform it into a department store, and thus a creation of their own making. In doing so they had driven the company into Indian territory. In 1969, automotive parts and accessories, Tire's stronghold, accounted for more than half the company's total shipments to its dealers. By 1976, that ratio had changed radically: now household hardware and leisure goods made up two-thirds of the company's total business. Automotive parts were solid things, but they weren't the stuff of glamorous retailing. The competition was not amused by Tire's trespasses into new markets. In the fall of 1977, Tire's enemies – notably Consumers Distributing, the Hudson's Bay Company, and Michelin Tires – reduced their prices and forced Tire to slice its profit margins by two points.

Strapped at the same time with the cost of Hobbs' store expansion program and Philbrick's computer gizmos, Dealerland panicked. A third of Tire's dealers were losing money. This had never happened before. Tire shares hissed from a high of $43 to a low of $25¾. Profits were hit hard: a 30.7 percent gain in 1974 sank to 13 percent in 1976 and 12.8 percent in 1977.

Not a loss, mind you; not even a profitless year. But for the
Canadian Tire Family, which had been weaned on growth,
even the slightest blip in the company's riches induced
paranoia. That fact was not lost on A.J. Billes and his cohort
from the Imperial Oil takeover rumor conspiracy of 1963,
Alan Warren.

Warren had made such a nuisance of himself as the dealers'
representative at head office in the early 1960s that Muncaster
and Hobbs had exiled him to a dealership in North Bay. North
Bay was a fat dealership but it was a long way from head office
and the caressing shores of Lake Ontario. A.J. had already bent
the dealers' losses into one more argument for profit-sharing
in Dealerland. For Warren, the losses reopened the door to
head office. That fall in Montreal at Dealerland's biennial
convention, Warren and others undraped a survey of dealer
opinion on head office's management team. Dawson came in
for his share of abuse, but the brunt was reserved for Richard
Hobbs.

"Alan Warren was always leading revolutions," Hobbs
would later say, "because he always thought he should be
running the company. . . . It was all politics . . . and it should
never have been allowed. If I'd been president, it wouldn't
have happened."

But Richard Hobbs wasn't president; Dean Muncaster was.
Hobbsy's attitude to the dealers, as Muncaster understood it,
was "if you guys were only a little smarter, you wouldn't have
this problem." Muncaster's answer was to placate them, to
extend loans and grants and reduce their rents. It was true that
within five years the "overstored" dealers would be Tire's
biggest moneymakers. But that was the future. Hobbs objected
to Muncaster's concessions so strenuously that, by late fall, he
had lost his footing at Tire. "The problem," Hobbs later
explained, "was, I wasn't getting enough support from Dean.
And that upset me, because I had always fought Dean's battles.
I'm not sure there wasn't some justification, but fundamentally I expected support and I didn't get it." Perhaps Muncaster

resented Hobbs' open desire to be president of Canadian Tire; if he did, he certainly didn't show it. Whatever the reasons, Richard Hobbs was no longer a shield between the family and his friend Dean Muncaster; Hobbs had become a liability. One morning early the next spring, Richard Hobbs walked into Dean Muncaster's office on the eleventh floor. "Dean," he said, "I don't need this bullshit."

Muncaster said very little in reply. Hobbs stared at him. Finally, Hobbs spoke. "I'm going back to my office to do my job. You talk to the board, and see what compensation you can come up with. Because you owe me." Hobbs, ever concerned with money, was drawing a salary of $125,000 a year – "totally ridiculous" – largely, he felt, because Muncaster was unwilling to ask the board for a raise for his senior managers.

Richard Hobbs and William Dawson left Canadian Tire that spring, in 1978. Years later their departure was often interpreted as the first crack in the Muncaster foundation. No one mentioned it at the time, of course. The boys in head office pooled some money and bought Bill Dawson a huge nylon tire in a stand as a goodbye present. It bore an inscription on the sidewall: *W.R. Dawson 140 mil. 900 mil.* – the size of the corporation when Dawson arrived and when Dawson left.

Tire's board was even more generous to Dawson: it granted him a dealership. Dawson always maintained that his move from Dealerland to head office had been the biggest financial mistake of his life. Pasturing unpopular executives out to Moneyland (as head office staffers called Dealerland) had been a Canadian Tire tradition for years. The creative friction between head office and Dealerland eventually destroyed the effectiveness of any vice-president of marketing, and a dealership was his safety valve, the guarantee that allowed him to do his unpopular head office job while he had it.

The board, however, and in particular, Hobbs believed, the Billeses, refused to extend a similar favor to Hobbs. Hobbs was too feisty, too much the independent, to be kept at bay in the ranks of the dealers. He was a symbol and a scapegoat: he had run the company as if it were his own, and that was a sin the Billeses couldn't forgive. Ownership had its privileges, however much Richard Hobbs tried to believe otherwise. In return, Hobbs never forgave the board – and particularly Fred Billes. "Those guys were brilliant," Arch Malcolm, A.J.'s petroleum man, and the survivor of half a dozen coups, said years later, "but they didn't listen. And that's why they aren't here anymore. They didn't listen. You can't do that. And Dean Muncaster, he's probably one of the smartest men in the country. But he couldn't handle conflict. Never could. And that's the bottom line."

Too true, Arch. Dean Muncaster had a nose for the line of least resistance. He was a dealer's son, and a dealer's son he remained to the end of his days at Tire. He couldn't challenge his father's crowd. There are some loyalties that are too deep to reach, too profound to change. The only question was, with Hobbs gone and no one left to fight the Billeses for him, how much longer could Dean Muncaster last? A truly rational man should have known the answer well ahead of time.

10

THE LION AND THE FOX

DEAN MUNCASTER WAS a wise and modest man, and not the sort to try to alter human nature. He played the cards fate dealt to him. Perhaps it is impossible to grow up in Sudbury, a company town, and not be that way. Muncaster did what he had to, and kept his hopes to himself. After Richard Hobbs banished himself from Canadian Tire, Muncaster calmly nominated one of his own best friends, John Kron, as Tire's new executive vice-president of operations. Kron was the most phlegmatic man on Muncaster's team; better still, the Billes family trusted him.

Shortly before the board meeting in December, 1978, at which Kron's appointment was approved by the company's directors, A.J. Billes called Kron down to his nest of an office, tucked away behind the mailroom. A.J. was still formally out of the management picture, still cooling his heels, still trying, behind the scenes, to wend his way back into the company's affairs. He was, however, Tire's founder, its president emeritus, and the company's internal figurehead, a living, walking inspiration to the line employees, who venerated the old man. It was considered good form to humor the old guy. "John," A.J. said, "I don't trust Dean. So we want you to be our main man." A.J. wanted Kron to be his mole in management.

"Well," Kron said, "if those are the terms of the job, I don't want it."

A.J. backed down, and Kron immediately reported the

conversation to Muncaster. Muncaster simply shrugged. What could he do? A.J. was a devious old man. Muncaster figured he was better off defending his performance as chief executive officer of Canadian Tire by speaking the universal language of results.

Dean Muncaster therefore applied himself to the task of making Canadian Tire his company in fact if not in name. To do so he began to steer the corporation into new and exotic locales. Crisscrossing Canada throughout the late 1970s to tout Tire's stock to financial analysts, Muncaster told and retold the same story: once Canadian Tire's network of dealerships reached 400 franchises sometime in 1981 – there were already 303 stores in the chain in 1977 – the company would be forced to expand beyond Canada. Growth was the lifeblood of retailing.

Muncaster had taken his first step toward an international empire in mid-June of 1979, when Tire bought five percent of McEwan's Ltd., the largest hardware chain in Australia, for $1.8 million. Muncaster had been attracted to Australia, an unusual choice of destination at a time when most retailers were looking south to the United States, by Tom Luxton, of the Luxton family who owned McEwan's. Tire's stake in McEwan's was to grow, according to a complicated series of advances and convertible debentures, to 36 percent, once the Australian foreign-investment review board approved the purchase. The threat of a takeover of McEwan's by a competing company, however, forced Muncaster and Alex Barron to push the acquisition of McEwan's past the Canadian Tire board without the benefit of Barron's four stages of approval. The sum of money was insignificant: as Muncaster pointed out, McEwan's was simply a practise run, a "toe in the water" of international expansion.

There wasn't much time, in any event, to think about Australia that busy summer in 1979. Within two weeks of the Australian purchase, Muncaster dropped more long-awaited news on the investment community. Canadian Tire was moving into British Columbia.

For many Canadians, Canada is an unlikely political entity, with very few good excuses for its existence. British Columbia has always been the unlikeliest member of that unlikely Dominion. Tacked on to one end of the country, isolated by the Rocky Mountains and exorbitant freight rates, and burdened by costly industrial real estate (up to three times that of Toronto, at the time) and costly labor (40 percent higher), British Columbia qualified as the retail equivalent of Rubik's Cube. When Don Graham and Vern Forster showed up in Dean Muncaster's office with a plan to open up British Columbia, everyone thought they had toys in their attics.

Graham and Forster were a pair of madmen. Graham was an MBA graduate from Western who had cut his teeth at IBM. Forster was a dentist's son and chartered accountant from Westmount, in Montreal. Both men had been made dealers in 1973, and both had won Dealerland's coveted Pacesetter Award in 1978. Other than that, Graham and Forster were as different as night and day. Graham was well-kept, thoughtful, rational, and a brilliant systems man. Forster wore a beard, was older, liked to shout and sing and tell dirty jokes, and was an equally brilliant salesman. Both men were devotees of military history. Forster was especially fond of Sir Winston Churchill: he often described his pell-mell manner of running a Canadian Tire store by invoking one of Churchill's war cheers, "Second Best Today!" A lot of dealers didn't understand what he meant. Forster liked to explain that he had started his Canadian Tire career in Nova Scotia. "If they're gonna give Canada an enema," he would then say, "that's where they should stick the hose in."

Muncaster had met Forster and Graham in 1973 when, still training to be dealers, the duo suggested a joint venture between themselves and head office to create a new sub-chain of Canadian Tire automotive specialty stores in Toronto.

Muncaster had handed the idea to Hobbs, who rejected it because 1. Tire didn't do partnerships with dealers; 2. dealers had never owned multiple stores; 3. Forster and Graham wanted to erect the new stores in downtown Toronto, in Fred Billes's backyard.[1]

Now, five years later, Graham and Forster had another plan: to open twenty-three Canadian Tire stores in British Columbia, *all of which Forster and Graham would own.* The resulting economies of scale were the only way to tame British Columbia's retailing eccentricities. They had conceived the idea over a bottle of Glenfiddich single malt scotch at Toronto's Royal Winter Fair in November, 1978. The Royal Winter Fair was not *un occasion* where one normally found Canadian Tire dealers, but Forster's daughter was mad about horses. They made their first pitch to the company in December, 1978. "It was almost like preaching to the converted," Forster remembered of selling the idea to Muncaster. In February, 1979, with Muncaster's support, Tire's board of directors unanimously approved the deal. Canadian Tire had reached the West Coast.

But Australia and British Columbia were small potatoes next to Muncaster's main course – expansion into the United States. Muncaster had talked publicly about growing south since 1977. Throughout 1979, 1980, and 1981, Muncaster, John Kron, and Gary Philbrick searched for a suitable company to acquire.

The marketplace was ecstatic, to judge from the reaction of the financial press and financial analysts at every major brokerage house in Toronto. A U.S. acquisition was roundly interpreted as Muncaster's next triumph. Beneath the praise lay a more profound hope: that the unbeatable Dean Muncaster would trounce the Americans at the retailing game.

---

[1]Thirteen years later, Canadian Tire decided that this freestanding auto store was workable after all.

Canadian Tire was to become corporate Canada's version of hockey.

The obvious place to buy a company, Muncaster told his eager audience, was in the southwestern United States, in the so-called Sunbelt, a region whose resource-based economy was growing as fast as the price of oil, which by March of 1981 had hit $40 U.S. a barrel and showed no signs of stopping. Everyone wrote that down. Even John Kron got into the act, predicting that oil would rise to $100 a barrel by 1990. Everyone wrote that down, too. Of course, John Kron was a conservative man: think tanks in the United States were predicting a price three times that high.

Finally, on November 17, 1981, Canadian Tire announced its intention to purchase White Stores Inc., a bedraggled eighty-one-store home- and auto-supply chain operating in twelve Sunbelt states. The price was $45 million, American, and was considered a bargain. White's was not a spectacular company: owned by Household Merchandising Inc., a finance company ("Never Borrow Money Needlessly . . ."), White's was little more than a source of customers to whom Household could sell credit. But Kron had visited the stores in the spring of 1981 and had declared them worthy, and by the fall Tire's board approved the purchase, again unanimously. White's wasn't making any real money, despite annual sales of $150 million, but that was because it didn't have the Canadian Tire system behind it. Muncaster predicted that in two years, with a $45-million makeover, White's would be one more shining star in the Canadian Tire universe.

It would take a whole year before the good news evaporated, but so far, whenever his chipmunk mug appeared in the paper, Dean Muncaster still wore a wide smile.

THE only hitch in Muncaster's expansion program, in hindsight, was not that it didn't work, though that would prove to be the case, but that it made him a hero. From the very

beginning, A.J. resented Muncaster's big moves. It seemed
that A.J. wanted to be the center of attention.

Of course he didn't put it that way. Instead, by the late
1970s, A.J. had begun to accuse Dean Muncaster of losing
touch with the company A.J. had given him to run. As A.J.
saw it, his adopted heir had become "wrapped up in his
own potential."

The difficulties Muncaster's expansion plans ran into
almost immediately did nothing to put A.J.'s mind at rest. The
fact that Muncaster and Barron had rammed the McEwan's
proposal through the board without the approval of all the
Billeses was only part of the problem. A.J. had visited
Australia. He and Muriel had been forced to walk through
the rain because the taxi drivers were on strike. That was
enough for A.J.: "I said that kind of a company I didn't want
to have anything to do with, because of the unions," he
later recalled.

Unlike White's and the British Columbia venture, which
were unanimously approved by the entire board, and therefore couldn't be blamed on Muncaster alone, Australia had
been Muncaster's idea – one that quickly came to represent,
in the family's mind, everything that was increasingly
wrong with Dean Muncaster and his management team.

In 1979, Tire's entire board of directors visited Australia. It
was quite a junket. Martha wasn't to join the board for a year,
but she went along as A.J.'s and David's representative. The
board was appalled by what it found. Everyone took a camera,
and Martha took a virtual book of photographs. Here she was
following the lead of Fred, who had taken an infamous earlier
trip to Australia. Fred had taken photographs of several
run-down McEwan's stores. Back in Toronto, Fred staged one
of his boardroom specials and set the pictures out on the
boardroom table. The managing director of McEwan's happened to be in the room at the time. Muncaster was furious:
for years afterward, he wished he had taken a few snapshots

of Fred's equally run-down slum of a store at Yonge and Davenport, and spread *them* out on the boardroom table.

Martha was no easier to contend with. She had lobbied Alex Barron, her father, and anyone else who would listen to let her join Tire's board since the early 1970s. Later she began to commute between Calgary and Toronto to care for her mother Muriel, who had developed cancer. Martha had barely taken her seat in the boardroom in the spring of 1980 when she began to make her presence known to Muncaster. One Martha was her father's daughter, a super-traditionalist committed to the values of the Canadian Tire family that had prospered under A.J.'s reign. The other Martha was a committed feminist who by now genuinely resented the fact that she had been kept out of the family company.

Her resentment leaked out in predictable and unpredictable ways. Her voice popped a register or two when she became upset, and sometimes she sprayed her invective very widely.[2] When her son Owen, whom she had adopted in February, 1970, was awarded a Canadian Tire pin for five years of part-time service, Martha was hurt: she didn't have a five-year service pin. Muncaster could get her going too. In Martha's opinion, Muncaster sometimes seemed less than comfortable around women, and he certainly wasn't used to Martha's questioning. For his part, Muncaster found Martha abrasive, but surprisingly powerful. Martha often went among the dealers to share her doubts about Muncaster's performance. As she was adamantly opposed to the Australian venture, the dealers reacted by placing bets on which way the board would vote on it.

In the end, the board voted against acquiring more of McEwan's and expanding into Australia, and decided instead

[2]Once, while reviewing portions of this book, Martha asked me: "Do you always list Fred, David, and Martha in that order?" She was keen that her name occasionally lead the triumvirate. That is how competitive she could be.

to sell its shares, in 1982, to another buyer for roughly $15 million, thereby recovering at least the book value of its investment, but suffering an actual loss. McEwan's inept management convinced everyone, Muncaster included, that the land of Bruce and Sheila was more trouble than it was worth. Muncaster half expected such an outcome. But the damage was done, and the family took advantage of the Australian retreat to react out of all proportion to the magnitude of the loss. By now Martha seemed convinced that Dean Muncaster was the earthly manifestation of Satan himself. As she later said, "Australia was what convinced the family that management was determined to have its own way no matter what the wishes of the controlling shareholders were."

WITH the Australian experience stuck in the family's craw, Muncaster's British Columbian expansion was that much harder for the Billeses to swallow. The company's move into Winnipeg in 1966 and into Saskatchewan and Alberta in the 1970s had taken longer to pay off than expected: the West's oil- and farm-based economy was less stable than Ontario's, and Tire was a newcomer. Nevertheless, by 1980, sales in Calgary were growing by 40 and 50 percent a year.

British Columbia was especially rocky ground. No sooner had Graham and Forster borrowed $20 million to finance their venture (the company provided another $9 million) than interest rates shot up from 11 percent to 13 percent, and then to 15 percent, and then to 22 percent. To make matters worse, Muncaster couldn't deliver on his promise to allow Graham and Forster to raise their prices above those set at head office. This would have allowed them to offset the hefty freight rates. "We thought we would break even in four years," Graham said recently. "It took nine." Meanwhile the company's retailing strategy in British Columbia underwent more physical changes than a fourteen-year-old boy. The stores were smaller, then bigger, and then smaller; sporting goods and automotive parts were emphasized, de-emphasized, re-emphasized. It was 1988 before Graham and Forster's little enclave earned its way to profitability, by which time it was doing $80 million of business a year.

But A.J.'s objections (and hence Fred's and Martha's) to British Columbia weren't only financial. A.J. decried Muncaster's tampering with Tire's holy "one man, one store" rule – and indeed, with all the rules by which Tire had become the pre-eminent retailing organization in Canada. A.J. couldn't countenance the thought of two dealers owning twenty-three stores; they had too much power at a time when A.J. considered even single-store dealers to be too powerful, thanks to Muncaster's lax ways. Graham and Forster were mavericks even by the wild-ass standards of Dealerland, and A.J. hated that.[3] When he made a trip out to the West Coast to promote profit-sharing – one of many such visits that caused no end of confusion among the dealers – the old man didn't even bother to visit Forster and Graham at their head office in Burnaby, on British Columbia's lower mainland.

But A.J.'s behavior on his philosophical safaris was tame next to Martha's. Martha would arrive on the doorsteps of Canadian Tire's western stores, and depart having left the dealers with the distinct impression that she considered them overpaid and underworked, and that Dean Muncaster's management team "was beginning to lose its direction."

---

[3]Jean Pigott, a Canadian Tire director before she was appointed chairman of the National Capital Commission in Ottawa, considered Muncaster's B.C. venture the source of his difficulties with the family. Pigott was familiar with the peculiar problems that beset family businesses: her own father had been a thorn in her side when she took over Morrison Lamothe Inc., the family's bakery concern. She had the following to say about Tire's B.C. set-up: "This is a family company that made money by doing the same thing year after year after year. I think Dean and the young management had gotten a little bored. And they wanted to try new things. But I don't think the family particularly cared about that. The family was trying to keep it a family business. And the new management team wanted a sophisticated international company."

If anything bothered Dean Muncaster – and he was a hard man to rile – it was this capacity of the Billeses to blame others for their own mistakes. The Billeses had approved the British Columbian expansion. Why was Muncaster the only one blamed for its problems?

Selective memory was certainly a characteristic of A.J.'s – one he had inherited from the collective gene pool of entrepreneurs everywhere. A.J. was devious, but he wasn't burdened with a complicating mind. He saw only what he wanted to see. His patchy consciousness was the source of his immense self-confidence and his energy as an entrepreneur. Like many successful businessmen who overcome human inertia and immense financial odds to create successful companies, A.J. had a quasi-religious view of the world based not on reason but on revelation.

A.J. thought as he talked – and talking to him was like listening to a psychiatrist's patient free-associate. He could say red was black, when that suited him, and then say in the next mental breath that black was red. He had only to say something often enough and . . . hey, presto, it was true! A.J. never felt much need to make two statements face one another. John Keats, the Romantic poet, defined a first-class mind as one that could sustain two contradictory ideas without having a nervous breakdown. A.J. didn't even admit his ideas were contradictory. Muncaster could see the contradictions in A.J.'s theories, but Muncaster was a manager, not an entrepreneur. His education had trained him to be a strategist. Muncaster was a fox, and A.J. was a lion. Entrepreneurs, like lions, prefer the power of will to education's formal rules, its systems of logic, its puny addiction to consistency. The lion in A.J. demanded only one thing of his employees: their complete and unquestioning loyalty. And there, Muncaster had failed him.

PROFIT-SHARING, more than anything else, ate away the bond between Dean Muncaster and his mentor. A.J.'s messianic crusade for profit-sharing had become a personal obsession. He had even been awarded the Order of Canada in 1976 for his pioneering work in the area. It continued to be his mission, even when, over Hobbs' objections, he had seen profit-sharing extended to Dealerland, beginning in the early 1970s and with increasing success over the next decade and a half.

By 1980, half of Tire's dealers offered their employees a cut of the take – itself a huge accomplishment, given the fiery independence with which the dealers ran their franchises. Under Dealerland's profit-sharing system – a system fueled by A.J.'s drive and modified into sanity by dealers Arch Brown in Barrie and Denvil Brown in Ottawa – a dealer paid half of one percent of his gross sales, or a percentage of his profits, whichever was less, into a pool for his staff. The corporation then matched the figure. A large, successful store of 180 employees run by a not-particularly-generous dealer could hand over $260,000 in profits – about $1,450 a year for each employee.

Muncaster was satisfied with the plan as it stood. But A.J. wasn't content. He wanted to see his own variation on the profit-sharing scheme, the so-called "fifty-fifty plan," adopted instead. In essence, A.J.'s new brainwave – and describing it was a trick, because A.J. changed the rules incessantly – guaranteed a dealer a minimum salary of $41,000 a year, or ten percent of his net profits, with the rest split down the middle with his employees.

The dealers thought A.J. was nuts. They knew it would mean less money for them, but because A.J. changed the terms of the plan more often than Wayne Newton changed his clothes, they were never sure exactly how much less. Nor did they react well to the suggestion that head office would tell them how to split the spoils of their labor. Of course that was the main attraction for A.J.: the dealers would turn their profits over to him in his warren behind the mailroom, and he would decide who got what.

A.J. tended to downplay such details. Instead,he praised the fifty-fifty plan in the phrases of a glistening demagogue. The great patriarch prepared videos that took dealers' wives to task for wearing fur coats. He pointed out that he himself, the founder of Canadian Tire, drew a $12,000 salary. He touted his plan as a way for dealers to "develop their own people" and combat the rapid employee turnover that plagued Dealerland. He ranted on about the evils of socialism, and hailed the satisfaction of working for just rewards. In short, A.J. saw himself as Robin Hood, taking from the rich to give to the poor.

Ironically, his railing was often sincere, because A.J. had fallen in love again. When Muriel Billes finally died of cancer on August 13, 1979, he was devastated. Shortly after Muriel's funeral, at which a two-foot-high framed color photograph of A.J. and Muriel was perched on top of the open casket – a nice touch – A.J. moved into Fred and Barbara's squat concrete mansion on High Point Road. There A.J. met Barbara's mother, Marjorie Kitchen. Gradually, he fell in love with his son's mother-in-law.

Yes! True! A.J. was dating his son's mother-in-law, and he married her in 1985. More than a decade his junior, Marjorie had grown up in St. Catharines in the pinched, humorless country of southwestern Ontario. Her first husband, Barbara's father, was a Baptist preacher. Marjorie had come up "the hard way," as A.J. put it; she had been poor, and she knew the value of a dollar. Marjorie loved A.J., and she loved God. She and A.J. came to know one another going to church together.

Come Sunday, A.J. would don a three-piecer, take Marjorie's arm and head over to the eleven o'clock service at the Melrose Avenue branch of the Fellowship of Evangelical and Baptist Churches, a tiny A-frame pre-fab building in the Tobacco Road section of north Toronto. A.J. liked the Melrose Baptist Church. The sign out front always bore a homily – "Life is Fragile Handle with Prayer" was standard fare – and the vestibule was loaded with instructional pamphlets with titles such as *Going Slow with God* and *Reconcilable Differences: Secrets of Overcoming Separation from Others and from God*. The church would haul in its devout and aging congregation in its blue and white bus, and the Reverend Barry Duguid would stand up in his light gray suit and crack jokes. A.J. liked Reverend Duguid, even if the Reverend was "just a little guy." A.J. and Marjorie would arrive at the church fifteen minutes early, to chat with other solid burghers of faith in the congregation, and then take their seats in the third pew from the front on the left-hand side of the church. Marjorie would deck herself out in her gray and celery silk houndstooth dress, say, and perhaps her pinky-blonde mink bonnet, and Rev. Duguid might pray for businessmen, "for the moral dilemmas they face," to "protect their minds from sexual immorality," and then A.J. would join in to sing "Have Thine Own Way, Lord (Thou art the potter, I am the clay)." A.J. could get into all that. He was in his eighties, after all. The Baptist Church's pietistic concern with hellfire and damnation has always had a special appeal for those approaching the quietus.

The dealers figured A.J.'s newfound religion lay behind his obsession with profit-sharing. The older he grew, and the closer he came to his Day of Reckoning – so the theory went – the more A.J. wanted Heaven's accounts of his moral goodness well in the black.

It was a nice theory, one befitting the uncynical middle-class optimism of Dealerland. It supposed a man was what he appeared to be; that A.J. was not a devious schemer but a visionary of supreme, if misguided, generosity. It preferred to ignore the fact that the fifty-fifty plan would turn the dealers, that unique brotherhood of intrapreneurial greed, into mere employees – the very specter A.J. had raised in 1963 when he lobbied Dealerland to protect Tire against an alleged takeover by Imperial Oil and Dick Billes. It refused to believe that the fifty-fifty plan was simply a scheme to put control of Tire's fortunes right back in A.J.'s hands. It refused to believe that

A.J. Billes, the father of them all, was a man who never gave up where power was concerned.

WHATEVER A.J.'s motives were, his fifty-fifty plan went nowhere because Dean Muncaster refused to support it, for the plain reason that (in Muncaster's words), "you're alienating your dealers because they're having to pay out half their profits by edict." Put simply, it was a bad idea. That drove Muncaster and his mentor even further apart. Dealers and executives alike tried to bring them together again, with no success. On more than one occasion after Muncaster had shunned him, A.J. showed up in the chief executive officer's modest office on the eleventh floor of 2180 Yonge Street, threw his keys on Muncaster's desk, and said, "I'm leaving." They were like estranged lovers.

A.J. felt lonely, tucked into his "office" behind the mail-room. Gradually his alienation soured into bitterness; the bitterness coagulated into complaints about Muncaster's performance. A.J. began to think Muncaster lacked backbone. "Muncaster never did say, 'You've got to do it, or else you'll lose your franchise'," A.J. complained by way of explaining why the fifty-fifty plan hadn't worked. "And you can't be a good president if you don't take a stand. Muncaster was a nice guy. But presidents can't be nice guys. You have to put your foot down and say, that's it, or else." From there it was only a step to the conclusion that Dean's success had gone to his head. "I'm not saying it did, but what else could it have been?" Neither Martha nor Fred had supported A.J.'s fifty-fifty plan on the board, but it was Muncaster's deaf ear that troubled him most. Muncaster, the perfect son, had betrayed his father-founder. "I never had the support of Muncaster," A.J. would say years later. "I was very much left out. Anything that I wanted just never took place. They never paid attention to that. The last ten years, he did a terrible job."

A.J. didn't care that Canadian Tire's core business was turning in results that made stockbrokers' eyes water with glee. In 1981, with the retail business in the doldrums and the rest of the economy suffering from pernicious anemia, Muncaster racked up $26 million in profits – an increase of 43 *percent* over the previous year. Inflation accounted for 18 percent of the rise, but his performance was still outstanding. Relations between head office and Dealerland had never been better, and Tire's shareholders were growing richer by the hour. Dave Antcliffe, Tire's toilet-seat expert, had bought his first block of Canadian Tire A shares in 1979 at $25 a share. The shares climbed $10 a year until 1983, when at $60 they split five for one. A $25,000 investment – not an unlikely sum for a ten- or fifteen-year head office employee to have stashed away in a profit-sharing plan – was suddenly worth more than $63,000.

But even strong results seemed to be losing their thrill for Muncaster. All the double-digit after-tax net-income figures in the world couldn't offset the effect of the united front of antagonism he faced from the Billeses in the boardroom. The children had been infected by A.J.'s bitterness. Fred restricted his complaining for the most part to his concerns as a dealer, but it was clear he felt compelled more and more frequently to question management's intentions. "I think that Fred is not very trusting of people," Muncaster observed. "He seems to think that he very often is getting a trumped-up story." Muncaster's forward momentum, his desire to modernize and expand, seemed to scare the Billeses. Muncaster interpreted their nervousness as a desire to return to the past and "a business they understood."

Others saw the dilemma differently. "When Dean was here," a company executive once explained, "it was Dean's company, Dean's show. And he more or less ran it as he thought it should be run." Even Dick Billes, Muncaster's ally, noticed Muncaster's high-handedness. "What they [Dean and his team] would do, would be to get . . . in a committee and decide what people were doing without even asking," Dick remembered.

Muncaster's autocratic ways were understandable. At the outset of his career, having watched his father struggle as a self-employed businessman, Dean chose the safer life of a salaried employee. But his success and his talent had gradually allowed him to think of Canadian Tire – the modern version, at least – as his own creation. Certainly, having grown up as a dealer's son in the working middle class, Muncaster could understand the dealers' aspirations more intimately than he grasped the peculiar concerns of a family of owners who inherited their wealth.

Muncaster's reaction to his conflict with A.J., characteristically, was to avoid it. That was a mistake. By 1980, as he set out to make Tire an international entity, his distaste for corporate politics was being interpreted at best as procrastination, at worst as "floundering." Muncaster found solace outside the office – in his half-dozen corporate directorships, in the affairs of Ontario Hydro, in his growing interest in international economics. His absence was noticed. "My real criticism of Dean" – this from one of his closest friends – "is that in the last five years he was president he acted like a chairman of the board. He was not a hands-on president." Even Dick Billes, Muncaster's crony by virtue of his distaste for A.J., saw Muncaster's commitment to Tire wane. "Dean started to ignore the business about the time of Australia," Dick said. "It was mentioned a couple of times." Dick would phone Dean with a problem, and it would take Dean four days to phone back, if he phoned back at all. "Dean's style of managing was simply to be measuring the results," Dick said. "Measure the results, measure the results. And I think he went overboard with some things, and lost touch. Oh, I knew why. He was getting bored."

There were several versions of reality at work within the corporation. The Billeses figured Muncaster was working for them. In Muncaster's opinion, they were mistaken. Indeed, Muncaster had considered a management-associated buyout of the estate's shares because he thought it would be in the best interests of the company and its shareholders. For at least seven years, beginning in 1975, Muncaster, Dick Billes, Robin Law, Alex Barron, and a rotating cast of investment community bigwigs (including Muncaster's Western pal, R. John (Jack) Lawrence, chairman and chief executive officer of Burns Fry, and his vice-chairman, Wilmot (Wil) Matthews) had pondered a host of strategies to see if they could "get the shares out of the estate," as Dick Billes described their conversations, "and keep them out of A.J.'s hands." They weren't trying to be duplicitous, or sabotage the company. Their intention was to neutralize, once and for all, the influence of A.J. and his family. Invariably the mutinists met in Law's or Barron's offices, away from Tire's head office where, as Muncaster has since admitted, "you were either on one side or the other. It didn't make very much sense to have Dick wandering in and out of my office."

It wasn't simply for himself that Muncaster sought to subvert the Billeses. "I was very much in favor of maintaining a balanced-control position," Muncaster explained. "It starts out from the two-tiered structure of the voting and non-voting shares. And trying to ensure that the non-voting shareholders were being taken into account, almost as if they were voting shareholders. . . . Secondly I felt that the company would be better managed if it did not have the pressure of a controlling shareholder coming in and saying, "I don't like the way you're doing this." Muncaster was no one's patsy. "They [the Billeses] knew that I was committed to the fact that all shareholders ranked equally, in my eyes, except as to their ability to elect a board of directors. And they didn't get much comfort out of me thinking of them as less-than-ten-percent shareholders. In a public company, all [voting control] lets you do is elect a board of directors. It doesn't give you any right to go fiddling around with the place."

If anyone was in a position to understand the difference between passive control and active management of a modern corporation, Fred and Martha were. But they chose not to sympathize with Muncaster's professional obligations and his subsequent dilemma; instead they seemed offended. Sometimes, as I contemplated Canadian Tire, I tried to imagine the Billeses' intentions – intentions they would never have articulated themselves. Sometimes, I thought I came close to understanding them. They were not founders of Canadian Tire, and had done little to encourage (or harm) its health. But they had *inherited the family business*. The very fragility and thinness of their claim to ownership seemed to fire and reinforce their passion to "control" it. The undeserving man, as the old saying goes, is the most jealous. How might they rationalize their jealousy? Simple. Muncaster, the princeling, had usurped their throne. "They had a proprietary feeling about the business that I can't think of a parallel for in any other Canadian corporation," Muncaster once explained. "It was 'their place.' I think the profile I had acquired over this long period of time meant that whenever anybody thought about Canadian Tire, they didn't think about the Billeses. I think that was pretty important to them." That, Dean Muncaster was about to discover, was the understatement of an understated lifetime.

11

CONTROL

NO ONE, least of all Norma Billes, would ever have called Dick Billes a social animal. As a teenager summering on Lake Simcoe, Norma had found Dick paralytically shy and, if the truth were known, quite boring. She had originally dated his older brother John. John didn't qualify as garrulous either, but at least he drank and knew how to have a good time. To Norma's mind, the Billes children's shyness stemmed from a collective inferiority complex brought on by the stringent distance their father, J.W. Billes, maintained from them. Both Norma and Betty, John's wife, were considerably less in awe of the old man, however, and they had stood up to him, and made a space around him in which his sons could draw a breath or two of their own. Norma knew she'd drawn Dick out of himself. After twenty-five years of marriage, she was willing to concede that Dick was "one-thousand-percent more outgoing."

Despite his politeness and his shy, halting manner, which many people who were only superficially acquainted with him diagnosed either as naïveté or that peculiar strain of social agoraphobia that afflicts the sons and daughters of the wealthy – despite that, Dick genuinely had learned to stand up for himself. He was immensely proud to have convinced the courts to raise the stipend he and his brother and sister received from his father's will from $15,000 a year to $48,000 a year. At work he had allied himself with Dean Muncaster's progressive management, overcoming A.J.'s cen-

189

sure to become a formidable force on Tire's board. He had transformed his role as trustee of the estate's shares – as the fulcrum of the balance of power at Tire, the counterweight to A.J. – into a personal cause célèbre, a moral position around which he could establish his character and define himself. "I think he really had a mission," a friend of Dick's once re-marked. "He really believed he was doing something great."

By the spring of 1983, however, it was obvious that achieving greatness was not an easy enterprise. National Trust had begun once again to harry Dick Billes and his mother, as trustees of the Canadian Tire shares J.W. left to charity. The charities wanted to sell their Canadian Tire holdings. For twenty-five years, and especially for the last six, Dick had stubbornly fought them off: the charities, Dick pointed out, had realized more than $11 million in dividends from their Tire shares, and the shares many charities sold off in the early 1960s were now worth $130 million. Dick wanted the charities to keep their shares because Dick's power at Canadi-an Tire grew out of his role as trustee of the shares. His father's shares were the crux of the checks and balances Dean Muncaster had engineered to cage A.J. Billes and his family.

Not that Dick was particularly happy being a trustee of the estate. He longed to wield the estate's shares as his own. That idea had grown along with his self-confidence. Dick Billes and Dean Muncaster had been trying, as mentioned, to secure control of the estate's shares since the early 1970s in order to maintain the status quo at Tire. But the discussions always came back to the Billes family agreement that gave Martha, Fred and David first dibs.

In the portentous spring of 1983, however, Dick's pleasant daydreams of owning his father's shares of Canadian Tire were challenged once and for all. On May 26, J.J. Robinette, National Trust's lawyer and the most famous advocate in Canada, applied to the Ontario Supreme Court for permission to sell the estate's shares. Robinette's argument was simple: it was simply too risky for twenty-three charitable organizations to have $80 million tied up in one company that yielded an anemic 2.5-percent return on the money.

The threat of a sell-off left Dick Billes with divided loyalties. As a director of Tire, Dick had responsibilities to the company; as a trustee, he had responsibilities to the charities. But as a Billes – as J.W. Billes's son – he had a duty to the Billes name and its rightful place at the zenith of the Canadian Tire universe. Everyone wanted a slice of Dick Billes, and he could feel his body tightening. That spring at his annual check-up, his doctor informed him his blood pressure was dangerously high.

What ensued in the summer of 1983 was one of the more bizarre chapters in Canadian capitalism. It entailed a takeover bid that never existed; corporate espionage of the highest order; the destruction of Dean Muncaster's power; and, in the end, the collapse of Dick Billes's only lifelong dream. Its one bright spot was a revelation, one that would finally show Dick Billes what sort of man he was.

DEAN MUNCASTER watched National Trust's maneuvering equally carefully in the spring of 1983, for different reasons. When, in mid-June, an Ontario court ordered J.W.'s estate to sell the charities' shares, Muncaster showed up in the newspapers declaring it a "virtual certainty" that Dick would either refuse to sell the estate's shares, or assign their voting rights to Tire's dealers and the trustees of the company's profit-sharing plan. Muncaster, handily, was one of those trustees. He played down the likelihood of a takeover. "I would like to see the present arrangement continue," Muncaster said. "It has worked fine up to now."

Which was a nice thing to say. In fact, Muncaster was so alarmed by National Trust's plan to sell the estate's shares that in January he hopped a plane to Montreal to visit Paul Paré, the chairman and chief executive officer of Imasco Ltd., the Montreal-based food, tobacco, and retailing conglomerate. Dean Muncaster wanted Paré to buy Canadian Tire.

Muncaster knew the chain-smoking Paré by reputation, and respected him. Imasco owned Shoppers Drug Mart, Imperial Tobacco, Hardee's Food Systems (the third largest fast-food chain in the United States), the UCS Group of Toronto (airport cigar stores), Collegiate Sports, and Embassy Cleaners. Imasco was the fiftieth largest company in Canada, and had sales of over $1 billion a year – sales built by the careful acquisition of companies started by others. Paré was known as a hands-off owner who let his managers run their own shows. Forty-five percent of Imasco was owned by B.A.T. Industries of London, England, but B.A.T. let Paré do as he liked. Imasco had cash to burn, the so-called "deep pockets" Muncaster needed access to, especially since White's, Tire's fledgling American operation, was now in considerable difficulty.

Paré in turn liked Muncaster and Canadian Tire. He saw a national institution with pre-tax profits of $22 a square foot, and sales per square foot twice those of its nearest competitor. More to the point, the chief executive officer of Canadian Tire was in Paré's office virtually begging to be bought.

Imasco had a good chance as a potential owner of Tire in large part because the legal strategist behind Imasco's growth-by-acquisition was not simply Paré, but Purdy Crawford. Crawford was a graduate of Dalhousie Law School and a senior partner at Osler, Hoskin & Harcourt, one of Toronto's bluest law firms. Crawford always looked as if he'd just spent the morning reading Dr. Johnson. He was one of the *lares* of Canadian securities law, and had virtually co-written Ontario's postwar securities legislation. One of Crawford's protégés was Peter Dey, another Dalhousie alumnus who, by the time Muncaster showed up in Paré's office, was on leave from Osler's (where Crawford had hired him) to serve a term as chairman of the Ontario Securities Commission. Dey and the OSC would have considerable say in any takeover of Canadian Tire by Imasco; Imasco was run by Crawford; Crawford was a friend of Dey. No one would ever suggest that the connections meant any thing, to be sure. But because everyone knew aforehand with whom they would be dealing, because they knew they could at least talk to one another, a slight feeling of confidence at Imasco's headquarters could easily have been forgiven.

Muncaster's approach to Paré was straightforward. "We're going to be owned by somebody else," Muncaster said, by the recollection of others in the room. "And we certainly think we can work well within Imasco." He spoke for the entire inner cabinet of Tire's management. Certainly Imasco would not cause Dean and his team the headaches A.J. and his family had – and would times ten, Muncaster believed, if Fred and Martha bought the estate's shares and thereby won control of the company. Muncaster's motives, as John Kron would later point out, "were not designed to attack A.J. Billes's family. They were designed to preserve the balance of power. Particularly when management's view was that the rationality of the family was open to some question. I mean, they were scary people." The fact that Tire's chief officer was on Imasco's side made the possibility of a friendly takeover that much greater. Nor was the prospect of Muncaster – one of the country's leading executives – joining Imasco's team lost on Paré and Crawford.

So there was Dean Muncaster – running a company for a family that had virtually raised him – thinking that it was in the company's best interests that its ownership be held as widely as possible, and suddenly trying to find ways to accomplish this. It was a weird space to be in.

There was only one hitch. Muncaster could not come out publicly in favor of the takeover. His role would have to be a secret. If the takeover failed and Muncaster were discovered behind the control panel, any alternative strategy to gain control of the estate's shares later on would be that much harder to mobilize. More to the point, if the Billeses found out Dean Muncaster wanted someone else to buy their company, he was dead meat. As a result, one Imasco insider explained, "we could never say that Muncaster undertook to say he could deliver the company to us."

THE very idea that an outsider might own part of Tire threw A.J. and his offspring into fits of spewing, foaming, eye-popping, lie-down-on-the-ground-and-have-a-temper-tantrum apoplexy. Imasco's attempted takeover of Canadian Tire was about to become the summer hit of Bay Street, and the audience watched the performances of A.J. and his kin with an enthusiasm normally displayed by paying customers at a carnival freak show.

The midway atmosphere was intensified by the fact that Imasco never made a formal written offer for the company. On the thirteenth of June, Dick Billes met privately with Paré, and Paré made an informal bid for the estate's shares. Nothing was in writing, and no announcement had been made. By the sixteenth of June, speculation about a forthcoming takeover bid for Canadian Tire was sweeping Bay Street. News travels like mercury in the Canadian investment community, especially when share prices are climbing on the strength of a rumor and there is a profit to be made. Bay Street and the financial press figured the takeover was a great idea. Analysts and journalists have never been fond of private companies, whose love of secrecy makes the job of predicting a company's future that much harder.

Four days later, on June 20, Paré got serious, and "approached" Alex Barron and Dean Muncaster. He was willing to buy all the Tire common shares tendered and the same percentage of preferred, or A, shares for $47 cash and three-quarters of an Imasco share. The package was worth $72 per Canadian Tire share. To lifelong employees of Canadian Tire, it meant an immense amount of money – the highest price the shares had ever attained.

Paré went out of his way to suggest that the takeover would be a friendly one. But without Muncaster's public endorsement, Paré had to win the family's approval on his own, mainly through the press. "If such support and endorsement are not forthcoming," Paré explained, "there can be no assurance that an offer will in fact be made."

Support and endorsement were not what A.J. and his children had in mind at all. They met every overture from Paré with a kick to the Quebec capitalist's head. Fred was the first to lumber into public view, and it was an exciting experience for all concerned. Fred planned to buy the shares himself! "It's quite different from what we thought was going to happen," he said, and his bewilderment was shared by anyone listening to him. No one knew what he was driving at. "We're not very happy about what's happening at all. We want to put together a big enough block so no one makes a run at us again. There aren't any negotiations going on with Imasco and there probably never will be."[1]

By June 21, Martha was tossing bombs as well. She was a lot better at it than Fred. If Fred objected to the offer, Martha seemed willing to do verbal violence to anyone who fiddled with Tire's destiny.

Martha was speaking to the world through her lawyers, and presumably speaking for her brothers Fred and David, who continued, nonetheless, to make their own statements; they were, Martha later claimed, "taking turns" as family spokesperson. To outsiders, however, it looked as if none of the Billes children could resist this long-awaited chance to shine in the limelight, to be seen, finally, as . . . yes . . . *the owners of Canadian Tire*. Speaking for herself and perhaps for everyone else, but then again maybe not, Martha rejected the offer outright. She seemed to take it personally, as if Imasco

[1]The battle wasn't all public. Barbara Billes, Fred's wife, took to calling Norma Billes, Dick's wife, to enlist her aid in fighting what she saw as management's insubordination. Barbara wanted Robin Law and Alex Barron fired. Norma was cool. "Barbara," she said, "this is my husband's company. And I think I shouldn't become involved in his business." Barbara never called Norma again.

were a reckless junior employee in the stockroom who had
had the audacity to ask for Martha's hand in marriage before
their first date. Martha had in fact talked to Paré and his team.
They were, as one Imasco executive remembered, "from a
distance impressed. She seemed to have more of a focus, more
of a business orientation than Fred." But Martha was still
straight-arming Imasco. "As far as I'm concerned," Martha
said of their generous offer, "it makes no difference. I'm not
interested in money. I'm interested in the corporation . . . I'm
in there for keeps."

It was not just Martha's sense of destiny that Imasco
challenged. Her pride, her notion of herself as the rightful
heir and owner of Tire, had been offended as well. Offended?
Martha was *pissed*. "Later on I was told – the old grapevine
bit – that Imasco had been studying Canadian Tire for a
number of years. Well, having done that, they should have
known better than to approach Canadian Tire through Alex
Barron. How many shares did he own?[2] They should have
approached the two sides of the family. Imasco made, I do
believe, all of us very angry." Imasco's subsequent decision to
forge ahead in the face of the family's demurral *really* got
Martha going. Her voice would jump a pitch or three, much to
the amusement of some of the lawyers involved. That these
tactics were everyday occurrences in the business world
didn't seem to cross her mind. Never mind that a public
corporation is supposed to resemble a democracy; or that
public companies, which in the past fifty years have fueled
the greatest economic growth in history, operate on the
principle that ownership of even the smallest shred of a
company entitles one to a say in its future. Martha did not see
the Billes family simply as a major shareholder of Canadian

[2]The answer was 215,000 common shares, or about six percent of Tire's
common stock, lodged for safekeeping in Canadian General Investments,
Barron's closed-end holding company. The purchase had been the result
of the many strategy meetings between Barron, Dick Billes, and Dean
Muncaster.

Tire: she presented herself and her family as owners, as a queer species of royalty, above the harsh laws that dominate ordinary lives.

Meanwhile, Dick Billes was trying, unbeknownst to Fred and Martha, to convince the dealers to support him. "Hindsight would tell us that we perhaps didn't do as good a job as we might have in communicating with the dealers," an Imasco insider later said. "They got the message, but only indirectly." The problem was A.J.'s influence in Dealerland. The Great Patriarch had only to raise the specter of Imasco selling off stores and turning the dealers into a troupe of managers, and the dealers were behind him. A.J. was ladling out the loyalty corn like a madman. "Our position has not changed one bit," he told the newspapers. "We have lived for the company all our lives." To allay the dealers' fears, Imasco had Murray Koffler, the founder of Shoppers Drug Mart (one of Imasco's prize purchases) in readiness, willing to proselytize for Imasco. But Koffler's influence was nothing next to the power of A.J.

Dick Billes figured it wasn't loyalty that motivated the dealers at all, but intimidation. Didn't he know that firsthand? Anyone who crossed A.J. Billes ended up suffering for it.

WITH the Tire offer topmost in mind, Crawford and Paré decided that year for the first time ever to hold Imasco's annual meeting in Toronto. Crawford's plan was to use the June 22 meeting, which would be covered by all the Toronto media, to publicize Imasco's offer. Within days, however, as Imasco's agents tried to round up shareholders willing to sell their Tire shares, it became clear that strange and irrational forces of loyalty were at work.

Muncaster's silence had finally been noticed by the press: first he was out of town, then he wasn't talking. The key to the Dick-Dean-Imasco strategy was Fred Sasaki. Sasaki and Muncaster comprised two of the three trustees who controlled the common shares owned by Tire's profit-sharing plans.

Muncaster knew which way he planned to vote. He believed Sasaki would consider the best interests of Tire as well, and he urged Sasaki to join him in voting the profit-sharing plan shares in favor of Imasco.

Poor Fred Sasaki. He felt as if he were being torn apart from his head and his guts. That isn't just gripping imagery. Dean Muncaster was his friend, his colleague, his boss. Imasco's generous offer was a temptation of its own, as well: Sasaki knew it would be a long time, if ever, before Tire's shares hit $70 again. But Sasaki was also Japanese – a loyal Japanese who had been saved from joblessness by A.J. Billes. "I was closest to A.J. because he's the one who hired me and gave me a job," Sasaki said recently. "I guess my heart was with A.J. My sentiments. I owe so much to him. I can't forget that I started at Canadian Tire. I've always been loyal to him. Though I always had the highest respect for Dean Muncaster." The sight of Sasaki pacing back and forth at lunch between Tire's head office and Eglinton Avenue two blocks north became a familiar one to Canadian Tire's employees, whose fortunes rested in Sasaki's hands. They began to call him "the samurai."

But eventually the pacing stopped, and Sasaki made up his mind by listening to his heart. He could not vote against A.J. Dick would have to successfully purchase the estate's shares before Sasaki would throw the weight of the profit-sharing plan's shares behind him.

Muncaster, ever the rationalist, didn't fault Sasaki: he had always understood the company to be a bucket of human instincts. Still, by June 24, Muncaster's hand had been forced, and fourteen Canadian Tire officers issued a press release in favor of retaining independence: Tire's employees would find it difficult to be close to as big an entity as Imasco, with the result that management could not back the Imasco bid. Muncaster did have kind words for the company, and pointed out that Tire's management was "not unmindful . . . that Imasco is a very fine, well-financed company, managed by a dedicated group of Canadian executives."

No one, save the insiders who knew the truth, would ever suspect Dean Muncaster had been behind the entire affair. That was as it was supposed to be. Three days later, Imasco dropped its bid. Paré played his part, saying he was "obviously disappointed with the reaction of the senior management group at Canadian Tire to our recent offer."

Obviously disappointed! Nice touch, Paul! An understatement of gigantic proportions that perfectly underscored the invisible workings of Bay Street. Public perception of what goes on within and between even the best-run corporations has always been extraordinarily superficial. If the real motives and actions of those involved were revealed, someone might begin to ask just what the hell was going on.

Had Imasco made its bid five years later, when shareholders' rights were almost as hot a fad on Bay Street as ornamental suspenders, a group of disgruntled pension funds that owned Canadian Tire shares might have sued Tire's board for not acting in their best interests. But the shareholders' rights movement was in its infancy, or at least in a lull, in 1983. More to the point, the critical balance of Tire's common shareholders – the people with the votes – were rabidly afraid of Imasco's bid. They still believed that the Billeses had their best interests at heart. In a strange way, their naîveté was quite touching.

WITH Imasco out of the way, the route was clear to sell the estate's shares to a private bidder. The Ontario Supreme Court had set 5 p.m., August 29, as the deadline for private tenders. Muncaster claimed he was staying out of it: the outcome was "not a management decision." In photographs in the newspapers, though, Muncaster looked tired and glum. Playing invisible games with Imasco and the family had exhausted him. He had been able to escape on his ketch on Georgian Bay only twice the whole summer.

Muncaster was still trying to maintain the balance of power at Tire – this time, as it happened, on Dick Billes's behalf. Dick had played his cards well during the Imasco takeover, even coming out *against* the takeover toward the end, presumably to keep his options open with Martha, Fred, and David. Little Dick Billes! Mister Strategy! Now he planned to buy the shares himself. First he had to convince the Ontario Securities Commission to exempt him from making a prohibitively expensive follow-up offer to Tire's non-voting A shareholders. Next he had to win the Ontario Supreme Court's permission to bid for the shares, even though he was an executor of his father's estate.

Then there was the question of paying for them. Dick had some ideas on that subject as well. By August, he had arranged to meet with Fred, David, and Martha at Fred's house on High Point Road. He approached them without a lawyer present – a decision his wife, Norma, would later deem "sort of naïve." Dick wanted to cooperate with the family in a voting trust, and he wanted peace in eternity within the corporation. "We were trying to do this on a cooperative basis in the naïve belief that A.J. would like to see me have control of those shares," he explained.

That afternoon at Fred's concrete bunker, Martha seemed to be on Dick's side. Dick and Martha were alike in a lot of ways: they were both redheads, shy, polite, intelligent, capable of toxic sarcasm, and allergic to publicity. There were those in the investment community, like Alice Bastedo, Dick's broker at Dominion Securities, who saw Dick and Martha as soul mates. "I could never figure out why Martha and Dick couldn't get together," Bastedo once remarked. "I thought their positions were similar. They were both a little on the periphery." Certainly Martha felt a bond with Dick. "I can't outfox Dick and he can't outfox me," she once said. "I understand him far more than I understand my two brothers."

Encouraged by Martha's warmth, Dick revealed his plan to pay for the shares that, in his mind, the foursome could then vote as a unit. The cost of the estate's shares might run as high as $90 million. Dick figured the family could borrow the money and, once the shares were in hand, split their common voting shares into one common and any number of non-voting A shares. The family could then sell the new non-voting shares to pay off its loan.

The plan met with the group's approval – Dick later considered he had given them the idea, though Martha disagreed. But Fred resisted the idea of a voting trust that included the investment community and management. That wasn't the family. "And if it had been just Dick, it would have been a hell of a lot easier," Martha said. Fred wouldn't work with Dick either, however. "Fred considered Dick an enemy," Martha realized. The ancient rivalry between the sons of the founders was still too hot to handle. Martha sympathized with Dick, but Fred – and therefore David – were against him. In the end Martha went along with her brothers, where her power lay.[3] "Cousin Dick approached the family and suggested setting up various forms of companies and voting trusts," Martha later recalled. "And from our point of view it did seem that they contravened the trust that we had and that we were better with the agreement we had." "They said 'we think we know how to run the corporation,' " Dick would remember of the meeting. "They were going to be the saviors of Canadian Tire."

Dick had arrived believing he might finally bridge the gulf of resentment between himself and Fred Billes. Leaving, he realized he was on his own. If he had any doubts as to the finality of the separation between the two branches of the family, A.J. put them to rest shortly thereafter. As word of Dick's opener to the family reached the old man, he publicly denied that he wanted Dick to own any shares. "I do not," he said. "My brother's will provided for his wife and family but expressly left the Canadian Tire voting shares to charity." A.J. thought Dick was simply backing Bay Street, which A.J.

---

[3]Four years later, after she and her brothers had parted company, Martha suspected her sympathy for her cousin Dick may have been "why we are where we are."

had begun to see as the enemy of everything he and Tire stood for.

A.J. was right. Dick's subsequent search for money to buy the estate's shares was warmly received by Bay Street. By the end of September, Dick Thompson, the chief executive officer of the Toronto Dominion Bank, had agreed to lend Dick's holding company $67.2 million, the full anticipated purchase price of the shares, at the prime interest rate. Thompson was being exceptionally generous: traditionally, banks lend takeover artists half of what they need, and seldom at prime. The bank also loaned Dick another $4 million to cover interest costs to April, 1984. Toronto Dominion planned to withhold $700,000 of the $4 million as its fee – and planned to pay $140,000 to Burns Fry Ltd., Tire's longtime underwriter. Burns took another two percent of the $700,000 fee if the loan were extended, and agreed to pick up 20 percent of any loss to the bank; in return the company got to be the broker in any subsequent sale of the shares. Burns had never done a deal like that, either. But Burns Fry had always been a pal to Tire's management: Jack Lawrence, the chairman and chief executive officer of Burns Fry, was a friend of Dean Muncaster's. Wil Matthews, the vice-chairman of Burns Fry, explained his firm's generosity by saying that Burns Fry wanted to help Dick Billes buy the estate's shares to "maintain the status quo." This was management's party line. But the structure of the deal suggested a different strategy: with an April deadline looming, it looked as if Dick Billes planned to sell the shares once he had them, possibly to Imasco. If he did, he would visit devastating revenge on his uncle and cousins.

BY Monday, October 3, 1983, the day of the auction, Dick's blood pressure was so high his doctors were alarmed. Norma spent the day in the office at Dick's store; Dick would telephone periodically to fill her in as the day progressed.

At first the news was good. Dick's contention to the Supreme Court of Ontario that he had a right to bid for the shares even though he was a trustee of the estate was successful. Years later, when Dick thought about that day, he recalled finding himself next to Fred in the bathroom after the court hearing. Fred seemed a tad put out. "Think of all the four-letter words you know," Dick remembered, "and he probably used them." Dick simply passed the time of day, and escaped to a telephone to call Norma. She was elated.

Round two took place at the Ontario Securities Commission in front of Peter Dey, its chairman. Gar Emerson, lawyer to Fred, David, and Martha, claimed Dick's byzantine loan arrangements were so insecure "that a buyer has to be found," and that any purchase by Dick was, in effect, a change in control. But Chairman Dey decided that a purchase of the estate's shares by Dick Billes would not amount to a change of control, since Dick was already the effective controlling shareholder of the estate's shares. Round two to Dick Billes.

By now there was only an hour and a half left before the deadline for private bids. Everyone rushed over to Blake, Cassels, where John Robinette was to conduct the auction. He claimed he was nervous. There were thirty people in the office, while others sat in the lobby, drinking coffee as they waited for the outcome.

The future of a sixty-year-old Canadian institution was up for grabs. The three lawyers for Fred, David, and Martha drew straws; Martha's lawyer won the job. (Later, when Fred was characterized as the spokesman for the family during the auction, Martha bristled: "Freddy was certainly *not* the point man," she said.) Martha, Fred, and David opened the bidding at $63 a share; Dick countered with $64. There were two Canadian Tire employee bids: one from the dealers at $60 (the dealers wanted to maintain the status quo at Tire, but wouldn't have minded owning it); and another from the profit-sharing plans at $65 a share if anyone other than the

Billeses won the bid. A secret offer slid in at $58 a share, via
Daly Gordon, a brokerage firm. Everyone figured Imasco as
the secret bidder.

The bidding was fast and furious. Muncaster and Fred Sasaki
sat at the auction table, a sealed envelope in their hands;
Martha presumed it was a bid from management, and
requested that the pair either participate or withdraw.
"Called their bluff," she later remembered. They withdrew.
When the price struck the $69 to $71 a share range, Dick
called time out and left the room to make a phone call. He was
back ten minutes later. The bidding resumed. But Dick was
out of money. With a final bid of $73 a share, Fred, David, and
Martha Billes took the company for a total of $76.7 million.
After a lifetime of wanting it, A.J. Billes and his children had
control of Canadian Tire.

Dick telephoned Norma from Blake's lobby. "We lost," he
said. Then and there, as she would for years afterward
whenever the subject came up, Norma Billes started to cry. "I
just thought if anybody was going to have it," she said, "Dick
ought to have."

NOTHING had changed, it was said, but in the weeks that
followed a subterranean wash of defeat seeped through the
executive offices at Tire. It wasn't simply that eight months of
planning by Muncaster and his team had evaporated; no, it
was the fact that Muncaster had spent *eighteen years* keeping
the company out of A.J.'s hands, remaking the corporation in
his own image – and now all that effort had disappeared down
the drain. The future no longer lay stretched out in front of
Dean Muncaster, cool and clean and rational and predictable.
Everyone knew it. In Owen Sound, Walter Muncaster heard of
Dick's defeat within hours of the auction, and he figured
October 3, 1983, was the saddest day of his life. "I don't see why
Dick couldn't have been in the picture," he said. For the Tire
family, the road to riches had just become a divided highway.

His son Dean kept his thoughts to himself: any hint o disloyalty on his part would now be disastrous. It was left to Alex Barron – predictably, for no one could doubt his integrity – to play Cassandra in discussing the impact of Dick's defeat. Barron did what he could to box the Billeses in. When Fred Billes revealed that he planned to do as Dick had naïvely suggested, and pay for his new common shares by splitting them and selling off the As, thereby even further diluting the extent of the family's holdings to less than four percent of the company's equity – Barron went straight to the microphone. The Billes family had used public money to pay for their shares, Barron explained, and they owned only a fraction of the company. "In effect," Barron tried to tell the newspapers, "this corporation is changing from a family-controlled corporation to a public corporation." It was a nice thought, in any event.

Martha, Fred, and David, on the other hand, felt proud of themselves. They had snatched Tire from the jaws of an international conglomerate. They had saved the Family. They wasted no time setting themselves up as the new *controlling* owners of Tire. Their first act was to write a letter. "TO THE CANADIAN TIRE COMMUNITY," it read:

> We believe that the policies which have guided the company so successfully to this point should continue. Canadian Tire is managed by Dean Muncaster, President and Chief Executive Officer, and our professional management team. In the past, the controlling shareholders

– a remarkable phrase in itself –

> left the day-to-day operations of the company in the hands of our management, and we fully intend to do so in the future. You can be assured that control of Canadian Tire is not changed; if anything, it is solidified.

So far, they were on their best behavior.

DICK BILLES never believed them. He could see the future. The following spring, at the first possible Canadian Tire board meeting, Dick resigned as a director. His cousins did nothing to stop him. Once again, Dick Billes was just another Canadian Tire dealer.

What he remembered afterwards was how hard the loss hit him. The maneuvering of the previous months had made him feel thoroughly alive. Somehow, amid the wrangling and negotiation, he had discovered an inner resilience in himself. And suddenly, at the height of his powers, his strength and vigor had been snatched from him. One moment he was headed for empire, and in the next instant he was hanging over open space, like a cartoon character who had just run off a cliff and didn't realize he was supposed to plummet to earth.

Dick plummetted. As he dropped, so did the aspirations of others around him. His daughter Anne's nascent plans to join the corporation had been demolished, as had his son Rob's. Nor did the letter – that goddamn letter! – make up for Freddy's behavior. When he thought about it, Dick realized that Fred believed he had a "moral right" to buy the shares. The very idea drove Dick crazy. "Who *did* have a moral right to buy them?" Dick would say whenever he rehashed the entire nightmare. "They were my father's shares. It was my father's company." Dick had believed Tire was too important to fight over. But Dick was wrong, and he had learned his lesson. Blood and money didn't mix. Money was thicker.

Two weeks after the auction Dick flew south to his condominium in Pompano Beach to recover. Pompano was perfect for recoveries. The Renaissance II was one of the two best buildings on the Pompano littoral, a gleaming white high-rise with black ironwork details and a shimmering pink marble lobby and thick oleander gardens guarding the driveway, all nestled between the Atlantic Ocean to the east and Florida's intercoastal waterway to the west. The Renaissance was slick, but it wasn't ostentatious. At the peak of the Florida condominium market in 1981, condos like Dick's had been selling for $250,000. From his sixth floor aerie on the southeast corner of the building – southeast corners were the most desirable units on the coast – Dick could look out his kitchen through ivory vertical blinds onto the beach, where a volleyball net had been abandoned in the breeze, and from there out over the water and the clouds puffed up like cotton balls on a cushion of hot air. The view from his apartment was strangely, soothingly . . . boring, really, the blue of the sea pasted onto the lesser blue of the sky, a flat concrete wall of blue. It was a good view to meditate upon, a constant against which Dick could turn his thoughts about the auction and his cousins.

As much as they resented the loss, Dick and his family resented the public airing Fred and A.J. had given the family laundry. The Billes name – hauled up from the psychological barren lands of Toronto's east end, nurtured through the adolescence of the company when the brothers were known as the Cut-Rate Boys, strengthened by the developing reputation of the corporation, and raised, finally, to the pedestal reserved for the great names in Canadian capitalism – well, the once-great Billes name was now, to Dick's way of thinking, the stuff of soap operas and family squabbles and gossip and greed. *If A.J. and his kids hadn't wanted so much, none of this would have happened.* Now whenever anyone asked if he was one of the Canadian Tire Billeses, Dick merely said, "Remotely." Now when he introduced himself it was simply "Dick."

But if for a while Dick was plagued by self-recrimination, of how he *might* have done it differently, of what might have happened *if*, such gnawing thoughts were soon replaced by a remarkable peace. There were those, like Alice Bastedo, who interpreted his new equanimity as proof that when all was said and done, Dick had lost Canadian Tire because he didn't want it.

"My feeling," Bastedo said, "is that, whether he consciously knew it or not, he did not want to do it. That there was some sense of *obligation*. . . . He wants friends who want to live in the same world he lives in. And it's a good world. I suspect he doesn't choose his friends because of their power. I think he chooses people because he likes them, and because they fit in with his picture of the world he wants to live in. And many people who have that sort of picture of the world do not become driving businessmen. He doesn't go for the jugular, you see. It's something you have to answer deep inside yourself. *Because if he had done it, he would have been no different from the others*. The others are like characters in English history: you've got somebody who has a claim to the throne, so what do you do? You kill him."

There was a lesson in that for heirs everywhere. Dick Billes had never owned his own life: he had been born into it, shouldered from birth with the legacy of his father. It was only fate and defeat that set him free. Unburdened, he was free to contemplate his history, his role in the past. In many ways the *memory*, the *idea* of power, was as pleasant as the real thing. The past, Dick realized, can be a possession too. The estate, the shares, none of that had anything to do with it. Nor was it just his twenty-seven years as a director of Canadian Tire, though Dick was justifiably proud of that act of servitude. The day Dick left Tire's offices for the last time, Dean Muncaster had presented him with an inscribed black marble triangle to commemorate all those years of his life, and Dick kept it on his desk in his office at his store on Kennedy Road, under the astrology clock.

The part of the corporation Dick still owned in his heart was more than that, something Fred could never steal. It was the private knowledge that J.W. Billes, Dick's father, had founded the most successful retailing empire in Canada. *Not A.J.; Dick's father*. There is something about the bond between a man and his father that is inviolable. The relationship does not have to be positive, thriving, or happy. Its strength is based on more than tradition and pride and generational history, and all the vague notions incessantly deified by the newspapers whenever they crank out yet another series on Canada's Founding Families. In many ways the essence of a son's bond to his father is biological, organic, communal, mythic, and unsayable. It does not matter if one's father was a great capitalist or a bum, a scrap dealer or a con man, a millionaire or a drunk, or all of the above. A father sits like a squatter in his son's memory, and never leaves. This is not because of pride or principle, but because of fate, love, resentment, and gratitude, all of which demand a reckoning, if not now, then later. The memory of one's father is a trick to beat back time – and with the memory of his father's accomplishments, Dick Billes salved his own wounds.

My father started this company. True, it was a quiet fact next to the hard shouting reality of owning shares. But it was a shard of the Truth About Canadian Tire. It was a fact that drove A.J. and Fred crazy, a fragment of truth they had tried to bury, but it was the Truth at least as long as Dick was there to state it. It was what passed for a cause in his life.

For years after he left Canadian Tire, Dick Billes carried the tall memory of his father wherever he went. He polished and maintained that memory the way he did the old store clock he kept in the basement of his house in Toronto. The clock had been the master timepiece that ran all the clocks at Canadian Tire back in the 1930s, including the slave clock that hung from the front of the store and was renowned throughout Toronto for its accuracy. The day he left Canadian Tire, Dick stole the clock and took it with him. *The master clock.* He never once let it stop ticking. A nice touch, that, the sort of quiet metaphor that was Dick Billes's specialty.

12

TEXAS

THE 1983 ANNUAL REPORT of the Canadian Tire Corporation Limited was remarkable for several reasons, not least of which was the plastic 45 rpm record bound into its pages. The record was an audio version of Dean Muncaster's report to the company's shareholders – a first, needless to say, in the history of corporate reporting. The flexible red disk had been Bernie Freedman's idea, down in the art department. Bernie was a flamboyant type who had spent most of his adult life working for Canadian Tire. Martha and A.J. had befriended him, and he had done well by the profit-sharing plan: now he lived alone in rich, self-designed splendor on the fringe of Forest Hill, with his framed photographs of Betty Grable and his huge projection television set "just like Martha's," except that Bernie had camouflaged his with mirrors attached with Velcro. Like many longtime Canadian Tire employees, Bernie displayed a certain childlike energy, undertaking company projects as if he were working on his high school yearbook. Bernie had sold the record idea to Dean Muncaster as "something different." Bernie was full of wacky notions: for one annual report, he even tried to create a pop-up photograph of the board of directors. He figured Canadian Tire was the most successful chain in the country, and could do anything it wanted. Of course Dean's speech on the record wouldn't contain many numbers. No one wanted to talk numbers at Canadian Tire in the spring of 1984, with good reason.

WHITE STORES INC., Tire's ill-fated Texas venture, had been a nightmare from the day Tire took possession of the run-down furniture-, appliance-, and hardware-chain in February of 1982. No one knew that better than John Kron, Tire's executive vice-president. Kron had been in on White's from the beginning. He had listened to Muncaster and Philbrick push the company as a takeover candidate in the spring of 1981, and he had flown down to Texas to investigate the company immediately afterward. He had voted in the board's unanimous decision to acquire the company. By the end of 1982, he was president of White's.

The keystone of the 300-store chain was 80-odd company-owned stores in Texas. Muncaster and Gary Philbrick figured Texas and Ontario were quite similar: their plan was to remake White's by transplanting the successful Canadian Tire formula in its entirety, profit-sharing and all, to the south.

To do that Muncaster didn't need a marketing genius: he needed a man who could follow orders. He had sounded out several candidates for the job, including William Dawson, the legendary Sudbury dealer, but Dawson had turned it down. "It would have wrecked my personality," Dawson declaimed, which was an interesting notion. Dawson was a superb marketer, but you never knew when he was going to wax independent and let fly at head office.

John Kron seemed a much safer choice. It was true, as Kron's envious colleagues in Toronto didn't hesitate to point out, that his marketing experience was slim. Instead he had an intuitive talent for organization and financial discipline; John Kron, everyone said, was "so tight he squeaks." He had built Tire's trucking operation, shaken up the marketing department, commissioned Tire's first (and highly successful) series of television commericals starring "Albert" the hockey player. He was also a loyal Muncaster man, someone the chief executive trusted to be obedient. Most important, Muncaster had shielded Kron from the family's politicking to the point

that the Billeses actually trusted John Kron. He had little of
Muncaster's smooth style, but he didn't use big words and
complicated concepts the way Muncaster did, and the family
found that reassuring. Kron was often referred to as Dean
Muncaster's successor at Canadian Tire.

Thus anointed, Kron embarked on a three-year voyage into
hell. Kron had three boys in university, and his wife wasn't
about to leave them alone in Canada to move to Texas. But
Kron loved his wife: he was one of the few Canadian Tire
executives married to the same woman he started out with. He
decided to commute between Texas and Toronto. Every
Sunday night, Kron crawled onto an Air Canada or an American Airlines flight to Dallas. That took three hours. He picked
up his car at the Dallas airport, and drove two hours to
Wichita Falls, where he rented an apartment a few minutes
from White's head office. Friday night, Kron would drive back
to the gridlock of the Dallas airport, park the car, climb
aboard Air Canada, and fly three hours home.

President of White's! It should have been such a proud
feeling for a boy from Kenora. Alas, from the day he assumed
the office, Kron didn't like what he saw. The company was an
open sore with the dimensions of a cancer: the worst of it was
invisible. Texas was in the middle of one of the biggest busts
in its busty history, thanks to a huge recession, the collapse of
the oil market, and a prolonged drought. All these factors
meant there was less money around for Texans to spend on the
things White's sold.

Or tried to sell. White's seemed to exist as a whim, a
sentimental creation with very little concrete connection to
the needs of its customers. "It was pretty chaotic at the time,"
Bob Hougham, Kron's righthand man in Texas, later said. "It
wasn't market-driven." To his friends Kron referred to White's
as "a furniture store that sold spark plugs." The place was a
mess, and the stores were losing $20 million a year. Texas was
no retail backwater, either. Muncaster & Co. had chosen to
stake a claim in the most sophisticated marketplace in North

America, the runoff zone for all the brilliant, wacko ideas and trends that burbled out of California, America's retail laboratory.

There were problems everywhere. One of the biggest was White's name. At Tire's head office a thousand miles away in Toronto, Muncaster, armed with inconclusive research, considered the name unimportant. Another school believed White's name had to be changed. White's, the theory went, stood for old stores, bad value, even – for there was a large black and Hispanic population in the southwest – racism. "The research showed that the name 'White's' had a negative halo around it," Gary Philbrick said. "And it did. All you had to do was go there. And my *strong* recommendation was to change the name as we refurbished the stores from White's to the American Way Stores." Kron trusted Philbrick, but he didn't want to spend the money for new signs. After all, the Billeses liked him because he was a penny-pincher.

Anyway, signs were only part of a greater problem with the stores' "presence." One of Tire's original reasons for buying White's was that its stores were the "right" size – some 25,000 square feet each. Up in Toronto that had seemed perfect, because Canadian Tire's stores averaged 25,000 square feet. But down in Texas? The Pep Boys chain, a specialty automotive empire out of the northeast now taking the southwest by storm, was building 100,000 square foot warehouse stores.

White's was also severely "understored" in every major city in the southwest. White's hadn't opened a new store in Dallas in fifteen years, though that city was one of the fastest-growing cities in North America. In San Antonio, a nice town with lots of culture and about 1.2 million people, White's had five stores to serve the whole city – one for every 250,000 residents, compared with one Tire store for every 25,000 to 50,000 customers in Canada. Furthermore, every time one of the old stores was closed for renovations, the chain lost sales.

Nor was the product mix at White's a glory to behold. Housewares and appliances, ripe with profit in Canadian Tire stores, were the toughest game in the United States. Everyone sold housewares and appliances. Tire's private brands – Motomaster and Mastercraft – meant nothing to brand-conscious Americans. Ninety percent of the shelves in a Pep Boys store were filled with car parts, almost twice the ratio at White's. When Kron slashed the prices of half his merchandise to draw customers, his profit margins evaporated.

And the locations! They were horrific, inner-city pits in undesirable areas. In Houston – maybe it wasn't Houston; in the end they all ran together in the mind – in Houston or wherever, once, Muncaster wouldn't get out of the car to visit a store. He was afraid to. "I was the only white guy in there," Philbrick remembered. "I was wearing a suit. They thought I was a cop."

Even Hugh Macaulay, a relative neophyte to retailing who was eventually to replace Alex Barron as Tire's chairman, realized that Texas was a foreign land. Macaulay had dropped in on a store in Fort Worth – on his first trip to Texas, no less – and asked the store's manager what hours he worked. The manager looked at Macaulay as if he needed his head read. "You're new, aren't you, to Fort Worth?" the manager said.

"Well, that's obvious," Macaulay said. Macaulay could be testy when someone suggested he didn't understand. "I'm from Toronto."

"Well," the manager said, "you see that road out there?" He pointed out the door at the street. Macaulay nodded. "That's the dividing line between the black and the Hispanic population. And you don't want to be here after dark. And neither do the customers. So we close before it gets dark."

But Macaulay's greatest revelation about Texas had come to him in Dallas. Macaulay had stepped out of a White's store, a hodgepodge of tires and blenders and bikes, and glanced down the road, and all he saw, for miles in a straight line, were auto-specialty stores: car-radio brokers, trim shops, auto-glass replacement outfits, electrical repairmen, quick-lube joints, muffler halls, specialty-muffler halls, tire stores – specialty upon specialty as far as the eye could see. Texas, the entire United States, Macaulay realized, was a market of specialists ten times the size of Canada, with ten times the sophistication, ten times as many niches and nooks and crannies. And the market was not only ten times more complicated; it changed faster, too. In a country that prides itself on choice – even has a name for it, the American Dream – a three-way, do-it-yourself store like Canadian Tire was little more than an oddity, the retail equivalent of tonsils.

Forcing White's to be Canadian Tire wasn't going to work. White's needed to start from scratch. But starting over was out of the question financially, especially with Martha and Fred on the board. In any event, many insiders felt Kron was the wrong person for the White's job, an operations man rather than the necessary marketer. One of the first things Kron did in Texas was replace White's aging truck fleet. It had worked in Canada; why not in Texas? Out in British Columbia, Vern Forster figured Kron was panicking, "regressing to his comfort zone." But Kron's move was understandable: White's problems were so immense, he had to start somewhere.

As 1983 faded, losses at White's reached nearly $29 million – three times the $9.6 million loss of the year before. Tire's Canadian income was up nearly fifteen percent, but White's not only wiped out that gain, it dragged the parent company's net income down another 16 percent. So far White's had cost $165 million. The loss was not recoverable. White's had been set up as a separate company, to render the Billeses' dividends untaxable when the company turned a profit. Unfortunately, that meant White's losses couldn't be used to offset Tire's Canadian income for tax purposes. That drove John Kron crazy, but the Billeses wouldn't go back on the original plan. Change seem to confuse them.

Nearly $50 million had been pumped into White's to shrink

its crippling interest costs. Meanwhile Tire's shares hit a new
low of $8.50, down from $14 that year and way down from
the $72 Imasco had offered. The slide hurt Muncaster as
much as anyone: he had $2 million tied up in non-voting
shares. But Muncaster and Kron were still suggesting that
White's would turn a profit by 1985.

It was never to happen. Even the best Canadian Tire habits
proved impossible to reproduce in the hot, dry air of Texas.
Kron wanted to install a hyper-motivated dealer team, but
candidates were hard to find: twenty-five Canadian dealers
had eagerly moved south in December, 1984, but Kron
needed eighty. He turned to Canadian Tire's B list, well-
intentioned men who hadn't made the cut as dealers in
Canada. "Some of them [the Texas dealers] were absolute
losers, in my opinion," Hougham said. Canadian Tire had
never permitted dealers to sell below the company's listed
prices, but in Texas a merchant had to be flexible to strike
back at a multitude of local competitors. For that matter, U.S.
law prevents wholesalers from forcing retailers to sell at one
predetermined price – with the result that, in April, 1985,
twenty White's dealers sued Canadian Tire for $25 million
for alleged violation of anti-cartel laws. It was only a detail,
but it suggested to Martha Billes that someone hadn't done
his homework.

Despite all these problems, Kron blasted ahead, conforming
rigidly to the Canadian Tire formula. By December of 1984,
he had redesigned, renovated, refitted, restocked, relabelled
and restaffed nearly all White's stores in Texas. But time had
run out. "We were much too optimistic when we started the
project," Kron explained to the newspapers in one of the
many interviews he and Muncaster gave to calm the jangled
nerves of Tire's shareholders. "We thought it would take two
and a half years to make the operation profitable, but now it
will take us three and a half years." The truth was, Kron and
Muncaster made promises they couldn't keep to keep the
Billes family at bay. It was a huge mistake. "One of the things

we shouldn't have done was go in all at once," Bob Hougham thought, remembering how eager the team was to produce results quickly. "We made the same mistake forty-one times."

MEANWHILE, back in Toronto, life was no easier for Muncaster. He had spent a lot of time since the spring of 1984 arguing with the Billeses. The Billeses had paid for the shares they bought from the J.W. Billes estate the previous fall by splitting their common shares into one common voting share and four new non-voting A shares; splitting their old A shares into five new A shares; and then selling off as many A shares as they needed to pay for the common shares. For agreeing to this scheme, Muncaster had won two important concessions for the company's non-voting shareholders. The first concession was "takeover protection." The protection took the form of a three-quarter-inch clause in eight-point type in the small print of the notes at the back of the company's consolidated financial statements in Canadian Tire's 1983 annual report. In other words, it was easy to miss. If someone bought more than 49 percent of Tire's common shares, the company's non-voting shareholders became voting shareholders. That meant they could approve or reject any offer for a majority of the company's voting shares; which meant no one could buy a majority of Tire's shares without buying the non-voting shareholders out too. The upshot? The next time a company like Imasco made a suitable offer, the Billeses would be powerless to stop it. (The protection did not, as would later become clear, rule out the possibility of someone buying less than 50 percent of the Billeses' shares. But with Fred, Martha, and David in control of sixty percent of the common shares, and united for life, that seemed an unlikely possibility.)

The second concession Muncaster won was the right of the non-voting shareholders to appoint three independent directors to the board. This was important, because Fred and Martha had used their newly won voting control to wreak huge changes on Tire's board in the spring of 1984. Dick Billes and Robin Law had been asked to resign, and Alex Barron was dismissed over the telephone. All three had been Muncaster's boardroom allies, and all three had supported the wrong team in the Imasco fracas. Fred was still so sore over that contretemps – he figured Dick had forced up the price of the estate shares by $10 million – that he refused even to take telephone calls from Dick Thompson, Dick Billes's pal at the Toronto Dominion Bank.

Even so, Muncaster managed to exercise considerable sway over the makeup of the board. By February of 1984, the board's nominating committee – Martha, David, Fred, and Muncaster – were plowing through lists of prospective directors suggested by each board member and by an independent head hunter. From that point on, into April, the committee interviewed a new prospective director every ten days.

The new lay of Tireland was not easy on Muncaster, accustomed as he was to running his own show. Barron had served as a heat shield between the Billes family and Muncaster. Muncaster knew that, if he was to accomplish anything under the new Billes regime, he needed to replace Barron with someone sympathetic to his goals. To that end, he recommended Hugh Macaulay as chairman of the board.

That was a story in itself. Macaulay seemed a wise choice. A journalism graduate turned car salesman, Macaulay had made a name for himself as a member of Ontario's Big Blue Machine, the loosely-knit cabal of political operators that had helped make the Ontario Conservative Party of the early 1980s the longest-running democratic government in the world. William Davis, Ontario's premier, had rewarded Macaulay with the chairmanship of Ontario Hydro, on whose board Muncaster sat. When Muncaster asked him to sit on Tire's board, Macaulay was running a committee set up by Davis to investigate the possibility of building a domed stadium in Toronto.

A handful of days after agreeing to Muncaster's request that he sit on Tire's board, Macaulay had a call from Fred Billes. Fred and Martha wanted to take Hugh out to lunch. "They, wanted to look me over," Macaulay later remembered. Dean Muncaster may have found Macaulay, but Fred and Martha could veto him. They were already flexing their new owner-ship muscles. Two days later, Macaulay, Fred, and Martha lunched upstairs at the Elmwood Club, a substantial down-town women's sodality that had come to represent, at least among females in Toronto in 1984, the emerging power of women in business. The Elmwood Club was a serendipitous choice, given Martha's emerging presence in the compa-ny – the sort of place a woman could be proud of, could use to make a point: *my territory*, it seemed to say, *not yours, Mister*. Fred and Martha described their plans for the corpora-tion. "They were keenly interested in the company," Macau-lay remembered. "They wanted to take a role in it." The siblings were worried about the United States and the losses they were absorbing in B.C., but felt they had a strong retailing company on their hands. They liked Macaulay.

A few days later, Fred called again. Would Hugh stand for chairman? Macaulay was surprised. Alex Barron was a good friend. "Well," he said, "you only need one. And you've already got one."

Ah, but they didn't anymore. As soon as Fred hung up, Macaulay phoned Barron and Muncaster. Muncaster con-firmed that Barron was on his way out of Canadian Tire after twenty years as its chairman. Bad Alex! He had backed the wrong team. It would be a great help to Muncaster if Macaulay would preside over the Canadian Tire All-Class Dog-and-Pony Boardroom Extravaganza. Muncaster may not have mentioned Fred's tantrums.

Macaulay thought about it for a few days, and decided to give the chairmanship a try. It was Fred he phoned with the news. "It was Fred who asked me to be chairman, and it was

Fred I replied to," the new chairman later explained. Hugh
Macaulay knew how to play politics, that was for sure.

THE departure of Barron – with but a single paragraph of
appreciation in the 1984 annual report in his memory – discouraged Muncaster profoundly. So did the daily presence of
Fred and Martha. Still, he made the best of a bad lot. In April
he agreed to a brand new board of directors that, in addition
to himself, Martha, Fred, David, and Macaulay, included
Pierre Côté, chairman of Celanese Canada Inc.; Derwyn
Phillips, executive vice-president of The Gillette Company's
North American operations; Jean Pigott, chairman of Morrison
Lamothe Inc. (itself a family-owned business); William Sobey,
chairman of Sobey Stores Ltd. (ditto); and Bruce Sully,
chairman and president of Champion Road Machinery Group.
While Fred and Martha personally approved each new board
member, Muncaster managed to present them with a list of
candidates he knew he could live with.

Two weeks before the annual meeting at which Macaulay
was elected to the board, Bernie Freedman's annual report
appeared. The record was a hit, and so, in a different way, was
the color photograph of the company's old board of directors.
On the left sat the Billeses. On the right were Dean Muncaster
and his management team. Dick Billes was still a director,
technically, but he had chosen not to be seen in the same
room with his cousins and uncle. Muncaster wore a peculiar,
restrained smile, as if he were sitting on a small but very hard
hockey puck. It was the last time his picture would appear in
the annual report, and he looked unhappy. All things considered, a pop-up board of directors would have been most
inappropriate.

IT was strange, sometimes, how naïve Dean Muncaster could
be. After the auction of 1983 and the share split of the
following spring, the Billeses controlled more than sixty
percent of the voting shares of Canadian Tire. But the split

also increased the number of Tire's non-voting shares seven-fold, to more than 76 million, and reduced the Billeses' slice of the company to a fraction (approximately four percent) of its total equity. Given that ratio, Muncaster expected the family to back away from trying to run the company.

But John Kron had no such illusions. By the fall of 1983, he could see trouble ahead. "And it wasn't White's. It wasn't anything, but that the family wanted to run the company. And Dean was in their way." That, at least, was the way Kron saw things. He was Dean Muncaster's friend, and always loyal.

The losses at White's infuriated the Billeses, even though, to Kron's recollection, "there was never a request put to the board about White's that was not supported unanimously." So why were they mad? Perhaps – and such were the speculations of executives and observers alike – because White's gave Fred and Martha a focal point for their vague dissatisfaction with Dean Muncaster. The new board knew very little about Canadian Tire and retailing; to them, Dean Muncaster was not an established hero who would eventually set the company right, but a chief executive officer with some serious explain-ing to do. On this new board of amateurs, Fred and Martha had loads of experience, and their opinions were valued as highly as Muncaster's.

They used their influence. At the behest of Fred and Martha, most of the directors visited Texas. "Just the fact [the direc-tors] were there was disruptive," Bob Hougham recalled. "It was kind of like the Big Brother syndrome." Even Barbara Billes, Fred's wife, flew down, and drove Muncaster wild by informing him – quite unnecessarily, Muncaster felt – that White's bug-laden computer system wasn't working. "In the very late stages," Muncaster remembered, "Barbara was cer-tainly anxious to be involved." But at least Barbara backed Fred, who for quite a long time believed White's might make it. Martha was a different story.

If Martha carried a torch for her father and an ax to avenge the years she had been kept out of the company, she also had good reason to be alarmed by White's. She resented her lack of control over what was happening. "We listened to the presentation of the corporation, John Kron in particular, and Dean Muncaster," Martha remembered of the original White's pitch. "And they were selling, and we were buying." She was too inexperienced to object. "I accepted it for what it purported to be."

She quickly developed concerns, however. She was troubled by the way Muncaster and his team changed their Texas gameplan. White's dealers fell into two somewhat obscure categories, the pure, Tire-style franchisees and another less formal group. One group were the 3000-series dealers; the other was 4000-series dealers. At every board meeting Martha asked which was which, but the answer never came clear. "The number of dealers never went up, but it was being severely curtailed. And they were the ones that weren't costing us anything." And every meeting seemed to present a new schedule for refurbishing White's stores.

The confusion did nothing to assuage Martha's fear, sown initially during the Imasco takeover bid, that Muncaster was planning to cut her out of the action. "We were always given a grandiose story about how different influences had affected the market, but that things were coming around," Martha remembered. Her father regarded John Kron highly, so Martha did too. "It appeared that Kron was doing an honest job. But it also appeared that something was wrong, that had started to bother me very early on. By the time the 1981 annual report was printed, I was downright scared. And I won't give an adjective for the 1983 annual report." Martha saw Canadian Tire's equity – *her* equity – running down the drain. "There was some sort of rot at the core, some force that we couldn't get a handle on. It was sort of self-consuming. Almost a death wish, it seemed to me. They were hell-bent on destruction. And I couldn't stop them. They just lost touch."

Muncaster had tampered with Tire's magic formula. (That was the phrase Tiremen used: "the magic formula.") He had also stopped talking to Martha, which did nothing to appease her. Martha was a shy woman, and she appreciated people who took the time to draw her out. "Muncaster took our opinion as inconsequential," she charged. "He took his opinion as the words that counted. Brother Fred and I were squawking about White's very early on. But it was a very long time before anything happened about White's. It was strange. It was always sort of a blank stare, the sweet smile, and then a total ignoring of what was going on. . . . I couldn't talk with Muncaster, either personally or about business. And I always thought it was a reflection of his relationship with people and the company. I was a woman, and I was a usurper in the boardroom." Sometimes, as Martha painted the story, it was easy to see Canadian Tire as much more than just a corporation: it was a Middle Kingdom filled with evil wizards and princelings trying to wrest power from an innocent princess.

Of course there were less surrealistic explanations for the antipathy between Martha and Muncaster. Jean Pigott had travelled by car through Texas with Fred and Martha, and she had seen them have "fifty fits" over the state of White's. "They intuitively knew what they knew," Pigott has suggested. "That I think was Fred and Martha's problem. They had been raised in the business so much, they couldn't show what they knew through research and computer printouts. So there was a cultural gap between them and management." That, if one need edit, was putting it mildly.

GRADUALLY, Martha lost faith in John Kron as well. When White's preliminary results for 1983 rolled in, the carnage was fantastic. The company was losing $1 million a week. The Texas recession had started late, in 1982. That was another lesson John Kron learned about the differences between Canada and the United States: when the Americans had a recession, they had a doozy. There were fewer social-assistance programs for unemployed Americans to fall back on. Or, as Kron explained it to the board on his trips back home to Toronto, the U.S. economy was much more "pragmatic" than the warm, safe, tiny Canadian one.

Back at home in Toronto . . . now there was a concept. On his frequent trips back to head office, Kron was beginning to experience a new brand of weirdness . . . strange, strange vibrations. They didn't stem from anything he could put his finger on: nothing so obvious. They were only suspicions, feelings whose very vagueness made them worse. At first when the feelings cropped up, in the fall of 1983, Kron thought he was paranoid, that his mind was playing tricks on him. By 1984, with the family in control of the estate's shares, he knew his paranoia was reality. Whenever he flew back to head office, that kingdom in Toronto that had *never experienced a loss in sixty years*, a subtle aura surrounded him, as if he were radioactive. Dependable old Johnny Kron, with four pens in his shirt pocket, his thick ankles peeking out over his short black socks and his dusty hard-working shoes, Mr. Reliable himself, was . . . you could hear the whispers . . . *no retailing experience . . . not a marketer*. John Kron was . . . *fucking up*. If there was anything Dean's boys didn't do, it was that.

Especially with the family lurking in the boardroom like a flock of vultures. "That close family feeling," as Kron called it, referring not just to the family per se but to the Canadian Tire family, executives and yeomen alike, everyone who owned shares whose value had plummetted, thanks to White's. It was quite a shock to them to encounter White's losses. But Kron's unease derived from more than anxiety over paper losses. It was as if his friends had started to abandon him, to make excuses. Kron could understand their feelings. "Well, the board was concerned, and I guess they had every right to be, with the losses. Had I been on the other side of the table, I might have been just the same way."

But he wasn't on the other side of the table. He was John Kron, president, White Stores Inc. He was . . . *fucking up*. Kron would come to the board and say, I need another $5 million, and they'd give it to him. But his blood pressure was sending telegraph messages to his heart, and there was the bloody commute. Three hours on a plane, two hours in the car, it was a long time to sit with nothing to do but stew about the goddamn company. . . .

That was when John Kron started to "verbalize," as the shrinks would say, to publicly express his doubts. He had first done so a year after he took over White's. Look, he would say to the board – to the board! Out loud! Like some snivelling self-fulfilling prophecy! – look, if you think I'm the problem at White's, please don't hesitate to remove me from this situation. "My exposure to marketing and all these things is minimal at best," he would say. By 1984, he was bringing it up at every other board meeting. *I'm the first to accept the fact that maybe it needs a better man than I.* He didn't mean it as an ultimatum: after all, he had never walked away from a tough situation. The answer, even at the board level, was always the same: no, no, John, we have complete faith in you. And yet, the next moment, out in the corridor, the subtle vibrations started up again. "You were no longer a part," Kron discovered. "Sort of, *he's here again.*" As if he were some grotty old sack of skin and rubbing alcohol who kept wandering in off the street, or some relative no one knew what to do with, the family failure. Maybe if we ignore it, it'll go away. . . . Martha noticed the pressure was getting to Kron. She said as much, on several occasions, to Muncaster, warning him that Kron was in trouble. "But Muncaster always said, 'Oh, he's okay.' "

Gary Philbrick sensed the pressure was getting to Kron. Philbrick had stopped working as a consultant on the White's venture by the early 1980s, following a disagreement over the company's computer systems. The family's lack of support for White's angered him, because Philbrick believed in White's; after all, he and Kron and Muncaster had discovered White's, had studied it and pushed it to the board. But without the financial support of the family, he could see White's was destined for failure. Still, he stayed in touch with Muncaster and the Silver Seven, and what he saw happening to John Kron troubled him deeply.

It was just a detail . . . probably insignificant . . . but all of a sudden Kron was showing up late for meetings, which wasn't like him at all. All those years on top, and suddenly . . . the weird isolated feeling . . . Philbrick knew all about that. He had suffered a severe case of executive burnout after he left Tire, and it was not a happy memory. "When I was very ill," Philbrick recalled, "it would take me fifteen minutes to decide whether to have a glass of milk or a glass of iced tea. And it was a wrenching decision. I couldn't even dial a telephone." Kron wasn't suffering from depression, but Philbrick sensed the pressure on him was intense. He wondered if Kron wasn't staying away from the confrontations that reminded him of the mess in Texas, of . . . say it . . . his *failure*.

Bob Hougham agreed with Philbrick's assessment. Hougham had blood pressure problems of his own when he finally resigned from Tire in September of 1984. It was funny, the way leaving Tire affected them all for months afterwards. Hobbs, Philbrick, Hougham . . . Hougham had never worked so hard and been under so much pressure in his life as he had his last months at White's. And yet when he left, the emptiness set in like quick-dry cement. It was partly because none of them had ever lost before, and partly that their natural competitiveness, the trait that made them superb retailers, also made them sore losers. They had measured their own worth by their performance, classic cases of outer-directed corporate ambition, and they took failure just as personally. "I had the feeling by the time I left that John Kron was going through the motions," Hougham admitted. "The horse was out of the barn . . . somebody just forgot to turn out the lights."

No one was terribly surprised, then, when late in the spring of 1985 Dean Muncaster made the announcement: by year end, the board would decide whether or not to sell White's.

White's had lost $55 million in 1984, dragging Tire's profits down by 41 percent from the year before. A forty-one percent drop! The staff at head office, the hard-working band of profit-sharers, might have reacted more dolefully to news of atomic war, but not much. The irony was that, by the final weeks, White's had finally begun to show some life. Kron had pushed the chain almost exclusively into automobile parts, accessories, and maintenance – the original Canadian Tire formula. Toward the very end, sales in one ten-week period rocketed up twenty percent.

But it was too late. The armchair quarterbacks and retrospective seers were already having a field day with their imagined postmortems on White's. The entire company was a morgue of theories. A.J. blamed Muncaster for letting his success go to his head; others accused Dean Muncaster of cronyism, making a pun on John Kron's name. "Muncaster surrounded himself with people who were on the same frequency," Vern Forster insisted. "And because he was a lonely person, or a loner, the people he did spend a lot of time with acted like a cocoon." Others saw Texas as a psychological inevitability. "Success breeds emptiness," a Canadian Tire executive once explained. "Your greatest strengths at the time become your greatest weaknesses." Muncaster's own laissez-faire attitudes had come back to haunt him, and White's had become shattering proof that Dean Muncaster was perhaps not the retailing genius everyone wanted to believe he was.

Or that Tire was the company invincible. The insularity and ease of doing business in Canada had spawned a false sense of security among Tire's executives. "I think a good question," an analyst once suggested – we were eating lunch in the Imperial Room at the Royal York Hotel, his favorite spot, and the analyst was on his fifth dinner roll and his second Heineken – "is, how good was Canadian Tire, and how lucky was it? Canada's not as competitive an environment as the United States. Canada has been an easier row to hoe."

If there's a lesson in the analyst's words, it's one Dean
Muncaster did not absorb until too late as he sought to eclipse
the Billes family's achievement by doing in two years in Texas
what had taken them sixty years in Canada. But he didn't duck
the blame when he realized his mistake. When the extent of
the White's debacle became apparent, Muncaster put it down
to overconfidence. "I guess we all thought we were pretty
smart up here," he said simply, "coming off this fifteen-
year success." What he couldn't expect at the time, though,
was how little those fifteen years would weigh against the
Texas misadventure once A.J.'s family made their own bid for
control.

▼

PART III

SKID MARKS

13

OURS

ONCE, AS I WAITED FOR David and Fred Billes to return from a meeting with their lawyers, Fred's wife Barbara asked me why writers have long hair. "Well," I said, "I suppose it's to be different. But musicians have long hair too."

"But musicians don't," Barbara said, peaking her eyebrows and speaking in the flutey, sing-song voice she seemed to use whenever she was confronted. "If you go to the Toronto Symphony, there's not one musician there on the stage that has long hair, except some of the women."

"That's true," I said. Barbara was always coming up with these logical cul-de-sacs.

"Even Murray McLauchlan doesn't have such long hair." This was from Donna Billes, David's wife, who was waiting with us. Donna was quieter than Barbara, and shy almost to the point of invisibility. Like David, she seldom spoke without seeming to think for an excruciating interval. Company lore held that Muriel Billes, Barbara's mother-in-law, had never been as fond of Donna as she was of Barbara.

"Or Liberace?" Barbara said, a trace of triumph in her voice.

It was true; not a long hair on him. "But what about the Beatles?" I said.

"Different era!" Donna said. "Flower power."

Flower power. Different era, indeed. Barbara and Donna were rooted in a different, simpler epoch, a frozen time zone in which all the Billeses seemed to live and think – the era of their father. Sometimes they seemed like dinosaurs.

No one knew that better than Dean Muncaster. In the spring of 1985, Muncaster celebrated nineteen years as the steward of Canadian Tire. Ironically, he had never felt less certain of his power. Working with Tire's new, Billes-seal-of-approval board of directors was a far cry from the solid days when he preached to a loyal board of his own managers. The new crowd sat with the family at the opposite end of the board-room table, staring down at Muncaster and his team. But the board was child's play next to Muncaster's real problem – the emerging ambitions of Fred and Martha Billes.

Muncaster saw the problem clearly. Muncaster believed that Fred and Martha resented the fact that his name was more clearly associated with Canadian Tire than their own, and wanted to run the company themselves. Muncaster objected. The Billeses did not represent a majority of the company's shareholders, and he certainly wasn't about to watch A.J.'s children dismantle the empire he had created. Muncaster had transformed Canadian Tire from a $100-million hardware store into a $2-billion Canadian institution. The Billes children, to his mind, had had very little to do with it.

In a strange way it was Barbara Billes who drove Muncaster craziest. By the standards of Western Business School, where Muncaster and his team had been trained in the art of High Rationalism, Barbara Billes was nothing more than a plump, dirty-blond housewife. But if her country upbringing had left her roughly finished – she had a habit of flooding a room with her emotion of the moment, for example – it had also graced her with a common touch. Barbara's Emotions of the Day were well known at Tire's main store at Davenport Road in Toronto, where she often visited her Freddy and chatted with his employees. Barbara made no secret of her affection for Fred: they often held hands in public. Barbara had taken lessons from Muriel Billes, Fred's mother, on that subject. "Barbara and Muriel were very close," a friend of the family has observed. "Because Muriel saw in Barbara a person who could strive to have Fred as the head of the organization. And it was Barbara who wanted Fred to be president." Whatever else she was – and irrational was a word that came up a lot – Barbara was intensely loyal to Fred.

Barbara was no intellectual, but she possessed an unpretentious middle-class confidence that was rooted in what she knew and liked and approved of. She had been affected by the enormous fortune she married, even if she told her children to play it down. She was terrified of kidnappers. She instructed her eldest son, Alfred, Jr., always to deny that the family had money. "I'm one of the poor relatives," he would say on meeting someone crass enough to ask if he was one of *those* Billeses. If someone asked where he lived, he replied: "In a house with a chimney and a front door and a back door, just like you."

This was a slight understatement. The house Fred and Barbara Billes lived in at 30 High Point Road, up on The Bridle Path near Conrad Black and Robert Campeau, where several major-league capitalists were vying to create the late twentieth-century Canadian equivalent of a Venetian palazzo – up there, on High Point Road, where the lawns were so vast and green they resembled a lush golf course, Fred and Barbara's house was an event unto itself.

The house had been built in 1977 by John C. Parkin, a well-known Toronto architect, for between $1 million and $3 million. Actually, "built" was entirely the wrong word: the house had been poured, for it was formed entirely of concrete. From the outside the thirty-room, 30,000 square-foot *objet* resembled a private research institute. That was from the front, where the circular drive and recessed banks of windows and four ventilation hoods and tiered brick entranceway and white and pink quartz-and-concrete walls – concrete! in a house! – blended into two and a half acres of landscaped shrubbery. From the back it looked like an office building.

But inside! Glorious! The drama began as one stepped across the massive threshold into a fifty-three-foot atrium foyer built around a waterfall which cascaded into a reflecting pool through a Babylonian garden of hanging plants. Sometimes Barbara covered the pool itself with a strong wooden dance floor when she held parties. The dining-room walls were sheathed in hand-painted Oriental murals that carried on right around the room. The living-room was forty feet long, about three times the length of a standard living room. Breakfast was taken in a room that hung over a two-and-a-half story indoor pool. There were balconies and sunrooms and five bedrooms. And hardware! It was as if Barbara and Fred had designed the house as a Canadian Tire Hall of Fame. Garages? Seven, all remote controlled! An eighth garage contained a workshop with hot and cold running water. There were wet bars, imported English antique mantelpieces, fourteen-foot ceilings, tinted sliding-glass doors, endless closets, powder-rooms, pot lights, top-hat lights, floodlights, skylights, a twenty-foot kitchen, Swedish chimney covers, Persian carpets, five-piece bathrooms adjoining living-room-sized dressing-rooms, five-foot-wide showers, whirlpools, bathrooms with electronically heated floors to warm the feet and aid in the evaporation of water, *en suite* this and walk-in that and walk-out the other, grasscloth, ceramic tile, quarry tile flooring, double washers and dryers, an upper hall "computer area," a built-in sewing-center, a family room *fifty-six feet long and thirty feet wide* (roughly four times the size of the average downtown Toronto condominium), a projection room, a dark room, an exercise room, a hydraulic elevator (for Fred's overburdened legs) with its own telephone, earthquake-proof ceilings suspended on springs for silence – earthquakes! In Toronto! Be prepared! – nine (9) furnaces, an individually-controlled thermostat in every principal room, integrated fire alarms, computerized security systems (Fred was very big on security systems), housewide intercoms, multiple phone lines, an underground sprinkler system, a sixty-ton central air conditioner, two dishwashers, two Jennair stoves, a trash compactor. . . . Though Dick Billes liked to say that from the outside Fred's house looked like a Canadian Tire store, it was inside where the comparison was most apt.

But the centerpiece of the entire glorious creation was the Pool. Swimming-pools have been a central icon of leisure capitalism for most of the twentieth century, a fact not lost on Fred and Barbara. The pool room was fifty feet long, thirty-two feet wide – about the same size as the family room – two and a half stories high, and glassed in on three sides. It gave onto a walk-out sun patio that sported its own gas barbecue. The pool room was the solar plexus around which the entire house was built. Fred could come home at the end of the day from the store and walk into the breakfast room and there could gaze down into the shimmering calm of the pool. The pool itself was astonishing. It was twelve feet deep and shaped like a B. B, for Barbara? B, for Billes? And if that were not enough, this shining monument to suburban leisure life carved in a swerving, majestic *beta* – as if that were not enough, suspended over the pool like charms on a bracelet were . . . Canadian Tire products, tail pipes and brake discs and tires, all in white enamel, a massive, life-size Canadian Tire mobile. It had been Barbara's idea.

Of course there were those who tittered and sneered at this monument, just as they tittered and sneered at the entire house and at Fred and Barbara Billes. Such people lacked the imagination to comprehend Barbara's vision. Fred and Barbara had never been known as creative or cultured, but Barbara Billes's house was a monument equal in its way to the greatest Medici cathedral, inasmuch as both were quintessential monuments of their own eras. Who needs Carrara marble and frescoes by Michelangelo when you can have hand-formed concrete living-room walls and a front hall like the lobby of

John Portman's Detroit Renaissance Plaza Hotel? Who needs centuries of learning when we have an eleven-hundred-square-foot master-bedroom suite? Who needs Botticelli or Dante or even Bach when we have, in the same master bedroom, a bed the size of a flatbed truck, topped off with a leather headboard that looks like a package of giant Swift's Premium Wieners fanned out like a poker hand? Number 30 High Point Road did not reek of culture or class as the stiffened brains of the Canadian Art-Lit Establishment claimed to understand it, but Barbara Billes wasn't interested in that sort of culture. Thirty High Point Road was a paean to the *middle class*: it was utterly original and unapologetic and unique. In the same way that the West Edmonton Mall is the Las Vegas of Canada – an entire world transformed into an indoor shopping mall – the Billes house was middle-class Canada's idea of Versailles.

Middle classicism! Such a rich and complex lust! For Fred's and Barbara's pride in the everyday objects of consumption was, in fact, a form of protective coloration. They had never appreciated the suggestion that their enormous wealth made them something special. Unexpected visitors to High Point Road, finding Barbara on her knees digging in the garden, sometimes mistook her for a hired gardener, an inhabitant, perhaps, of the servants' quarters in the concrete bunker. Barbara seldom set them straight. She told them Mrs. Billes wasn't home. Fred did the same thing while he tinkered with the engine of his huge cruiser, the *Puba*, and was mistaken for some mountainous grease monkey rather than its owner.

It was one of the games they played. Anonymity was a way to escape the demands of "being a Billes," a way to escape being "more" or "better" or at least something other than what they were. Fred took his just-another-guy-in-the-street act to inspired lengths. On one spectacular occasion, a Forest Hill couple invited Fred and Barbara to dinner. The hosts had heard that Fred drank only champagne and so had ordered several bottles of Dom Perignon, at $65 a bottle, for the occasion. Fred showed up with a white plastic grocery bag in his hand, which he proferred at the front door. "I don't know whether you've heard," he said, "but I only drink this." Inside the bag were two bottles of Bright's. That night over dinner Barbara entranced her hosts with stories of how hard it was to run her household on the tiny budget Fred allowed her.

But Fred and Barbara Billes's thrilling lack of pretension, their joy in being ordinary denizens of the middle class, had a dark flip side. *We are no different from anyone else*, it suggested, *but no one is any better than we are, either*. As a result, Fred and Barbara found it difficult to see Dean Muncaster as anyone special, as someone whose priorities or visions were any wider or more far-sighted than their own. It was clear to many observers that in this regard Barbara "had an enormous influence on Fred."

Thus Barbara thought nothing of making her presence known throughout the company: after all, she had as much right to do so as anyone else, and then more, because her husband "owned" it all. After the share auction of 1983, Barbara called Lynn Cox, Muncaster's assistant, incessantly. Barbara was full of suggestions about what charities and interest groups the company ought to support. (Polo was one enthusiasm.) Her requests drove Muncaster wild. John Kron, who was out of the direct line of Barbara's fire, watched in wonder. "I don't know," he once observed. "I guess there's a God up there. Because somehow he made Barbara and Fred a match." Barbara, of course, was simply being protective; she guarded her family as fiercely as a thrush does its family and its nest. "But thank God I only saw her for an hour a month. . . . She had very, very great difficulty separating personal life from that of the company."

Barbara didn't hesitate to tell Muncaster why the computer system at White's wasn't working properly. And she made it perfectly clear she thought Fred ought to be the president of

Canadian Tire. For a while, at least, until he ran smack into his sister, Fred appeared to share her fantasy.

BUT we are getting ahead of ourselves. As the fall of 1984 thawed into the spring of 1985, Muncaster's relations with the Billes family had deteriorated to the point of no return. There were those – Martha, for instance – who believed that the relationship had begun to sour the day Muncaster assumed the presidency in 1966. "Muncaster had a change of character," Martha said, remembering the "kitchen cabinet" conversations at 24 Old Forest Hill Road after A.J. got home from work. "Muncaster severed a tie." Certainly Hobbs' departure hadn't improved the atmosphere. But the spring of 1985 brought a new twist: Now, A.J. and Muncaster had stopped talking. Their differences over profit-sharing and nepotism – whether dealers could pass their stores on to family members, as A.J. insisted – had become a wall between Muncaster and his mentor. Muncaster also objected to A.J.'s appearance on the board, once again, that spring. Until then A.J. had been an honorary director, but now Fred wanted his father back in the boardroom full-time.

Muncaster and A.J. had barely spoken in a year. Denny Brown, a dealer in Ottawa and a longtime friend of both men, tried to soften Muncaster toward A.J., to convince him to share information with the old man.

"No, I don't want to," Muncaster would reply. Muncaster didn't relish the thought of another six-hour conversation about fifty-fifty profit-sharing. "You know, he takes all day when he gets into a problem area."

"You know what to do with that. Have the meeting begin at four-thirty."

"I represent all the shareholders, not just them. I don't have time for a minority."

"Nothing wrong with that," Brown said. "But when you're playing with the founder. . . ."

Or, Brown might have added, when you're playing with

your father. For A.J. Billes was Dean Muncaster's professional *pater*, just as Muncaster was A.J.'s adopted son, the son who had made good. The split between them was deeper than policy, or control. It was, in any other context, a profoundly Oedipal conflict, with Mother Tire as the prize. A man willing to deal in the currency of emotions might have yielded, but Dean Muncaster wasn't the type.

No one was more offended by this standoff than Martha, Muncaster's corporate sister. Martha had joined the board in 1980, forcing A.J. to step down to make room for her. "He [my father] made room for me, where others [Fred and David] wouldn't." Her father and brothers had kept her out of the business, but she seemed to blame Dean Muncaster. Her desperate desire to connect with her father, to speak his language and be recognized by him, had by now become a crusade to return to A.J.'s basic principles and practices. Martha had become her father's champion. Anyone who opposed A.J. was an enemy. Muncaster was no longer content to be a hired gun, Martha believed; he wanted control. And control, as Muncaster knew, was something the Billes children had been trained to think of as theirs alone. The more Martha went after Muncaster – with "facts," as she called them – the more Muncaster pulled his team around him for protection; the more Martha felt cut off and left out, the more she sniped. The all-Canadian, self-perpetuating, corporate neurosis. A psychoanalyst would have had a field day.

Alas, there was less and less of a team for Muncaster to take cover behind. Muncaster's managers were like a band of rebels under siege, slowly dwindling in numbers. Hobbs had been gone seven years, but there were other, more recent casualties. Philbrick had been forced out of the company as White's went down. Kron was fighting for his life in Texas. Barron was gone from the board, Robin Law was no longer a director, both victims of the Imasco scrap. As for the new band of directors, they were understandably too new on the scene to think of Dean as a hero.

As the new year of 1985 dawned, Martha moved in for the kill. During the last week of January, Denvil Brown, the longtime Ottawa dealer, received a telephone call. It was Martha. Brown was vacationing at his double mobile home in Pompano Beach, Florida. On the telephone, Martha said she wanted to go across the country visiting Tire's directors, to deal with what she referred to as Dean's "problem with procrastination." She wanted Brown to go with her.

Brown hung up and immediately called Hugh Macaulay, Tire's chairman. Macaulay was in his own condominium further up the coast of Florida taking a well-deserved vacation from his chores as chairman of the board. Despite the tension on the board, Macaulay was, to Muncaster's mind, performing his duties admirably. Muncaster trusted his chairman. But Macaulay was a political animal, and now he was faced with a classic political dilemma: Muncaster versus Martha, management versus family, brains versus power. Would political wisdom – something Macaulay knew a lot about – not demand that he let the opposing forces fight toward the middle, toward compromise? How could he know, with but a year's experience at the corporation, that there was no middle ground left? Or perhaps he did know: it was hard to tell with Macaulay. Macaulay told Brown that he didn't agree with Martha, but that Brown ought to do as he thought best.

Brown went with Martha. He was a dealer, after all, with a dealer's nose for opportunity. He believed the balance of power at Tire lay among management and the family and the dealers; this was the dealers' chance to stake some power within the new family-dominated company, and perhaps to restore peace. Travelling with Martha, Brown got an earful of her life stories: how she had been educated in Jewish schools, and looked down upon as a Gentile; how she had been scorned by her demanding, workaholic father; how Freddy, the favored son, had been sent to any school he wanted. "What I saw," Brown recalled, "was a girl who dotes on her father, really wants to please her father. And her father was

really using her as his whipping boy, so to speak. But Freddy
was the one who was bitter to his father, because his father
would not let him become president." Brown sensed that
Martha still didn't trust anybody. He also saw her pull rank
when she needed to shore up an argument. "She's a Billes,
which she plays up a bit."

Martha's cross-country tour further galvanized the board
against Muncaster. The directors Muncaster had tried to win
over now resisted him outright. Pierre Côté, in whom Muncaster originally heard a voice of reason, was busier and more
aloof than Muncaster had hoped. Jean Pigott had left to take
over the National Capital Commission. Derwyn Phillips had
resigned from the board after a year, claiming the excuse of
other responsibilities. William Sobey had been forced to
leave – "broken-hearted," Martha recalled – because the dealers believed Sobey's own retail business created a serious
conflict of interest.

The buffers between Dean Muncaster and the family were
falling away. By the spring in 1985, Muncaster was meeting
with the board's executive committee – which meant with the
family and Macaulay – before every board meeting. The purpose of the meetings was to discuss "substantive issues" such
as the sale of White's, John Kron's performance, quality
control, and the company's newspaper advertising program.
Martha, at least, figured this was what an executive committee
was supposed to do. When Martha had first joined Muncaster's
"management" board in 1980, she never heard talk of
financial details; instead, operational issues, shipping, receiving, were the order of the day. In 1984, under the influence
of Martha and Fred, the board was suddenly populated with
professional directors, most of whom were retailing rookies. A
good percentage of formal board meetings were taken up
educating the new directors. That left the executive committee to discuss substantive issues. "We were simply doing what
they'd done before," Martha said.

That wasn't how Muncaster saw it. The family suddenly had

concerns that Muncaster considered management issues, and therefore outside the province of the family, whose role on the board, he believed, was largely ceremonial. But of course the issues themselves were beside the larger point: Fred and Martha Billes were countermanding Muncaster's authority, and attempting to influence the running of the company they controlled. Muncaster's standard answer in the past had been to play the Tough Man: this is my answer, if you don't like it, find a new boy to run the company. The Billeses had always backed down. But now they were insistent. They especially wanted to be out of White's – so they said, at least – and Muncaster disagreed. But gradually the disagreements were wearing him down. "You might have won in the short run," Muncaster later recalled, "but in my view they were so committed to this course of action, which meant doing without me."

MAY 2, 1985, was a Thursday, the regular monthly board meeting. Shortly after the session began, Hugh Macaulay asked Muncaster to step outside. John Kron joined him. Macaulay suggested the two men wait in Dean's office across the hall from the boardroom on the eleventh floor – the office Dean had always maintained, down there among the operational people – while the board deliberated. Macaulay would call them when they were needed.

By ten o'clock, as they sat in Muncaster's office, Muncaster and Kron knew they were waiting to have their fate at Canadian Tire decided for them. Robin Law, who was still the company's lawyer, joined them intermittently. The trio were running back and forth between Muncaster's office and the boardroom as if they were playing a child's game, a pretend Inquisition. Kron found the entire affair bizarre. Twenty years at a company, and suddenly he was being treated like a three-year-old who had broken a vase and pooped his pants and was waiting for Daddy to come home to spank him.

Kron and Muncaster knew there was no just reason for the

board to dismiss them. But reasons were irrelevant, and easily manufactured: what mattered, they figured, was that Fred and Martha wanted them out. Earlier that year, in January, Kron had discovered that the board was secretly trying to replace him as the head of the Texas operations. No one had informed Kron of the fact, and no one, at least as far as Kron knew, had told Muncaster. Kron had always been a loyal company man, the most obedient of dogs, and in return he expected loyalty from the company.

Life within the cozy world of the Canadian Tire family, under the benign protectorship of Dean Muncaster, had evidently blinded him to the fundamental ruthlessness of corporate life. Now, the board's perfidy frightened him. "That's the sort of thing that destroys a company," Kron later said – preferring not to mention the effect it could have on a man's life and psyche. He had been particularly chilled, that winter, when the human resources committee of the board hired a psychological assessment outfit to run a full profile of each member of management. Kron – the man the board wanted to replace – came up as the only person capable of replacing Dean Muncaster. Muncaster passed the test with flying colors as well. But the board had ignored the tests.

Ten-thirty. What the hell was the board doing? From the window of Muncaster's office, the trio could see spring leaking into the air. A change of season always gave a Tireman a jolt: his mind immediately jumped to shipping schedules and store refurbishing, to planning for the influx of Tire's new seasonal merchandise.

Today, however, a charming day in May, Muncaster and Kron could be forgiven their preoccupations. As the minutes ticked by, snatches of good and bad news filtered out of the boardroom. The good news was that Kron didn't appear to be a topic of conversation. The bad news was that Dean Muncaster most certainly was.

More flitting back and forth. What the hell was the board doing in there?!?

More time passed. Every once in a while Macaulay would poke his woolly head into Dean's office and say, "You'd better wait another half hour," or some such thing.

Then the news started coming, via messengers. The board was forming a special committee to assess the future of White's, and to arrange the orderly dismissal of Muncaster. The special committee had been granted the full power of the board! The bad news was, Dean Muncaster wasn't on it. "And that," John Kron recalled, "was when the shit hit the fan. It was very upsetting to Dean."

The Billeses weren't on the committee either, but that was arguably a legal formality. Certainly the Billeses approved the committee. As Muncaster and Kron saw it, the board's mission was to get rid of Dean Muncaster and anyone else who stood between the Billeses and effective control of a company the family did not own.

The Billeses had effectively engineered a coup d'état in which the future of one of the country's largest public companies was suddenly taken out of the hands of its duly and legally elected board and officers, including Dean Muncaster, the chief executive officer of the company. Fred, Martha, and David Billes had effectively seized control of Canadian Tire. Even by the roughhouse standards of Canadian business, this was hardball. A coup! And it was invisible to the public and a majority of the company's shareholders.

Muncaster hired a lawyer the next day.

Hugh Macaulay went along with these events. Kron wasn't surprised. He, for one, didn't share Muncaster's high opinion of the former chairman. Kron referred to Macaulay as "just a used-car salesman" – a common, if unfair, assessment of the chairman. Like most of Dean's crowd, he couldn't help comparing Macaulay with Alex Barron, who had run the board back in the golden days. Kron had travelled with Macaulay on several occasions, visiting banks to raise money for the company's Texas venture. "You get to know a man, and a chairman should support his people," Kron said. Kron did not feel Macaulay had been sufficiently supportive. Kron had suggested to Muncaster early on that Macaulay might let them down. Now Kron felt vindicated: Macaulay had permitted the special executive committee to be formed. "It was odd," Kron allowed. "And legally, it was questionable."*

Kron flew back to Texas to resume his duties, but Muncaster had other things to think about. Legal negotiations over a severance agreement bogged down. It was not the amount of the settlement that was at issue – Muncaster was eventually granted the standard two years' salary, or roughly $1 million. One of the sticking points was a gag order the Billeses wished to impose on Muncaster to prevent him from talking about Tire or his dismissal until June, 1987 – or, "depending how you read it, never." Gag orders are standard issue in corporate termination agreements, but the Billes clause seemed particularly rigid. Muncaster had a theory about it. He believed the Billeses wanted him to sign the gag order to ensure that he would not talk publicly about his dismissal, to ensure that he would not disclose any information about the creation of the special committee that eventually fired him – a committee on which Muncaster did not sit, that was arguably not in the best interests of the shareholders, and whose propriety Muncaster questioned. If Muncaster wanted his separation agreement – and he needed the money: his A shares were worth a fraction of their original value, thanks to White's – he had to agree to keep his mouth shut. If he kept his mouth shut, no one would ever find out how the Billes family operated. Such tactics were no surprise to Muncaster. He expected as

*Kron wasn't the only executive to question the legality of the special executive committee; Muncaster had a few concerns of his own. Neither man considered their case strong enough, however, to take the company to court. Premature, quite possibly; high-handed, perhaps; standard cut-throat corporate behavior, most definitely. But not illegal. Still, an executive in Kron's or Muncaster's position could be forgiven for thinking that it might be illegal. Canadian Tire, after all, was their life's work. They expected better treatment.

much from the family. "They're very strange people," he explained.

The wrangling over Muncaster's settlement was so intense that it was eight o'clock in the morning on June 6, the day of the company's annual meeting, before a deal was struck. Muncaster's imminent departure was known only to a few people inside the company. As the annual meeting fell quiet, Macaulay told the assembled multitude that Dean Muncaster had "relinquished" his position. He refused to say why. "The board of directors has a responsibility to carry out the affairs of this company in the best interests of the shareholders and employees," Macaulay said. That was a nice fat irony.

Then Muncaster stood up. "While the circumstances surrounding my appearance before you here today are substantially different than on the previous eighteen occasions" – a nice shot, Dean! Go for the understatement! – "I do wish to take the opportunity to review with you the current operating conditions of the company." Just like Dean! The results man to the very end! Even so, he cried. The crowd gave him a standing ovation. "If you want a definition of class," Hugh Macaulay said, "there it is." The only sneak attack Muncaster launched was to tell the shareholders he had not known he would be leaving until that morning – a statement that, while true, cast the Billes family in a most unflattering light.

And then it was over. Dean Muncaster was gone.

BOTH his secretaries cried when they heard the news. He didn't waste time leaving. Within two weeks he had disappeared, having declined to help the company find a successor. He escaped to Georgian Bay, climbed aboard his thirty-nine-foot Kemper Nicholson ketch, and made plans to marry Brenda Bell, his third wife, to design a new home, and to have a son.

In his absence, the newspapers set about "explaining" his departure. They put it down to the disaster at White's. The company had cost about $225 million, and had lost $10 million in 1982, $29 million in 1983, and $41 million in 1984. When asked directly if he left willingly, or had been pushed by the Billeses, Muncaster replied "a little of both." It seemed that White's was simply an excuse, a smoke screen. The Billeses wanted Muncaster's job, his glory, his reputation. "They kept him on long enough," Dick Billes maintained, "to make it look like something else."

But those views, while accurate, were only part of the reason why Dean Muncaster, one of the finest businessmen of his time, had been fired. His departure was not just about the failure of White's, or about his waning interest in the company, or about having spent too long in the presidency, as A.J. believed, or about the Billeses' lust for power, or even, as Muncaster later theorized, about the Billeses wanting "a business they understood." Muncaster could say, "I thought my problem was that I was trying to take them too far into the eighties too quickly," but the cause of his dismissal went beyond that too.

The reason for Dean Muncaster's corporate death lay in capitalism itself, in the myth that a company could be a lasting home for the aspirations of an ambitious man. All companies pretend to create a family for their employees. They promise security in return for a life of devotion, but seldom deliver because the aspirations of the best men are by nature too rough and wild and individual to be contained by organizations that in the end value conformity over fresh dreams. It was no accident that Dean Muncaster and nearly every other member of his management team, once they left corporate life, turned to small businesses. The ordinary ambitions Dean Muncaster had voiced to Arch Brown at the time of his appointment as president in 1966 had come to haunt him. *"I would never belong to a company that I couldn't eventually be head of."* The company had encouraged him to think that way, but in the end its encouragement was a lie.

"Family businesses have two problems," Jean Pigott once

explained. "One is [for the family members] to know their place. They should be interested in policy, long-term planning, quality. They should always be looking for success. But they should let managers manage. And set up rewards. And managers should be smart enough to make sure that family members get trained and brought along. But it's a very difficult thing to know when to stop being a hands-on manager and let professional managers take over.

"Muncaster had something of the same problem. Because he didn't make the jump. There's no ifs, ands, or buts about it. He got mixed up. He got confused. Was he one of the family? Or was he professional management? See, he enjoyed being in the family business. He enjoyed being part of the family. Until all of a sudden it wasn't A.J. anymore. It was the three kids."

Dean Muncaster was paid $500,000 a year to mind the store – something he told himself twenty-five years earlier he had no interest in doing. He had made the leap from shopkeeper's son to corporation executive, and was hailed as one of the best business minds of his time. But in the end the power he had been lent was repossessed by the family that had owned it all along.

Perhaps there is no crime in that. Occasionally, as I tried to decide if the Billeses had acted fairly, I imagined I was Dean Muncaster. It wasn't that difficult, and I like to think I became quite good at it. I imagined myself shorter – a shade under five-foot-ten – and shyer, a man whose enthusiasm for women surpassed my attractiveness to them, and whose innate shyness and introversion made me polite and unassuming and yet remote at the same time. I relived his decision, as the young Dean, to go to business school, to leave behind the insecurity of self-employment, so well known to his father, for life as a corporate hired hand. I imagined taking refuge from the pain of human interaction in the harder, more reliable currency of results. I imagined my growing sense of self-worth as I became more successful and celebrated. I imagined being committed to fairness, and I imagined being taken advantage of, as Gary Philbrick, who knew Dean well, said Dean often was.

Sometimes I felt powerful and clever. More often, and strangely, especially as I watched Muncaster's end draw near, I felt an overpowering loneliness – a feeling I suspect is well known to the heads of large corporations, but seldom talked about. I imagined analyzing and re-analyzing my own motives. I imagined regrets as well. I saw Dean Muncaster looking back on his life at Tire, sometimes feeling pleased, and sometimes thinking, to his surprise, as we all do, that it wasn't what it had seemed at the time.

14

FAMILY FEUD

FOR TEN MONTHS after Dean Muncaster was fired, Canadian Tire had no chief executive officer. Such a situation would be difficult for any company, but a leaderless Canadian Tire was not merely like a car rattling down a highway at ninety per with no one at the wheel: it was like a car rattling down the highway at ninety per with twenty drivers. There were plenty of contenders for Muncaster's throne. In that atmosphere, it was easy for Fred and Martha Billes finally to decide they didn't like each other.

Fred and Martha seldom, if ever, talked about the source of their disagreements – they found it difficult to separate business and family – but the tension between them affected every important dilemma the company faced. The decision to sell White's was no exception. By August, 1985, two months after Muncaster's resignation speech, the board had fired John Kron, and Fred was spending a lot of time in Texas. He had been hired and given a salary by the board to help Arthur Andersen, the consulting company, assess White's. Fred still believed White's might succeed, albeit in pared-down form, as a chain of automotive specialty stores.

Martha disagreed. Like her father – indeed, because of her father, who despised the Texas venture – Martha had been convinced Canadian Tire had no business in the United States. "We didn't know the land," she said later, "and we didn't understand the people." The board supported her. Fred tried, but the same difficulties that had plagued John Kron – the super-competitive Texas market, the lackluster quality of White's dealers – plagued Fred too. But he hung on.

Martha sometimes wondered why. She thought she had the answer, too. Martha believed Fred wanted to use White's to qualify as Tire's next chairman or chief executive officer, thereby earning the crown his father had denied him twenty years earlier. "Freddy perhaps coveted a more prominent role in the company," Martha said. But Martha had no enthusiasm for the idea of Fred as Tire's chief executive officer. She believed his rambunctious ways were responsible for the lawsuits White's dealers had brought against Tire. But the *intensity* of Martha's feelings toward her brother was just as important. Martha didn't hesitate to tell me, for instance, quite voluntarily, that her brother had a drinking problem, and that this was a reason she was against his running the company. (A.J. made the same claim.) Whether or not it was true – and I encountered no evidence either way – it was a startling claim for a sister to be hurling publicly at her brother, especially when they both sat on the board of their family company. Whether or not it was true, Martha believed it to be true, and the upshot was the same: no one, Martha claimed, was taking the idea of Fred Billes, President, White Stores Inc., very seriously – to say nothing of the quaint notion of Fred Billes, chief executive officer of Canadian Tire.

The tension between Martha and her brother was nothing new, however. It had first surfaced openly prior to Muncaster's departure, and it concerned the composition of the board of directors. In the spring of 1984, Martha and Fred had agreed easily on the makeup of their first board. The second board, assembled in the spring of 1985, was a different story. Martha was keen to install women as directors of the company. "One of my criteria," Martha said, "which my brothers did not get along with, was that there was a lot more to Canadian Tire than tires; that there were a lot more to our customers than the males. Stock markets are more than males.

And women have brains too." That was the way Martha expressed herself on the subject: she didn't restrict herself to Tire, but instead scattered her shot widely, taking on the entire corporate world. She had a legitimate complaint, but she also seemed to be exacting revenge on the favoritism A.J. had shown Fred all his life. At the company's annual meeting that year, Tire's board sported two new members, both of whom were roughly Martha's age: Maureen Sabia, an outspoken lawyer; and Lynne Hall, a brilliant and highly articulate American-born consultant who was president and chief operating officer of F.S.G. International, her own firm. Later, Martha made less of the conflict. "They [my brothers] didn't think it was necessary. But I wanted it, so they went along with it." Sometimes when Martha described life at Tire she made it sound as if she were running the whole show.

By summer, the acrimony beween the two siblings was alarming. Martha no longer kicked Freddy under the boardroom table when he launched into one of his rants, or dropped a pen on the floor as a private signal. Now she stood up and fetched herself a cup of coffee and let him fry himself in full view of the other directors. Canadian Tire had been Fred's life; now Martha planned to make it her life too. She resisted him. Sometimes she had no constructive ideas to suggest as alternatives to Freddy's, but to have offered recommendations was not Martha's way.

For instance: the executive search firm hired in January of 1985 to find a replacement for John Kron as president of White's had turned up several candidates. One of them was Dean Groussman. Groussman, the son of a small-time discount retailer from Utah, had tried out several colleges and worked his way through the retailing world, eventually presiding over 160 discount drug stores in Texas, owned by Zale Corporation. By the time the search firm found him, Groussman had resigned – the owners refused to make him president of the company's jewelry division – and was president of The Fine Jewelers Guild, another vast Zale outfit operating under thirty-nine different trade names.

Groussman knew White's from his years in Texas. He wasn't interested in running it, however, until he learned that Kron and Muncaster had been dismissed. Hugh Macaulay and Pierre Côté, one of Tire's board members, interviewed Groussman, and asked him to meet Fred. Groussman and Fred hit it off. They both agreed that John Kron's latter-day improvements to White's had to be more extensive, that White's could make it as a chain of automotive-specialty stores. They also shared a disdain for MBAs and business theorists. Later, in Dallas, Groussman met Martha. If Fred knew there was no hope of convincing his sister and her supporters on the board to make him president of White's, Groussman was his next choice; Martha agreed. Groussman went to work as the president of White's in October, just as the subsidiary's losses bobbed to $2 million a week.

Which was fine, except that two months later, the Western Auto chain made Tire's board an offer for White's that it couldn't refuse. White's was a dog. Groussman, on the other hand, displayed a number of desirable qualities. He had experience as a retailer, but he was also a newcomer. He bore no loyalties to any faction within the Canadian Tire community, and no resentment toward the Billes family. He got along well enough with Martha and Fred that in mid-January, 1986, the board asked him to move to Canada to be Dean Muncaster's replacement as Tire's chief operating officer. Groussman accepted.

Here again, Martha displayed what, to an innocent bystander, seems like less than enthusiastic support for management. What else is new? It was true that she had, in the end, supported the decision to hire Groussman. Hugh Macaulay remained both acting chief executive officer and chairman. Martha thought of him as "a chairman." With Groussman as chief operating officer, that left the chief executive officer's office empty. Alternately, if Macaulay became chief executive, the chairman's position would become vacant. And both Fred and Martha considered taking the position for themselves.

Yes . . . chairman of Canadian Tire! Glory! Fame! The Billes name in lights, or at least at the top of the list in the annual report! In fact, the idea had occurred to a number of people. Several dealers had suggested Fred for the job. At the same time, Martha maintained, "there were a number of longtime employees who came to me and suggested, why don't you become chairman of the board? And I said, without a strong CEO, there's not much point."

But did Martha ever declare these feelings openly to anyone? No. She tended instead, as the psychologists say, to be "passive aggressive." She seldom revealed what she wanted, as Muncaster had learned, but she stood silently in the way of what she did not want. Fred would speak his mind; he was a realist, and he was mainly interested in money. Martha preferred power, and silence. Martha's tendency when she was confronted with an idea she disliked was to dream up a counter-proposal. At one point in her negotiations with Fred over who the company's chief executive officer and/or chairman ought to be – negotiations that required at least ten months to resolve – she suggested the company have not one, not two, but three presidents. "So that nobody would know who was in control," R.B. (Biff) Matthews, Fred's lawyer, noted. "She wanted the family to have control, so she thought that by having three presidents she could keep them all off balance."

Martha's talent for sabotage seemed to be the product of her past. Think about it. She thought of herself as a practical woman, but it was Freddy who "got" the dealership. She was articulate, but it was Freddy who was seen, publicly, as the family spokesman. She wanted to sit on the board, but it was Freddy who had the "experience." Martha's reaction, her recourse to power, seemed to be to withhold her approval from an initiative until it imploded from lack of movement. Maybe it was a trick she had learned from generations of disempowered women before her, and from her father, A.J., who taught her a lot of what she knew about corporate life. Whenever A.J. ran into something he couldn't fight – such as Muncaster's trained rationalism – he went underground.

Martha knew A.J. was the source of it all, the progenitor of a classic sibling rivalry between a daughter who wanted to be recognized by her father and a son who wanted to replace him. "I guess we all wanted to prove ourselves," Martha once said, "not just to our father but to the world."

Whether Fred and Martha could sort out these dynamics was unfortunately beside the point: they simply didn't talk about them. It wasn't the Canadian, white Anglo-Saxon Protestant thing to do. Siblings could despise and dislike each other, but one didn't mention such things. For years afterwards, whenever someone asked one of the Billeses why the family had disintegrated, no one could precisely identify the cause. Martha knew what had triggered it, but she wouldn't say.

So who could be surprised that by the fall of 1986 Fred was tired of wrangling with his sister? He was less worried about the future of Canadian Tire, having found Groussman to run it; he was still concerned, however, that all his money was tied up in its shares. Martha was becoming dominant; the board was displaying a distressing tendency to independence; why fight it? Why not get out and disappear on a big boat to some hot place in the tropics where the name Billes meant nothing to anyone? Barbara, furthermore, was afraid Fred would have a heart attack. In short, Fred was Tired out. For twenty years his family had fought to control this company; once they did, it turned out to be too complicated for a family to run. Fred wanted to be left alone. He had spent his entire life living Tire, breathing Tire, thinking Tire, being defined by Tire.* Now he openly bad-mouthed his sister. Fred would walk into a restaurant and see a dealer at dinner with

* How proprietary was Martha? In May of 1989, I read this sentence to her, to check its accuracy. The words were my own, culled from Fred Billes's testimony before the Ontario Securities Commission, from conversation

Martha – Martha would be complaining that she didn't have a man in her life – and Fred would walk up and ask, "Martha buy you dinner? How the hell did you get her to pay for your dinner?" The idea of them running the company together was understandably out of the question.

By the late fall of 1985, a common share of Canadian Tire was worth nearly $20. Encouraged by Barbara, nagged by Martha, discouraged by his inability to seize the leadership of the company, Fred had reached the end of his rope. He wanted to sell. David would come with him. But Martha – well, Martha was her father's daughter, and her father didn't want anyone to sell the dream he believed he had co-created. Thus it was that Fred and Martha Billes began the nimble dance known as the rites of takeover.

LATE in March, 1986, as the price of Canadian Tire's shares nuzzled $24, Fred received a telephone call from Gordon Carpenter, the president of Shane Morgan Investments Limited. Carpenter was a little-known business broker – a deal-maker – telephoning on behalf of Carling O'Keefe Limited, the brewery. He wanted to take Fred out to lunch. Carpenter informed Fred that Carling O'Keefe had figured out a way to pay the Billeses, over a five-year period, three times what their shares would fetch in the stock market.

Fred was interested. He had been approached many times over the years to sell his shares. Carling O'Keefe was the first acceptable buyer to offer an acceptable amount of money. After discussing the offer with David and Martha, Fred wasn't sure the family would sell, and he wasn't convinced about the price. But the discouragements of the fall made him susceptible to the overture. Fred telephoned Biff Matthews, his lawyer.

with Barbara Billes, and from interviews with half a dozen dealers who knew Fred well. When Martha heard the sentence, she blew a fuse. She claimed the words were from a speech *she* had given. "Don't you dare put those words on Freddy," she said. "They're mine. I have proprietary rights to those words. They're *mine. Mine, mine, mine, mine, mine* !"

Matthews was the right man to call. Like A.J., Fred displayed no sustained desire to be part of the Establishment, but he understood how and when to use the Establishment. Matthews was the son of Brigadier Beverley Matthews, the grand old man of McCarthy & McCarthy, Toronto's largest law firm. At McCarthy's, Bev's nickname was "God." The first Canadian Matthewses were members of Upper Canada's Family Compact. Biff had attended the right schools – Ridley College, Oxford and Dalhousie for law – but he had no desire to ride his father's coattails, and he did his best to make his own way up the ladder of corporate law. On being called to the bar in 1974 he had started his own firm, which later amalgamated with the firm of McMaster Meighen. He moved to McCarthy's only after his father had officially retired.

Under the direction of Matthews, Senior, McCarthy's had begun to transform itself into a "national" law firm with branches across the country. Nevertheless, it was a traditional firm. Most McCarthy partners dutifully represented the same handful of corporate clients for the bulk of their careers – as Robin Law had represented Canadian Tire, for instance. They were loyal legal dogs.

That sort of life was fine, but it wasn't exactly the good life the young legal Turks of the postwar generation envisioned for themselves. Biff Matthews was a member in full standing of the postwar generation. The Canadian businessmen who had seen the last action in the Second World War were now in their sixties and cruising into retirement. The financial revolution of the 1980s – the fastest-growing, most ambitious, and, some would say, most profligate period in the history of Western capitalism – was led by men for whom the war was at most a distant childhood memory. The new breed was better educated, but without a war to temper its character, its members turned their attention, as men always have in times of protracted peace, to waging war among themselves in politics and business.

The head coach of McCarthy's post-war crowd was a highly respected lawyer named Peter Beattie. With young bloods such as Biff under his wing, Beattie was trying to transform McCarthy's once again – following the lead of law firms such as Tory, Tory, DesLauriers and Binnington, and Davies, Ward & Beck – into a new species of legal animal known as the transactional firm. Transactional firms still served regular clients, but their new specialty was one-time deals such as takeovers. By the early 1980s, any law firm worth its letterhead possessed an elite squad of corporate hit men, paper entrepreneurs who for purposes of gentility were known as the mergers and acquisitions (M&A) department. To be a hot young lawyer doing M&A work at a big-time law firm in the 1980s was the peak: you just couldn't be any hotter. Biff was a prime example of the breed. Young (forty), tall, dark, strikingly good-looking, impeccably dressed, tremendously articulate, immensely hard-working, and preternaturally discreet, he seemed to thrive on work and risk. When he wasn't engineering takeovers, he liked to ski on mountain glaciers. An M&A specialist learned to handle risk like a highball, rinsing the glass with one hand while keeping all his options open. Multiplying your options was the sine qua non.

It was natural that Fred would phone Biff with the O'Keefe news. Fred was a good client, to Matthews' way of thinking. "He knows what he wants in the most general terms. He's willing to accept advice. And he's willing to take a chance." Fred was a shrewd businessman, but he played the part – perhaps as camouflage – of an unsophisticated yokel, an act made more convincing by his tremendous size. Some of the lawyers at McCarthy's thought of the act as Fred's trucker persona. Shades of his father?

It was May 12, 1986, however, before Matthews talked with Fred in person about selling his shares. Two days later, convinced Fred was serious, Matthews introduced him to Peter Beattie and Rene Sorell. Beattie had been called to the bar in 1958, and as the chairman of McCarthy's commercial group was the Holy Father adviser of the firm's young M&A squad. Sorell was a few years younger than Matthews, but already famous for his legal creativity: he could always dream up a dozen ways to solve a single legal problem. While Beattie and Sorell listened, Fred recounted the reasons he wanted to sell.

Two weeks later, on June 2, they met again, this time with Alfred Billes, Fred's son, in attendance. Matthews reviewed Tire's articles of incorporation, and noted the coat-tail, the so-called "takeover protection" that Muncaster had extracted from the Billeses three years earlier in return for allowing them to split their A shares to pay for control of Canadian Tire. The coat-tail, that tender little passage!

> Should an offer to purchase Common Shares be made to all or substantially all of the holders of Common Shares, and should a majority of the Common Shares then issued and outstanding be tendered and be taken up pursuant to such an offer, the Class A Non-Voting Shares shall thereupon be entitled to one vote per share at all meetings of shareholders.

The coat-tail had been dubbed "takeover protection" for good reason. If a buyer seeking to control the company bought more than half its common shares, without buying the non-voting shares that made up 96 percent of the company's equity, the transformed A shareholders could then vote against the deal. Thus anyone who wanted to buy Canadian Tire had to buy the whole thing. That was an expensive proposition.

Carling O'Keefe wanted to buy the entire platter, A shares and the Billeses' common shares alike. McCarthy's, however, had another idea, a product of Rene Sorell's hyperspatial mind. He had studied the coat-tail. He realized the coat-tail came into effect if a *majority* of Tire's common shares changed hands. If someone bought less than a majority – say 49 percent – the coat-tail didn't apply. In 1983, when Matthews drafted the coat-tail, it had seemed to cover all imaginable circumstances. If one of the Billeses wanted to sell his twenty-percent chunk of the company, he or she could do so without triggering a total buyout. But if all three Billeses sold their collective sixty-percent block – that is, if control changed hands – the A shareholders cashed in too. Matthews later claimed he had never contemplated Sorell's scenario back in 1983, but now, in 1986, he found it fascinating. Fred had never contemplated it either. Still, it was another option to consider. After the meeting, Matthews sent a letter to Fred, reiterating what had transpired at the meeting, as was his usual practice.

David and Martha found these notions interesting enough to meet three days later, on Thursday, June 5, at five o'clock, at McCarthy & McCarthy's offices on the forty-eighth floor of the Toronto Dominion Bank Tower in downtown Toronto. Matthews was there, and so was Rene Sorell. The group discussed Sorell's unusual 49-percent option before looking at the Carling O'Keefe proposal. Fred was impatient to make a deal – he'd waited nearly five decades to capitalize on his inheritance. However, Matthews urged the Billeses to hire a financial agent anyway, to determine the value of their control block, and to flush out other offers. Fred readily agreed, seeing the possibility of both maximizing his return and finding a suitable buyer for his family's firm. David agreed wholeheartedly; and Martha, while she played her cards close, was equally eager to find out how much her shares were worth. All three siblings agreed to hire their own lawyers.

A handful of Carling O'Keefe executives visited Fred at his concrete house on High Point Road the following week, leaving Fred even keener to sell. Come Wednesday, a group of Bay Street financial men travelled to Fred's rambling store at Yonge and Davenport at nine o'clock in the morning. Peter

Beattie from McCarthy's led the troupe, which included Duff Scott, vice-chairman of Merrill Lynch; William Biggar, a senior vice-president; and Allan Crosbie, Merrill Lynch's senior specialist in mergers and acquisitions. The trip to a Canadian Tire dealership made a pleasant outing for the Bay Street boys.

To prepare for the meeting, Biggar looked up Tire's share price in the morning's *Globe and Mail*. What he found surprised him. Tire's common shares were trading at a price a third again as high as the company's non-voting shares – even though they received the same dividends. That was unusual. Biggar went in search of Tire's annual report. Bingo. It was the coat-tail. Within minutes Biggar realized that a buyer could buy less than a majority of the common shares and not trigger the coat-tail. Investors must have realized the same thing; that was why the common shares were more expensive. Thus Biggar became the second person to see a way around Tire's takeover protection.

Fred did most of the talking in the meeting at his store that morning. Someone wanted to buy his company. He wanted Merrill Lynch to determine the value of the family's shares and solicit offers if the Billeses decided to sell. (He also wanted to know how much Merrill Lynch was going to charge. That was just like Fred.) Fred knew his family had one thing to sell: voting control of Canadian Tire. He wanted to know how much that control was worth, the value of what the Bay Street boys called a "control premium." Fred also said he wanted a buyer who wouldn't tamper with the company or the dealers or its profit-sharing plans, and who would leave Dean Groussman and his new management team alone. Fred thought Groussman was doing a good job.

Fred also mentioned Rene Sorell's forty-nine-percent trick. It had a strange fascination for him, for good reason. By the summer of 1986, the ownership of Canadian Tire's common voting shares broke down as follows:

SHAREHOLDER	COMMON VOTING SHARES		NON-VOTING A SHARES	
	NUMBER	% OF TOTAL	NUMBER	% OF TOTAL
Alfred W. Billes	700,384	20.3	1,528,071	1.8
David G. Billes	700,383	20.3	1,329,127	1.6
Martha Gardiner Billes	700,383	20.3	1,978,932	2.3
Deferred Profit-Sharing Plan	419,280	12.2	7,226,716*	8.5
Dealer Holdings	582,790	16.9	709,800	0.8
Others (Public, etc.)	346,788	10.0	71,780,691	84.9
TOTAL	3,450,008	100.0	84,553,337	100.0

*The deferred plan is the largest of Canadian Tire's three profit-sharing plans. Together they owned 9,498,176 non-voting A shares, or roughly 8.9 percent of the outstanding total.

Together, Fred, Martha, and David controlled slightly more than sixty percent of Tire's voting shares – solid control. At bare market prices ($24 a share at the time), their block was worth $50 million. Voting control was worth a premium, however, and could easily double the price. But buying the sixty-percent control block would trigger the coat-tail – and to buy sixty percent of the A shares at even $18 a share would cost a cool $1.2 billion.

But if a buyer bought two percent of the company's common shares on the open market . . . and made a formal bid for only forty-nine percent of the Billes block . . . and didn't trigger the coat-tail . . . that buyer could still pay Fred and David and Martha a huge premium (say $99, four times the share price) . . . and thus buy control of Canadian Tire for $105 million – a real bargain.

So Fred informed the gentlemen from Merrill Lynch that he would consider selling 49 percent of his shares at, say, four times their market price, roughly a third again more than

Carling O'Keefe was offering. He said he wanted to keep his dealership, where he was grossing an estimated $1.7 million a year, and remain a director of Tire. He added that both his son and his son-in-law were in the business. He was asking for the earth, but why not? He and his brother and sister owned *control*. By the time the visitors left, they were most impressed with Fred Billes.

The next day, Crosbie, Sorell, and Beattie met again to discuss the deal. They chatted on, as lawyers do, about arcane considerations: Fred's children (they wanted to stay in the company), the business broker (an unknown, but representing a very creditable buyer), details of securities law. They also discussed the dynamics among the three Billes siblings. Peter Beattie had been a businessman too long to ignore psychology. He felt that Fred and Martha might go their separate ways, although for the moment everything seemed okay. As Beattie saw it, Martha wanted an auction for her shares. He also believed that she held considerable sway over her brother David. Fred, on the other hand, was a realist. It wouldn't take much, Beattie said, to get the friction going again between the three of them. If Martha decided not to sell, the brothers had only 40 percent of the company to sell. Forty percent wasn't control, and it wouldn't command a "control premium."

For the next two weeks Biggar wrestled with various ways to find a buyer for the company. It was clear that Sorell's 49-percent end run around the coat-tail was gaining favor among the Billeses: it kept coming up at meetings. But it presented huge problems. Biggar had realized that on the evening of June 23, when he placed a call to Tull Gearalld, the managing director of Merrill Lynch's mergers and acquisitions department in New York. Even though he had never heard of Canadian Tire and knew nothing of the coat-tail beyond what Biggar described over the telephone, Gearalld saw the problem instantly. If a buyer purchased less than a majority of Tire's common shares simply to grab control of the company, 96 percent of the company's shares would be left out of the offer. The "optics," as M&A men referred to the superficial appearance of a deal, were not good. "Skimming value from the Class A shares to get more for the common . . . underscores the problem," Gearalld said. "Clearly the class As are intended to have takeover protection." Merrill Lynch's lawyers had said much the same thing.

But Sorell's idea was a germ that would not die. As sworn testimony before the Ontario Securities Commission would later show, on June 25, two weeks after their meeting at Fred's dealership, Duff Scott and Bill Biggar from Merrill Lynch met with the three Billeses and Rene Sorell, Biff Matthews, and Peter Beattie from McCarthy & McCarthy. The Merrill team was adamant: the 49-percent route wasn't a terrific idea. Scott said it best: "We don't think that any purchaser is going to be terribly interested in getting into controversy." The potential for controversy was quite clear: if the deal sneaked around the coat-tail, there was a good chance that everyone would wind up in front of the Ontario Securities Commission, and that the OSC would nix the deal for being unfair to the non-voting shareholders who were supposed to be protected by that coat-tail. Scott was concerned that a controversial bid would attract fewer bidders.

Before the issue could be resolved, however, Martha added a few thoughts of her own. She objected to Fred's dealership being included in the price of his shares: it might be considered a special consideration to one party. There was something to this, but several lawyers in the room believed that Martha simply resented Fred's dealership. Or perhaps she wanted to buy Fred and David out, and needed a clean financial evaluation of her brothers' shares and nothing else. Whatever it was she wanted, by the end of the meeting, Biggar agreed to put a price on the company. It was also agreed that no one would tell anyone at the Corporation what was going on.

Within a week Biggar had decided Canadian Tire was worth

anywhere from $1.6 billion to $2 billion. Still the Billeses stalled. Meanwhile the Carling O'Keefe deal was falling through. Rod McInnes, the late president and chief executive officer of Carling O'Keefe Ltd., was on the verge of making a bid when he discovered that the Billeses had engaged Merrill Lynch. That was enough to make him pull out.

On September 25, Biggar presented the Billeses with a rough draft of the information packet he intended to send out to prospective buyers. To everyone's surprise – and to no one's – Martha threw a minor tantrum. She wanted Merrill Lynch to estimate the value of the family's shares – nothing more. She did not want them to look for a buyer. Clearly, Martha was having second, third, and fourth thoughts about selling.

Then again, maybe she wasn't. That was the trouble: no one knew what Martha wanted. One day she seemed to be selling, the next, buying. Early in September, McCarthy's had pre-pared a press release to announce the Billeses' plans to sell. The press release had been delivered to Robin Law when Martha objected. The release was killed. By now it was late September, and Martha was communicating almost entirely through John Stransman, her lawyer at Stikeman Elliott. Stransman was a young man in his early thirties. He seldom spoke, but he was a funny man. He was also not one to telegraph his hand.

By then Martha was driving the lawyers at McCarthy's batty. Martha, according to one lawyer, was "always in or out depending on her whim." She was hard to understand, too. At one of the earliest meetings the family had attended together, back when the sale of their shares was first being considered, Martha had suddenly sailed into an analogy. Fred had used it several times too: but Martha rolled it out far more frequently. "We keep getting words of interest in my gold watch," she told the room. No one knew what the hell she was talking about. "And I don't even know if my watch is for sale. But there have been expressions of interest in my watch. I don't know if this is a gold-filled watch, a knock-off, or what. And until I know, I'm not interested in hearing the expressions of interest. But if someone is willing to pay me a large amount of money for my watch, I may decide to sell it." So: did she want to sell, or not? Martha now claimed she didn't. "I was interested," she said afterward, "in hiring Merrill Lynch to find out how much I might have to pay for the other two-thirds of that watch." At the time, though, Martha did what any shrewd horse-trader would have done, and kept her intentions to herself.

But she still hadn't declared any desire to own the company. "As things progressed," one lawyer observed, "it became more and more clear that she enjoyed being courted. The more courted she was, the more she enjoyed it." *Martha was always looking for someone to want her.* The lawyers watched her, and sometimes – as might be expected of a bunch of smart businessmen who found themselves stymied at their own game by a woman – well, sometimes, they thought they saw a woman driven by an intense rage and resentment toward men. They saw a woman out to prove, with the help of Lynne Hall and Maureen Sabia, her fellow female board members, that – and these were Martha's words – "men couldn't rule the game anymore." (Needless to say, this went over on Bay Street like chicken-fried brains sold out of a corner hot-dog stand.) Fred seemed to be the largest target for her rage.

The end of September rolled around. Still no sign from Martha. Despite the absence of firm evidence either way, both Fred and Biff Matthews figured that Martha's watch was no longer for sale. Matthews was convinced that Martha still hoped the family would put aside their differences and work out a mutually acceptable way to control Canadian Tire. But she never actually said so. By the second of October, John Stransman was attending meetings for her. The following day, he informed Fred and David that their sister would no longer be part of the deal.

Finally! Fred went ahead regardless. Biggar informed the two brothers that their 1,400,767 common shares (40 percent of the company's voting shares) were worth between $67 and $91 each – anywhere from $94 million to $127 million. Fred settled on $99.95. That was Fred's kind of math – exactly four times the market value of his shares, the price he had wanted from the outset. Biggar had urged Fred all along to ask for a lot of money for his shares: the windfall would have to compensate Fred and David for handing the company over to their sister to run as her own.

By October 15, Biggar was actively looking for buyers. He had already mailed out between fifty and eighty copies of a report bearing the hep title, "Canadian Tire Corporation Limited: A Business Acquisition Opportunity." That same day, Fred and David Billes announced publicly that they were selling their portion of Canadian Tire. The company was "in play." They visited Hugh Macaulay that afternoon, and walked next door with him afterward to repeat the news for the dealers. The news made the front page of business sections across the country, and the shock of the Canadian Tire community could be felt throughout the land. Their father was outraged.

Martha immediately phoned Dick Billes down in Pompano Beach to tell him the news. Dick couldn't believe his ears. Martha had seen the news in the *Globe and Mail*, clipped the story, and attached it to her fridge while she spoke to Dick. Two and a half years later, it was still there, a reminder of her divided loyalties.

Two days after the brothers' announcement, Bill Biggar received a telephone call from Alan Warren, the chairman of Canadian Tire Dealer Holdings Limited. He wanted to talk.

15

THE TAKEOVER DANCE

WHILE THE BILLESES were navigating the waters of buying and selling, one important group of common shareholders had been left in the dark: the good citizens of Dealerland. Not, of course, that the dealers hadn't heard rumors. The Canadian Tire Dealers' Association convention of 1986 was held in Halifax, in the balmy month of September. The convention continued to be one of Dealerland's most important tribal events, a gala powwow where dealers from coast to coast gathered to say hello to Home Office, to talk rebates and marketing strategy, and – most important – to reaffirm the values that made the middle class a wonderful place to be.

Martha and Fred Billes took care to be on hand at the convention, which seemed to give the lie to any rumors of an impending sell-off. Martha, at least, seemed pleased to have the opportunity to show the family colors. She had even had her hair restyled, trading in her schoolteacher's do – itself a vast improvement over the ringlets she had worn as a young woman, which had given her a strong resemblance to a maddened stepsister in one of George Cruikshank's copper plates in Dickens's novels – for a hipper and more luxurious neo-pre-Raphaelite look. She looked younger, and several dealers said so. Martha was a good-looking woman when she gave herself a chance. She'd lost a lot of weight over the years, as if her ever-larger public role in the company required an ever-slimmer profile. At dinner with a handful of dealers the night before the convention, neither Fred nor Martha had mentioned anything about their plans for the future. That would come in their speeches to the dealers the next day.

Martha had been planning her speech for a year; she wanted the dealers to know who she was. It turned out to be an evangelical rouser in the style of her father, in which she reaffirmed the cardinal virtues of Canadian Tire, Trust, Cooperation, and Working Hard to Do Things Right. Fred's speech, by contrast, had been shambling, or, as several dealers later described it, "half-assed": much of what he had said, as well as nondescript, was inaudible through his mumble. Both Fred and Martha had implied they were in Canadian Tire for the long term, and a lot of dealers had believed them.

Two weeks after the brothers' offer went public, Martha had a conversation with Denvil Brown, the dealer who had accompanied her on her director-by-director campaign to undermine Muncaster the year before. Brown was a dealer of twenty-five years' standing and a personal friend of the family. He remembered the conversation, too, but claimed it took place two days after the dealers' convention, in September.

No matter; the import of the conversation was obvious. On the telephone, Martha sounded agitated. She often sounded nervous and forthright at the same time, as if she were overcoming her natural shyness by a sheer force of will.

"Remember you asked me at the convention if something was going on?" Martha warbled. Brown had been one of the dealers at her table. "Well, there was. Can we raise some money?"

"Why?" Brown said.

"We may have to buy the boys out," Martha said.

"Martha," Brown said, "who'd have control?" He always got straight to the point.

"Well, I'd have control."

"Martha, that's not going to work."

Within hours the rumors had spread anew across the country.

TO say the news was shocking does no justice to the panic that raged through Dealerland like impetigo. Panic of that magnitude was hard to imagine unless you'd grown up within the Canadian Tire Family. The dealers were competitive men. Now their congenital suspiciousness made them paranoid. The thought of a new, unknown controlling shareholder made them break out in collective hives. How would the newcomer pay for the company? By cutting into the dealers' profits? By reducing margins? By – heaven forbid – disbanding Dealerland altogether, and transforming their stores into a chain of company-operated branches?

This was the darkest evil Dealerland could imagine. The dealers were barons in a kingdom powered by the pure fuel of material acquisitiveness – the North American Good Life, circa 1986 – whose rewards were boats, cottages, cars, trips, Rolexes, the freedom to run their own businesses, and, most of all, the feeling that they mattered. All that was now threatened. "Here was the dilemma," Arch Brown, the dealer in Barrie, explained. "Say Canadian Tire was bought by Sears. And let's say the vice-president of Sears made $300,000. How would he feel about several dealers making over a million dollars? That was what concerned the Canadian Tire dealers. . . . We didn't know of any buyer who would want to keep that. We didn't want to take a chance on somebody coming in and not accepting that philosophy."

In past crises, the dealers had turned to the Billes family for help. Come to Daddy! But that was the past. The dealers already knew how low Martha's opinion of their work habits was (overpaid! underworked!). As for Fred . . . Fred Billes had not admitted publicly or openly in Halifax that he planned to sell, even though he had been considering selling out for at least six months. When the dealers discovered that little fact, no more than six weeks after the Halifax convention,

Dealerland's sixty-year-old trust in the Billes family evaporated instantly.

Tire's head office management team didn't make the dealers feel any better. Dean Muncaster's successors weren't part of the Canadian Tire Family. Dean Groussman was a *discounter* and an *American*. Hugh Macaulay had been a *car salesman*. In the fall of 1986, Groussman and Macaulay hired two new executives – Jim Williams, a former *financial man* from Dominion Stores, an expert in winding up dying organizations; and Clive Minto, the former head of Pepsi-Cola Canada, a hugely ambitious man known for ruling Pepsi's bottlers (the equivalent of Canadian Tire's dealers) with an iron hand. None of these men had any experience running a store. None of them had the Tire faith. Groussman and his team were *professional managers*. Groussman felt no need to apologize for the fact.

It wasn't just the men Groussman and Macaulay hired that troubled Dealerland. It was how they hired them. Macaulay and Groussman had compensated for their lack of familiarity with Canadian retailing by creating an extra level of executive vice-presidents. This was standard management practice, but it was radical for a company that prided itself on direct lines of communication. To make matters worse, Groussman and Co. installed themselves on the eighteenth floor of the company's head office at 2180 Yonge Street. Muncaster had worked on the eleventh floor, next to the accounting department. The new eighteenth floor – the Taj Mahal, as A.J. called it, or The Ivory Tower, the epithet employees at head office preferred – was dusky rose-pink, broadloomed from here to eternity, and replete with sconces and glass and brass. Not that this was any great luxury for a $2-billion corporation. It simply insulted Tire tradition. Employees saw wall-to-wall carpet, and immediately computed its cost to the profit-sharing plan. And a whole new level of management! And the titles! "We ran the business and built it to be a billion-dollar corporation with three or four guys," said Bill Dawson, the former vice-president of marketing who later became a dealer. "Now they had a fucking army down there." The old corporation had revered the dealers, considered them partners. The new corporation seemed to think of them as cash-flow deliverymen.

Up in Owen Sound, where he was living out what was left of his admirable life, Walter Muncaster, the uncle of them all, watched the spreading bonfire in Dealerland with what by the late 1980s was a rare and valuable emotion: chagrin. "That just makes you sick, what's been going on," Muncaster said. "We had good fellowship." As of October 15, 1986, the days of good fellowship were over.

A WEEK after Dealerland's convention, the board of directors of Dealer Holdings Limited, the business arm of the Canadian Tire Dealers' Association, held an emergency meeting at the Four Seasons Hotel in Toronto. The purpose of the meeting was to appoint what would later be known, with considerable derision, as "the point team." The point team would become the sole voice of the dealers. It was well known, as Vern Forster, the mad dealer of British Columbia, observed, that "you can't get two dealers to agree on the time of day, never mind how to run the company." The point team consisted of four dealers: Alan Warren, the chairman of Dealer Holdings and a Tire dealer in North Bay; Paul Weber, of Windsor; Grant Wallace from Calgary; and Ian Van Norman from Saskatoon.

They were a curious group of men to lead a takeover, and they did not enjoy universal support. Warren was by far the most controversial. A short, neat, gray-haired motor-mouth, Warren began life at Canadian Tire behind the counter in A.J.'s store at Davenport and Yonge. He eventually became a dealer and Dealerland's self-appointed representative at head office in the early 1960s. Warren loved head office, loved office politics, and openly coveted an important position at the mother corporation. It was Alan Warren, you may recall, who had made life unpleasant for Muncaster's management team in 1977. It was Warren whom Muncaster and Hobbs eventually banished from court in Toronto and made a dealer far away in North Bay.

Everyone had an opinion about Al Warren, and no one was surprised to see him on the point team. He was variously described as "a non-stop talker," "a man of huge, huge ambitions," or, less frequently, as "the hardest-working, most dedicated dealer in the dealer organization." He had enormous energy, and an almost endless concern for the health of Canadian Tire. There was plenty of evidence that Alan Warren wanted to serve on the board of Canadian Tire, and there was plenty of evidence that many dealers could imagine nothing worse. Still, he was persuasive enough to rise to the top of Dealer Holdings. Like the other members of the point team, Al Warren was one of the new breed of businessman-dealers who made the older generation of merchant-dealers nervous.

Van Norman and Weber and Wallace, on the other hand, were widely respected. Weber knew the Billeses; Van Norman was a dealer's dealer, a devout Free Methodist who, with donations from fellow dealers, had built a hospital in Haiti, which was a huge success, as well as a real estate development in Corpus Christi, Texas, which was not. At one point, Van Norman's Texas deal stood to lose more than $2 million, a fact that alarmed several dealers once he joined the point team. Grant Wallace was a straight-ahead trout fisherman who had worked at IBM for twenty years and now enjoyed sales of $21 million a year at his dealership in Calgary, where he was involved with the Olympics. Van Norman, Weber, and Wallace were less openly ambitious than Warren, but ambition is a relative notion. If the dealers took over the company, it would need a new president – one chosen, perhaps, from the point team.

Such ambitions were still in their infancy, however. As of October, the dealers were engaged in a defensive, rearguard action. Ever since Imasco had taken its run at Tire, the dealers had been quietly buying common shares. By the fall of 1986 they owned 17.4 percent of the company. In the event of a takeover (so went the rationale), the dealers could play kingmaker to a potential buyer, guarantee themselves a few seats on the board, and protect hallowed Dealerland. But no one, the dealers included, considered them potential buyers. Such an idea offended Dealerland's middle-class modesty.

Even Biff Matthews was surprised when he learned on November 3, two weeks after Fred's and David's shattering announcement, that the dealers had hired Gordon Capital Corporation, the most aggressive financial institution on Bay Street, to look into takeover strategies. Obviously the dealers had something in mind. Meanwhile, the Billeses had other prospects. Matthews knew Dean Groussman had been talking to Gerry Swartz of Onyx Capital and to Wood Gundy about the possibility of Tire's management buying the company as well. That gave Fred and David at least six options:

1. They could sell to the dealers.
2. They could sell to management.
3. They could sell to a third party.
4. They could sell to the dealers and a third party jointly.
5. They could sell to the dealers and Martha jointly.
6. (The least likely and least desirable scenario) Martha and the dealers and Tire's profit-sharing plans could unite their common shares – roughly half the total – in a control block, thereby preventing the brothers from obtaining the premium a buyer would pay for voting control of Canadian Tire.

ON Wednesday, November 5, having heard nothing from the dealers, Matthews returned to his office at half-past four to learn that Fred Billes was upstairs in the Toronto Dominion Bank Tower with Bob Fung, a partner at Gordon Capital. Fred wanted Biff to come up. Fung had been meeting secretly with Martha as well. Matthews still wasn't sure whether or not

Martha was going to sell her shares. If Fred and David sold, she might sell, but given Martha's habits, that was anything but a certainty.

Over the course of the next two hours, Fung laid out the dealers' plans. Al Warren, Paul Weber, Grant Wallace, Ian Van Norman, and Denny Brown listened. The dealers were more interested in stability, Fung said, than they were in buying control. They didn't want all the Billeses' shares. They wanted an arrangement. Fung wanted to know what it might take to keep Fred from selling.

Fred said he wanted his children and children-in-law to be able to own Canadian Tire dealerships. He also wanted the right to institute more favorable policies for the dealers. In short, he wanted more control over the affairs of the company – control his sister had apparently denied him.

Fung then suggested a plan. Fred and Martha could each buy half of David's shares. The dealers would agree to vote their shares with Fred. With the dealers' 17.4-percent block, that gave the Fred-dealer team close to 50 percent of the common shares, considerably more than Martha's measly 20 percent. The plan left Martha in the cold, but no one was too concerned about that. As Fung pointed out, he had no desire to form an alliance with Groussman and support management's leveraged takeover. Furthermore, the dealers preferred dealing with Fred to negotiating with Martha. Fred was one of their own. Fung wrapped up his presentation with the observation that no matter who bought Tire, the funds would eventually come out of the company, and the dealers would wind up paying for it. So the dealers were a natural purchaser.

Fung's plan, alas, required a rapprochement between Martha and Fred. Fred figured that might be possible – perhaps on another planet – but it was unlikely. His mind was already made up. In the end, he decided he wanted to sell more than he wanted to remain the controlling shareholder of Canadian

Tire. The fate of Canadian Tire seemed to be out of the dealers' hands.

WHILE the dealers contemplated new options, Fred and David urged Merrill Lynch (whom the Billeses had now hired) to find other buyers for their shares. David may have shared Martha's shyness and educational background, but he also shared Fred's distaste for complication. Without Fred to look after his interests at Tire, David's connection to his father's company became even more tenuous. David didn't want to argue about company policy, he wanted to build high-performance engines.

But the brothers' mandate to Merrill Lynch wasn't easy to fulfill. The so-called Aldamar agreement, for starters, was a big pain in Merrill Lynch's neck. The 1983 pact between Fred, David, and Martha gave each of them first crack at the shares of the others if one of them decided to sell. If Fred or David wanted to sell their shares for, say, $10 million to Sears, they had first to offer them to Martha at that price for ten days. Sears could buy them only if Martha turned the offer down or if the ten days expired.

Merrill Lynch quickly discovered that Martha's "right of first refusal" troubled potential buyers. Any offer they made could become a set-up, at their expense, for Martha to swoop in and grab the company. No one knew what she was going to do, nor how many shares a potential purchaser would want to buy. At the same time, Fred and David wanted $140 million for their shares, no matter how many they sold. The objective – and it was bewildering in its complexity – was to determine a price for the brothers' shares that would earn them $140 million, no matter how many shares were purchased, even if the buyer were Martha.

To accomplish this Biggar hauled out his MBA algebra and devised a formula to determine share value for the purposes of divestment. It was a wonderful piece of work:

$$\text{Price per share} = \frac{\$140 \text{ million} - \$12 \ (1,400,767 - X)}{X}$$

X was the number of shares sold under the offer; 1,400,767 was the number of voting common shares the Billes brothers owned. Any shares not sold under the offer (1,400,767 - X) would automatically convert into non-voting, or A, shares, which would then be bought for $12, just under the market price of A shares at the time. *Abracadabra!* The formula made a buyer pay the same price for any number of common shares: one share cost $140 million, and 1,400,767 shares cost $140 million. The formula guaranteed that any buyout would be a total buyout of the brothers' voting shares. The formula also forced Martha to pay $140 million if she wanted to exercise her prerogative under the Aldamar agreement.

Armed with the formula, Matthews drew up a notice to Martha of her brothers' intention to sell, as he had to under the Aldamar agreement. She had until November 20 to reply, at which time the brothers were free to sell elsewhere. The notice was delivered the next day, November 8, a Saturday. The dealers learned of these developments the next day.

By now the dealers were in the thick of it. Gordon Capital had indeed galvanized them into action, in keeping with its reputation as a strict mistress. Fung and Neil Baker, another partner at Gordon Capital, told the dealers what to do, and when to do it. "The dealers," one lawyer explained, "were not organized to do something like this. The dealers were pretty naive when it came to the M&A world on Bay Street. So they took their lead from Gordon's." To make sure they did, Gordon Capital forced all the dealers to sign a gag order forbidding them to talk about the deal.

By the middle of November, the point team and one or both of Fung and Baker were crisscrossing the country to convince dealers to sign promissory notes worth some $290 million; the notes in turn were used as collateral for a bank loan from the Canadian Imperial Bank of Commerce. The dog-and-pony shows the point team staged with Gordon's were like religious rallies. Dealers were regularly signing loans for $1 million. The point team's plan wasn't sold on the basis of taking Canadian Tire to broad new sunlit plains – to be Churchillian about it – but simply to maintain the "status quo." Control of the company was merely a means to an end. There were very few dissenters. Still, Vern Forster and Don Graham, the two notoriously independent, self-confessed maniacs who ran Tire's operation in British Columbia, couldn't believe what they were seeing. "They [the point team] were acting as if we were selling our souls for Christ," Forster said. The point team leaked information about the deal in dribs and drabs; the more suspenseful the drama became, the more willing the dealers were to resolve it, and the more they wanted to buy the company.

But the meetings did what they were supposed to do. By November 19, the day before Martha's notice under the Aldamar agreement expired, the point team informed Biggar that if Martha were not a buyer, the dealers would be, at the same price. Biggar was thrilled.

Two days later, on November 21, between half past five and six o'clock in the evening, Fred and David visited Gordon Capital to discuss the offer the dealers might make. There was a new face among the lawyers – that of Peter Dey, now one of the top securities lawyers at the law firm of Osler, Hoskin & Harcourt. Dey had been urged upon the dealers by Gordon Capital (as co-counsel with Davies, Ward & Beck, Gordon's usual lawyers, who were helping out) and had been sold to the dealers as the most experienced and expert securities lawyer in all Creation.

Dey was the dealers' ace-in-the-hole. Young (forty-five), energetic, vastly successful (estimates of his annual salary began at $350,000 a year), Dey had recently climbed down as the chairman of the Ontario Securities Commission to re-enter private practice. He *was* the best-known securities lawyer in the country, and he knew how the OSC operated. If the deal landed the dealers in front of the OSC for circumventing the coat-tail – and the lawyers for the dealers and the brothers all knew it might – a lot of people figured Dey stood the best chance of winning the case.[1] Ironically, during his tenure as OSC chairman it was Dey who had championed – often against the wishes of the financial establishment – the creation of the shareholders' rights that led to Tire's coat-tail. The dealers' offer was Dey's most controversial case since his return from the OSC. Certainly a win would enhance Osler's profile among serious transactional firms on Bay Street, up there in the firmament next to Davies, Ward & Beck and Tory, Tory, DesLauriers and Binnington. Furthermore, Dey considered he could win the case for his client.

None of these possibilities, except the last one, was a concern of the point team. The dealers looked to Dey and Gordon Capital as sophisticated men of Bay Street who knew everything there was to know about the terrifying business of takeovers. The more the Bay Street power-brokers insisted the dealers could own Canadian Tire – and urge them they did, persistently, insistently, telling them the deal was so close they could "taste it" – the more the dealers began to believe it. They weren't provincial yokels any more! No siree, they were in the big leagues! Indeed, it seemed that perhaps the point team's ambitions had gone to their heads. "There was a lot of lip service paid to the idea of maintaining the status quo and the balance of power," one dealer noted. "But in the end, power corrupts, and absolute power corrupts absolutely." Warren in particular seemed to have changed. "As he went along," another dealer observed, "perhaps the spotlight became a little awesome." Yet, thanks to Gordon's gag order,

---

[1] Gordon Capital's respect for Peter Dey was profound: the firm had offered Dey a job when he left the OSC, but Dey had turned it down. Despite his dashing presence, he was a careful man. He wasn't one to rashly leave the security of a law firm like Osler, Hoskin & Harcourt for the rough-and-tumble ways of Gordon Capital.

there was no way to test the reality of the point team's vision against the hard pavement of public opinion.

The blinding big-league Bay Street spotlight: you could see it from North Bay, where Al Warren had languished, frustrated by his own success, and from Calgary and Windsor and Saskatoon as well. The spotlight beamed out from Toronto, announcing a Frank Capra movie, directed by the Chamber of Commerce, produced by Greed, and starring the four horsemen of the point team: Mr. Dealer Goes to Bay Street. The big leagues were seductive. Even the lawyers' offices were seductive.

The offices of Gordon Capital and Osler, Hoskin & Harcourt, Peter Dey's firm, where the point team frequently met, couldn't have been more different from the makeshift over-the-store-floor hovels that served happily – until now! – as offices in Dealerland. There were a million dollars' worth of paintings hanging in the hallways! And the elevators . . . the elevators in the soaring white marble lobby of the Bank of Montreal's First Canadian Place that transported you to the upper limits of Canadian capitalism, to the lawyers' lairs, didn't ping and groan their way upwards. These elevators made no sound at all: you simply soared ever higher and faster, the swoosh of your rise ever so slightly terrifying, until suddenly a light box lit up at the sixty-fifth and sixty-sixth floors, Osler, Hoskin's floors – two floors! In an office tower in downtown Toronto ! How much had that set them back!? – and a little discreet bell went (((bing))), just once, the same reserved tone as the old closing bell at Eaton's, and suddenly there you were, in corporate Heaven again, deep in the hypothalamus of the business brain where rules were made to be broken. It was enough to make the lowliest dealer feel like one of the blessed.

You stepped off the elevator and the first thing that hit you, like a reprimand, was the name of the firm, OSLER, HOSKIN & HARCOURT, all in fat cast brass letters, the serifs off-center and just right, the classic we've-been-here-for-generations look, the letters so thick and permanent and heavy it was a wonder they stayed attached to the wall.

The floors of the lobby at Osler, Hoskin were a deep green malachite marble, and there was a spiral staircase in the middle of the reception area. No one raised his voice here, no PA systems rang out with snow-shovel or lawnmower specials. The receptionists seemed to have taken their clothes right out of the Holt Renfrew box and they spoke in X-ray tones that told you that they knew that you had as much business being up there on the sixty-sixth floor as a distressed muskrat. Even the telephones rang with a discreet blip, so as not to disturb the Big Legal Thinkers who at that very moment were closeted away deciding the future of western capitalism. The whole place reeked of weight and roots and money and power and class.

Neil Baker, of Gordon Capital, was the first to speak at the meeting on November 21. The dealers, he explained to Matthews, were prepared to make a generous offer to Fred and David for their common shares. The question was what form the deal would take. It was only toward the end of the evening that the point team raised Rene Sorell's 49-percent route. Dey had come up with it on his own at home over the weekend, "sitting and fiddling" with the coat-tail. Dey believed the deal would not be stopped; if anyone got reprimanded or sued as a result of skipping around the coat-tails, it would be the Billeses, not the dealers. The 49-percent plan was controversial, but the lawyers involved seemed to consider that the potential reward outweighed any possible risk. How could so many big-league law firms be wrong (said the small-town logic of the dealers)? And, to be fair, the Ontario Securities Commission had not stopped similar transactions, at least according to the lawyers' reading of the relevant legal authorities. Still, there were lawyers at McCarthy & McCarthy, lawyers working on the Billes team, who were amazed that the dealers bought it.

Then Biggar dropped his bomb: his clients, Fred and David,

wanted the dealers to pay a deposit for the Billeses' shares. "It wouldn't be prudent for our clients to go into a deal . . . unless there was a sizeable deposit," Biggar maintained. A deposit would commit the dealers to the purchase. And, he added, a deposit was standard fare on Bay Street. Biggar called it "earnest money." Earnest meant anywhere from $7 million to $15 million, cash. A lot of cashola! But if that was the way the big leagues did it, that was the way it would be.

Some bickering still followed. Fred's lawyers opted for the high end ($15 million) as a *non-refundable* deposit, to be forfeited if the offer wasn't accepted by five in the afternoon on December 8. By November 27 the amount was still in dispute, but Fred and David had agreed to make half of the deposit refundable if the Ontario Securities Commission intervened. This was not a giant concession on the Billes boys' part; everyone knew the deal was risky. At the same time, the sheer size of the non-refundable deposit meant that Gordon Capital, Peter Dey (and therefore – yes, sir! – the dealers) figured the company was theirs. The dealers gave themselves four-to-one odds in favor of the deal going through.

In the midst of these negotiations, two other bids material-ized. The board of Canadian Tire was still trying to firm up its offer to buy the company, and was meeting regularly to discuss the matter. As usual, A.J. was in the thick of things. What would happen to the corporation if the dealers owned it? Who would they favor? Themselves? And how would they pay for it? Out of profits? And would it not be better if they were to implement . . . yes!!! Here it was!!! . . . the fifty-fifty plan!! Tire's board members could see the old man coming a mile away. But the company's offer was still in its early days, despite the efforts of C.E. (Ted) Medland of Wood Gundy Inc. to organize it.[2]

---

[2]Canadian Tire's offer did not surface until December, by which time it was too late to be considered.

A second offer surfaced in mid-November when Cara Foods Corp. (now Cara Operations Limited), the well-known chain of airport concessions owned by Paul Phelan, informed Merrill Lynch and Matthews of its desire to amalgamate with Canadian Tire. It was a bizarre idea, but that was nothing new at Cara, where Phelan was always acting out his oversized passions and enthusiasms. Phelan loved well-run family companies. Cara's plan was worth $60 a share. Merrill Lynch rejected it as insufficiently generous.

It was also too late. On November 27, at eight o'clock in the evening, Biff Matthews, William Sheridan (David Billes's lawyer), Fred and David Billes, Bill Biggar and a host of others met in the boardroom at Lang Michener Lash Johnston, Bill Sheridan's firm, to finalize the agreements. Barbara Billes was there too, as she had been at several meetings. If anyone wanted evidence that Barbara had a hand in what was happening, there it was. The group planned to head over to Osler, Hoskin at nine to sign the deal. Just before they left, Sheridan received a phone call from John Stransman, Martha's lawyer. Stransman said A.J. Billes was in his office with Martha, and that A.J. wanted to talk to Fred. Over the speaker phone, A.J. told Fred that Stransman had prepared a document for Fred to read.

Fine. Sheridan sent a lawyer over to Stransman's office to pick it up. He was back by 9:30. There was an envelope for Fred from Martha, and various others for everyone else. Martha's instructions were that Fred was to read his first, before the others were opened. Matthews found the scene a little like Christmas Day. He was close. In fact it was Fred's birthday. Martha's package was a birthday present of sorts, and a last-ditch attempt at a reconciliation with her brother. The other packages contained copies of a letter dated November 27 – seven days after the notice given to Martha under the Aldamar agreement had expired – informing the brothers that their notice failed to comply with the agreement, whatever that meant. Everyone found the letter quite odd.

Fred (and therefore David) was in no mood to entertain a final flurry of creativity from Martha. They went ahead and struck a deal. The contract was a quarter of an inch thick. For the opportunity to buy control of Canadian Tire, the dealers would pay Fred and David a deposit of $15 million, half of which was non-refundable, period. If the dealers didn't make their bid by five o'clock on December 22, or take up and pay for the shares by January 16, the other $7.5 million became non-refundable too. If the OSC intervened and stayed the bid, the dealers got half their deposit back. If the deal went through, the dealers paid Fred and David another $125 million. But it wasn't the end of the world if the deal didn't go through: with a stroke of the pen, Fred and David Billes had just earned themselves $3.75 million each – whether or not they sold their shares. No one could say Biff Matthews and William Sheridan weren't looking after their clients' interests.

Of course, if anyone had walked up to a dealer and asked him to pay $15 million for a load of lawnmowers that had a twenty-percent chance of not being delivered, the dealer would have laughed the supplicant out of the room. But that was the power of the spell of the big leagues, and of the lawyers who dominated them. They were the experts.

EVEN so, the most ferocious and entertaining negotiations were yet to come. The next day, the point team mailed a similar offer to Martha. They offered her a $7.5 million deposit of her own, half of which was non-refundable.

Once Fred and David agreed to sell to the dealers, Martha was in a bind: without her brothers, her slice of the Billes control block was considerably less valuable. On the other hand, her block, joined with any other, represented a considerable challenge to the dealers' control, which gave her bargaining power. John Stransman used it to reject the dealers' offer in favor of a $15-million deposit for Martha – *none of which was refundable under any circumstances*. Martha was making twice as much as her brothers, just for putting her shares up for sale. And she didn't have to share her deposit with anyone.

Even for $15 million, however, she hadn't made it easy. Thanks to the details of their offer to Fred and David, the dealers had to commit Martha to their deal by one o'clock in the afternoon on Friday, November 21. The negotiations with Stransman were protracted, and by noon the papers had yet to be signed. Fred and David extended their deadline until later in the afternoon. But Martha was up at her home, the former Billes family estate on Lake Simcoe outside Barrie, a good hour-and-a-half drive north of Toronto. By now Dey was going crazy with work: in addition to the Billes deal, he was immersed in a public financing for another client. Stransman, Fung, and Dey decided they had to fly to Martha's by helicopter. They commissioned one out of Buttonville airport just north of Toronto and headed north. Dey assumed the dealers had given Fung a map, but – no! No one knew where Martha lived. By three o'clock the whirlybird was blasting up and down the coast of Lake Simcoe, looking for a big house. They had to find it soon, because the pilot was licensed to fly only by visual flight rules, and it would be dark by five.

Finally, the team spots Martha and Dennis Gardiner Billes, her husband, waving from a dock. The helicopter finally lands. But . . . Martha does not sign! Attagirl, Martha! The papers went back to Toronto to be reworked. (Dey later became a director of the helicopter company.) Finally, by December 2, Martha was in.

Which was all well and good, except that by now the competition between the brothers and their sister – to say nothing of the gamesmanship among their lawyers – knew no bounds. When Fred and David learned that Martha's deposit was twice as big as their own – and completely non-refunda-ble – they were miffed. But the dealers needed the brothers to extend the closing of the deal to March 31, 1987, to conform to securities law. In return for that concession, Matthews forced the dealers to make the boys' entire $15-million deposit non-refundable, just like Martha's, except that they had to split it.

But the deal was set. Three hundred and sixty-one Canadian Tire dealers had borrowed $290 million – between $300,000 and $750,000 each – to buy 49 percent of the Mother Corporation. On the ninth of December, 1986, they announced their offer to the world. They already owed the Billeses $30 million.

It felt *good*. Security, the hallowed status quo, had been preserved. Unfortunately, the very next day, the Ontario Securities Commission made an announcement of its own. There was going to be a hearing.

16

THE HEARING

THE MATTER of the *Securities Act*, R.S.O. 1980, Chapter 466, as amended, and Canadian Tire Corporation Limited, C.T.C. Dealer Holdings Limited, Alfred W. Billes, David G. Billes, and Martha Gardiner Billes – to use its official name – was convened at a quarter to ten on the morning of Thursday, December 18, 1986. There weren't enough chairs to go around. The Harry Slocomb Bray Hearing Room, which resembles an airport waiting-lounge, is the largest chamber at the Ontario Securities Commission's headquarters on the seventeenth floor of the south tower of the Eaton Centre in downtown Toronto. But the prospect of the secretive owners of Canada's largest retailing concern being thrust for the first time under the spotlight of public attention had drawn a bloodthirsty crowd. The early birds who arrived by nine were predicting the proceedings would be "better than 'Dynasty.' "

The Ontario Securities Commission (commonly known as the OSC) was not a place where one expected to be entertained. The Commission was a non-judicial body that had been created by the Ontario government in the 1930s to regulate Canada's adolescent capital markets. Securities cases were often too complicated to be decided by juries or judges; the OSC was to operate as a board of experts. For the first forty years of its life it had served mainly as a rubber stamp for the wishes of the Toronto financial establishment. Its role was discreetly veiled by a thick dust of Baptist reserve compared

287

to the U.S. Securities and Exchange Commission, the OSC's counterpart in Washington, which flaunted itself as a tough cop catching bad guys in the stock market. In Ontario the enforcer worked things out without making headlines.

That changed when a rash of takeovers in the late 1970s heralded the dawn of the financially profligate 1980s. By 1984 the OSC was one of the two most powerful financial regulatory agencies in North America. As soon as the middle class began to gambol in the roiling waters of the stock market, the stock market became a more public place, and thus the OSC did too. Ermanno Pascutto, the OSC's youthful executive director, had been appointed to his position in October, 1984, at the age of thirty-one. He was the son of an Italian construction worker, and something of an angry young man. His mandate was to build a team of rebels who would make the OSC more aggressive and interventionist in the course of creating new public policy.

One of those rebels was Joseph Groia, the OSC's associate general counsel, and the man responsible for handling the Canadian Tire case. Groia had graduated from the University of Toronto law school in 1979 (Dean's Honour List, Chief Justice of the Moot Court), and had gone straight to work for McMillan Binch, one of Toronto's most eminent law firms. Unfortunately there were twenty trial lawyers in McMillan's litigation department; after four years at the firm, Groia was eleventh in the pecking order, and he wasn't moving. Trial lawyers, the ones who stand up in court and do the talking, are the most competitive, the most egotistical, and sometimes the brightest minds in the profession. Groia had wanted to be a trial lawyer ever since – well, since he was a boy watching Raymond Burr on the television series *Perry Mason*. True! The number of trial lawyers in Toronto who traced their love of the law to *Perry Mason* was astounding. But as for working twelve and thirteen hours a day (plus weekends) for six or seven years as an assistant to some status-encrusted senior partner until the firm deigned to take him into the fold

. . . no way. When Ermanno Pascutto approached Groia at a summer jurisprudence course at Harvard University in the summer of 1985 and asked him to be the Commission's associate general counsel, Groia jumped. He was thirty years old.

Joe Groia was not a fool. He was aware that, with the economy on high boil, a few years in the public eye at the Ontario Securities Commission, taking on established financial interests in the name of justice and the public good, was the fast track to a national reputation. More importantly, a stint at the OSC would offer a deeper, more thorough legal education than was available at a downtown law firm, where, Groia was convinced, business and making money were now more important than the once-hallowed practice and protection of the law. Groia was a purist. He earned less at the OSC than he did at McMillan Binch – $65,000 a year, compared to $100,000 in private practice – but his hours and his cases were his own. Groia was thus lured to the Commission from McMillan Binch for a year or two. "For a person of my age and stage," Groia explained, "it was the same kind of game, but all of a sudden the players were a lot older and better. . . . At McMillan Binch I would have been the fifth lawyer on the Canadian Tire case. I wouldn't have gotten within a hundred yards of the microphone." Instead, Joe Groia was about to take on the most important case in the history of Canadian securities law. From the OSC he could leap directly into a partnership at a major downtown law firm – McMillan Binch had already offered him a job – provided he didn't irritate too many of his legal colleagues on the other side of the fence.

What mattered just as much to Groia, however, was the fact that the OSC's new interventionist mandate reflected his own personal and political philosophies. On the wall of his office was a cartoon entitled "The Rebel." It depicted a man being hauled off by the authorities for painting his house an unorthodox color. Groia sported a beard and horn-rims, and he wore red waistcoats. He looked like an enlightened *consigliere* in a Bertolucci movie set in the 1920s. The image meshed well with his background. His grandfather had emigrated from Italy to work as a shoe-shine boy. His father was a bellhop at the Royal York Hotel, where he had lugged the bags of Canada's capitalist class for thirty years. His mother toiled in the post office. Their son had advanced into the professional classes (losing a marriage on the way), but there was a side to Joe Groia that was happy to wreak revenge on his parents' masters.

Groia worked as a lawyer for the Ontario Government, but deep inside he considered himself an outlaw. It was a common fantasy among the young corporate climbers of his generation, with whom he shared many characteristics. Sometimes, for instance, he felt guilty about his material success. He believed, for another instance, in telling people what was good for them, rather than letting them decide for themselves. He believed happiness was as much a collective good as it was an individual one, and that it could be – *ought* to be – legislated. To that end, he thought lawyers had responsibilities that went beyond the simple wishes of their paying clients – a notion distinctly out of synch with the values that prevailed in the M&A departments of many big downtown law firms. ''I don't see us – the legal profession – as being highly paid whores,'' Groia maintained. His concern was not honor: honor was a ''generational word'' that was not part of Groia's lexicon. ''I think I would call [it] an ethical standard.''

What made the Canadian Tire case so perfect was that it set many things that offended Joe Groia against many things he held dear. The Billeses, three scions of inherited wealth, had used the money of ordinary shareholders to take control of a firm. Now they were trying to sell the company for a huge profit, with no thought of buying out the ordinary shareholders. The family had hired the best legal talent money could buy to accomplish this, a fact duly noted by Groia. In the end, what got both Groia and his opponents going was that the Tire deal presented an enormous *intellectual*

challenge. The battle about to take place in the Harry Bray
Hearing Room was more than a controversial takeover bid. It
was a battle between two generations of lawyers, two establishments, and two distinct legal camps: the traditional anti-
government school, on the one hand, that believed in the
strict letter of the law and the responsibility of the individual
to look out for himself, and a newer school that was willing to
subjugate the letter of the law to a new, amorphous, and
potentially dangerous notion: the public interest. The side
that won this fight would make the rules on how business was
done in Canada for years to come.

Groia knew that instinctively. Normally a case like Tire
would have been the province of the Commission's enforce-
ment division, but this was too big, too important, too
prominent a transaction to leave for drab civil servants who
resented the likes of Groia. He had heard rumors of the
Canadian Tire deal two weeks before the offer was made
public, and he immediately set out to make the case an
important one. Investors were already calling the OSC with
complaints about the dealers' offer. Groia and Pascutto told
the staff to clean off their desks; this was going to require
everything the Commission had. The OSC's notice of hearing
was typed up and ready to go the day before the dealers' offer
was announced.

That was quite unusual, but to anyone familiar with the new
OSC, it was predictable. Groia and Pascutto were aggressive,
and ambitious, and they had a mission – to bring the Billeses
to justice.

AT the press conference held to announce the hearing, Groia
gave himself a fifty-fifty chance of winning the Tire case. Even
odds were the only fair way to reflect the reputation of Stanley
Beck, the OSC's chairman. A short, trim, round-headed fifty-
two-year-old with reddish brown hair, a taste for handmade
suits, and a mind of pure titanium, Beck had a somewhat
accurate reputation as a strict black-letter lawyer, and a

completely accurate reputation as an independent legal think-
er. Stan Beck made up his own mind. As dean at Osgoode Hall
Law School, and later as a member of the OSC, Beck saw the
OSC performing a strict, elevated, almost judicial function. As
commissioner, he wasn't afraid to take an unpopular course of
action. In his opening remarks the first day of the Tire
hearing, Beck had characterized the proceedings, with wry
scorn, as "the OSC's very own Christmas pageant." Among the
overwrought OSC staff, more than one junior lawyer believed
that if anyone saw the merits of the dealers' offer, it would be
Stanley Beck.

Looking out from his vantage point on the raised dais where
he sat with three fellow commissioners and two guests from
the Quebec Securities Commission, Beck could easily have
concluded that Canada's business affairs were controlled by a
handful of lawyers – a small club of paper entrepreneurs.
There were twenty-nine of them working on the Tire case.
Most of them were hauling down $2,000 a day. There were so
many minor conflicts and intermarriages in the room that it
resembled a small town in Tennessee where everyone has the
same last name.

To Beck's left sat Groia and the Commission's staff, including Jim Turner, a lawyer who had been seconded from Tory,
Tory, DesLauriers, and three junior lawyers. Behind them
was Sheila Block – also from Tory, Tory – who was acting for
Canadian Tire.

Behind Block sat the sadly aggrieved Class A Shareholders
Action Committee, who collectively owned more than 20
million non-voting Canadian Tire A shares. Groia referred to
them as "the A Team," and included himself among them.
The committee's counsel were Stanley Fisher from McMillan
Binch, and Jack Geller, a Pickwickian securities lawyer from
Campbell Godfrey. Geller had represented Dick Billes during
the 1983 National Trust auction.

The Shareholders Action Committee had been formed by
William Allen and Stephen Jarislowsky. They had first worked

in concert in the late 1960s when British Petroleum tried to buy SuperTest; in the intervening years they had emerged as a unique species in the securities world – investment counsellors who made a good portion of their handsome livings defending the rights of oppressed shareholders. The institutional clients of Allen's firm, the Allenvest Group Limited, had phoned Bill Allen the day the dealers' offer went public. The institutions were furious, and justly so: as non-voting A shareholders, they were being cut out of what was in essence a takeover bid for control of Canadian Tire. Allen had been in the investment business since 1948, and he shared his clients' indignation. "A third of a company's share value is the control factor, " he stated. "And that is the area that major corporate groups trade in." He also admitted that taking on public causes like this one was terrific free advertising for his firm: "[It] gets us more business. The last thing I would ever claim to be is some altruistic thing. That's claptrap." Strategically, however, do-gooders like Allen and Jarislowsky were important allies for the OSC. "What we did," Allen later said, "was provide outraged institutions and provide a focal point" for the OSC's case. In return, Allen and Jarislowsky charged the institutions they represented a little under two cents a share – some $420,000, the largest portion of which, Allen claimed, went to McMillan Binch.

Stephen Jarislowsky did not join Allen on the first day of the hearings. In fact, he seldom attended hearings at all, though he was considered one of the most influential investment counsellors in the country. By the phlegmatic meat-and-potato standards of Bay Street, Jarislowsky was a rare and eccentric bird. Born in Berlin in 1925, he had been educated in Europe, the United States, the U.S. Army (where he studied Japanese), the University of Chicago, and the Harvard Business School. Fond of art and enormously learned, he had been raised a Protestant, schooled in Catholicism and Buddhism, and often worked his religious views into his criticism of the opposite side of whichever issue he happened to be riding.

He had started his company, Jarislowsky, Fraser & Co. Limited, in 1955. As of the fall of 1986, it owned $4.5 million worth of A shares – one of its less spectacular investments that Jarislowsky was now trying to protect by championing the public interest. The following year, in 1987 – the year of Black Monday – his personal take from his company's investments, after taxes, was $6.3 million. And that was "a bad year."

Father Jarislowsky was never at a loss for an electrifying quote. He had no particular love, for example, for minority shareholders – "they're a waste of time," he said, "I don't make any money off them." Still, he preferred them to owners who tried to cut him out of the action. "These guys aren't just normal control shareholders," he once said of the Billeses. "To me, there's no law against a company being taken over. If people want to control a company, let them put up the money and buy all of it. Not control it with two or three percent." The case before the Commission, Jarislowsky believed, concerned "the question of whether greed is stronger than decency."

Stacked up like logs on the right-hand side of the room were the lawyers for the dealers and the Billeses. Front and center was Peter Dey, of Osler, Hoskin & Harcourt, who was acting for the dealers and Gordon Capital Corporation, the dealers' financial agent. Dey looked relaxed, but then he always did. Dey was so relaxed he was known as the Perry Como of the Toronto legal community. He was also critical to the dealers' case. As previous chairman of the Ontario Securities Commission, he knew his securities law backwards. He also knew Stan Beck. One of Dey's last acts as chairman of the OSC had been to recommend Stan Beck as his successor. "I take personal credit," Dey once said, "for making Stan Beck one of Toronto's most influential citizens."

Canada is a small country, its legal community particularly so. The securities fraternity is tinier still. Many of the same lawyers of necessity act in the most prominent cases. It was during Peter Dey's tenure as chairman that the Commission had established most of its policies protecting shareholders' rights. The same policies now formed the spine of the OSC's case against Dey and Dealerland – an irony Groia did not hesitate to point out. But the inter-connectedness of the legal community working on the Tire case drove the Commission's junior staff lawyers to previously unscaled heights of paranoid theorizing. That was understandable: the staff saw itself as the underdog, taking on the all-powerful Establishment. But the theories! They were fabulous. The OSC staff speculated that Dey had taken the Tire case on in part to prove he could play with equal aplomb from both sides of the regulatory fence – as a good lawyer should. That's what the law is all about, rational argument. By the time the case was under way, however, the OSC's junior lawyers had taken that idea and blown it up to magnificent proportions. Gordon Capital had hired Dey, staffers now believed, because Dey was a big name in securities law. If Dey were representing the dealers, it meant the case was an important one, which meant Stan Beck would feel compelled to sit on the panel, which meant the staff would have to work especially hard to convince him to stay the deal. Stan Beck, for his part, considered these theories utterly witless, while Dey ignored them. He figured the odds of winning the case were running three to two in the dealers' favor.

Sitting next to Dey, and also acting for the dealers and Gordon Capital, was Dennis O'Connor, from the prominent law firm of Borden & Elliot, counsel to Dealer Holdings. O'Connor was an unflappable trial lawyer known for his fluid intelligence and his eye for compromise. Next to O'Connor was William Gula, of Davies, Ward & Beck, Gordon Capital's favorite law firm. The Beck of Davies, Ward & Beck was Stan's brother, Howard, who had helped put the dealers' offer together. The joke on Bay Street was that Howard told Stan "just enough to let him do his job" as chairman of the OSC. It was a weak joke, however, because Stan Beck was no one's patsy and every lawyer in the room knew and respected the fact. True, Stan was in the bizarre position of judging a deal his brother had worked on. The fact that no one publicly mentioned the potential conflict of interest, however, was a testament to Beck's independence – not to mention the assembled lawyers' reluctance to set fire to Beck's moral indignation.

Behind the dynamic O'Connor-Dey duo were Tom Heintzman, a tall, thin, sharp-nosed litigator from McCarthy & McCarthy who knew his law backward and forward and was there to represent Fred Billes; Donald Wright, Heintzman's counterpart at Lang Michener, for David Billes; and John Stransman from Stikeman, Elliott, Martha Billes's lawyer. At thirty-four, Stransman had already established himself as a brilliant deal-maker, thanks in large part to the way he had negotiated Martha's $15-million down payment.

Behind Stransman, in two neat rows, sat anywhere from six to fifteen Canadian Tire dealers, including the "point team," neatly dressed in their best $900 suits, every immaculate hair in place. The dealers weren't allowed to say anything: the Gordon Capital gag order was still in force. Together they resembled a warren of well-behaved rabbits.

To the rear sat the focus of everyone's attention, the Billes *frères* and their wives. Fred looked calm enough, if older than his fifty-one years. He was wearing a wrinkled blue suit and his French detective mustache. He needed a haircut; his gray duckbill was showing yellow at the edges. On his finger was a ring the size of a small faucet. He sat with his arms folded across his stomach, as if he were carrying an armful of firewood. He often closed his eyes. Every once in a while he coughed like a small volcano. His only show of emotion during the testimony was an occasional nod or shake of his massive head. Sometimes he tapped both his feet at once, as if dreaming. Rarely, very rarely, he would write himself a note, moving the pen languidly, as if it were tied to his finger. For some reason he conjured up images of Oscar Wilde.

Barbara Billes, Fred's wife, conjured up a different persona. Everyone assumed she was sister Martha – this despite the fact that she and Fred were holding hands, and that she was protecting her escort like a wolverine. (If a reporter approached Fred, Barbara would turn on the intruder: "Are you press?" she would say, her voice quavering with emotion. "Oh, yeah, just distorting everything. Don't trust them, Fred.") Barbara was nothing like Martha Billes, though they were equally forceful personalities, and the comparison offended her, not least because Fred and his sister were no longer speaking.

Barbara didn't look anything like her sister-in-law. Barbara wore half-glasses, a tattersall jacket, and just a touch too much red lipstick. Her brown hair was streaked blond, and she was pleasantly plump. She looked like a mother out for a day of shopping in the city.

Actually, Martha wasn't even in the room the first day. And when she did show up, in contrast to Barbara, she was openly sexy, even brazen. She went for trendy purple wool-and-leather knits and gold gabardine dresses and black leather skirts and her great-grandmother's jewelry and her grandfather's watch chain. Barbara found her eccentric. For one thing, Martha lived in Calgary.

Groia had decided not to call Martha as one of his side's witnesses because she was "a wild card." But that didn't stop some of the press from assuming that Barbara was Martha. During the first break in the hearing, one of them had tried to photograph Fred and Barbara standing by the telephone. Fred backed his bulk into the camera to spoil the shot. "Oh!" Fred said, his voice booming with innocence. "Sorry! I backed into him."

"You hit me!" Barbara shrilled, holding a newspaper up in front of the camera. "Yes, you did!"

"Excuse me!" Fred bellowed. He was suddenly trying to get out. "I want to get out. I want to get out."

"Stop hitting me!" Barbara was saying. "Stop hitting me!"

In front of the elevator, the dealers' lawyers were watching in wonder. "Did you see Billes dealing with the photographers?" one said.

"Yeah," said another. "It's great."

Great? It was marvellous! And all here in the Harry Slocomb Bray Memorial waiting room! Better than "Dynasty" for sure. Even better than Dogpatch.

AFTER a morning of procedural wrangling, during which Fred's lawyers disposed of a video camera taping the proceedings, and unsuccessfully tried to deny the Shareholders Action Committee standing in the proceedings, Joe Groia and Jim Turner were ready to present their case.

Groia and his staff had assembled an impressive array of evidence, some eighty different documents now collected into two three-inch-thick plastic-bound books. This evidence had been culled in three mad days of fishing and rooting through the files of Canadian Tire, the Billeses, their lawyers, and their associates, past and present. It represented a level of disclosure unparalleled in the annals of Canadian business, and it made for a strong case.

"In the view of the staff," Turner told the assemblage, "[this case] is fundamentally about the abuse of the rights of public shareholders." The key was Canadian Tire's "takeover protection," the coat-tail that promised the A shareholders would be bought out if a buyer purchased a majority of Tire's common shares. The dealers' offer, Turner went on, "has been structured in an artificial and technical way to avoid the operation of what we are referring to as the coat-tail provision," and entailed "a huge premium payable to a very small number of insiders of Canadian Tire Corporation." At stake were profound questions about the right of the Commission to become involved in such matters, the use of non-voting shares, the duties of controlling shareholders and directors, questions of secrecy and disclosure. This was a hearing, in other words, about the nature of capitalism itself.

But it was mainly about money. If the dealers' offer went through as planned, the Billeses made a fortune, and the A shareholders made nothing. But if the coat-tail was deemed to be operational, Tire's non-voting A shareholders stood to share a major windfall. Consider the following scenarios:

TAKEOVER SCENARIOS

Buyer	Offer	Price per share common/As	Gross profit		
			Billes family	Total A shareholders	Per 1000 A shares
Dealer Holdings (coat-tail does not operate*)	49% of common	$160.24/nil	$165 million ($55 million each)	nil	nil
Dealer Holdings (coat-tail does operate)	49% of common, 49% of As	$160.24/ $160.24	$165 million ($55 million each)	$6.6 billion	$81,722
Theoretical Carling O'Keefe bid	51% of common, 51% of As	$60/$20	$64 million ($21.2 million each)	$864 million	$10,200
*Roughly equivalent to Dealer Holdings bid.					

It was mid-afternoon by the time Groia called his first witness, Alex Ethelred Barron. At sixty-eight, the former chairman of Canadian Tire had been retired since Martha Billes ousted him two and a half years earlier. Groia considered Barron his most important witness. Everything about Barron, from his distinguished fifty-year career in the investment business to his thinning silver hair and his handmade glen-plaid suit and waistcoat, spoke to his character, to his reputation on Bay Street (former chairman of Burns Fry, the brokerage firm) and to his role as the representative of a time – so Groia depicted it, at any rate – when principles mattered as much as profits.

Groia's plan was to start in 1983; establish the intentions of the executives who drafted the coat-tail; and then move into 1986, to demonstrate how the dealers' offer betrayed those intentions. As Barron explained it to him – and as John Kron and Dean Muncaster concurred when they subsequently took the stand – the coat-tail clause that was now in dispute had been created within an atmosphere of trust. "I think one of the important points," Barron said, "is, at least to me, that in the period 1966 to 1983, basically what we had in Canadian Tire was a balance of power. . . . And no one controlled the board; it was basically an independent board and operated that way up until 1983 when the shares changed hands."

When Fred, Martha, and David bought the J.W. Billes estate's shares in 1983, they did so with the intention of owning the company forever. The takeover protection clause had been designed with that in mind. If control ever changed hands – if the Billeses ever sold their shares, which they claimed at the time was not about to happen – the A shareholders would be paid back for helping the Billeses buy control of Tire. It was an *understanding*. An offer like the dealers' had never been contemplated, Barron insisted, and would not have been considered proper.

Only toward the very end of Groia's questioning did Barron display any sense of having been betrayed by the Billeses. "After the re-organization [after the auction in 1983] was completed and the placements [of the Billeses' A shares, which they sold to finance the purchase of control] were carried out," Groia asked, "how long did you remain on with Canadian Tire?"

BARRON: I can't remember precisely, but it would be a few months, but no longer.
GROIA: Do you know why it was that you were not asked to stand for re-election?
BARRON: Yes. [*Such restraint!*]
GROIA: Would you be willing to tell us?

BARRON: Well, the members of the A.J. Billes family advised me that they were not prepared to recommend me in the future as a director of the corporation.

GROIA: Did they tell you why that was?

BARRON: Well, they said I hadn't supported them.

GROIA: Who had you supported?

BARRON: As far as I was concerned I had supported the corporation, the shareholders generally. I wasn't trying to take sides with anybody.

GROIA: I don't think I have any other questions, Mr. Chairman.

The lawyers for the Billeses and the dealers – the B Team – were not as gentle with Barron. Their case was based on one fact: that the dealers' offer did not contravene a literal reading of the coat-tail, and therefore was entirely legal. The coat-tail clause said that a bid for less than a majority of Tire's common shares – say, 49 percent – would not trigger the coat-tail. The coat-tail in dispute was triggered by a *majority* of shares changing hands, rather than a change of corporate *control*, which is not the same thing, as it is possible to control a company without owning a majority of its shares. The lawyers for the Billeses made a great deal of this distinction. But with the three Billes children acting in concert, as they were in 1983, and therefore controlling sixty percent of the common shares, the two terms effectively meant the same thing.

Thus, the lawyers insisted, the dealers' bid conformed to the coat-tail, as written, and the Commission had no right to interfere.

The lawyers for the Billeses and the dealers believed the Commission's case was the result of "industry pressure" – true enough – from financial institutions that had knowingly bought non-participating shares and now wanted in on the takeover premium to which they had no right. Each day of the hearing, the lawyers claimed, cost the Billeses $100,000 in lost interest. It was a terrible hardship. The only thing that

worried the B Team was that the Commission might balk at
the huge figure the dealers were paying the Billeses for control.
Apart from that, they figured their case was open and shut.

The warm aura of integrity Groia had established around
the reputation of Alex Barron quickly evaporated when
Donald Wright, David's lawyer, began his cross-examination
of Barron. A tall, wiry man with a nasal voice, Wright was
famous for his surgical ability to extract exactly the evidence
he wanted out of even a hostile witness. Reading a transcript
of Groia's direct examinations of a witness was like reading a
novel: Groia would cast a question like bait, listening for
anything that might come up, and the answers would flow,
page upon page of solid type. Wright's cross-examinations, by
contrast, read like dialogue: crisply framed questions to
which the only possible answer was a simple yes or no.
Listening to Don Wright was one of the genuine pleasures of
the hearing – the spectacle of a first-rate mind manipulating
another to its own invisible purposes. Wright's words had the
ring of nails being hammered into a coffin.

Having set the older man up as a self-professed investment
expert, Wright forced Barron to admit that he owned a
substantial number of A shares – thereby suggesting, though
never saying outright, that Barron had an ulterior motive in
appearing as a witness. Wright then began, subtly, as if
playing a secondary theme in a sonata, to undermine Barron's
mental credibility.

It was wonderful to watch, in a sick kind of way. Wright
would ask Barron to look at a document – and then, almost as
an afterthought, would add: "Do you see that?" Every time
Wright asked the question, the invisible taunt sunk in a little
deeper: *Can you see the very words on the paper in front of
you, you retired old fool? Do they not say what they say as
clear as day?* "Would you not agree with me then," Wright
asked, "what this calls for is 49 percent of 3,345,000 shares
would be tendered and taken up pursuant to the offer; is not

that what this is dealing with, under the plain meaning of the words?"

BARRON: I suppose you are correct there, but you are avoiding the facts of life.

WRIGHT: I beg your pardon?

BARRON: You . . . avoid the facts of life. I mean, if somebody said to me, "We are going to tender 49 percent and then buy 2 percent in the open market," I would say, "You are buying control."

WRIGHT: Is there anything about control in here, sir?

BARRON: No, there is not.

WRIGHT: Why do you talk about control? We are talking about majority, are we not?

BARRON: Yes.

WRIGHT: Are you identifying that in your own mind with control, is that the difficulty you are having?

BARRON: I'm having no difficulty . . .

WRIGHT: Isn't the point you were making that you can have control with less than a majority of the shares?

BARRON: Certainly you can have control with less than a majority.

WRIGHT: Thank you.

Leading Barron through document after document in which the takeover provision was stated clearly, Wright drove the point home that the dealers' offer conformed to the "exact words" or "letter" of the coat-tail. Finally he came to a report prepared by Burns Fry – Alex Barron's own company, for Chrissake! – in which the coat-tail was laid out in full. He also read from the Canadian Tire annual reports Barron had signed.

WRIGHT: They haven't said anything about control changing in there, have they?

BARRON: No.

WRIGHT: And this is a widely respected investment company, is it not?

BARRON: Yes.

WRIGHT: And then did you read the financial statements of the company regularly as they were issued?

[*Asking the chairman if he had read his own annual report! Asking Alex Barron!*]

BARRON: Yes, very definitely.

WRIGHT: And again, they made specific and accurate reference to the anti-takeover or the takeover protection in each year, did they not?

BARRON: Yes, that is correct.

At 6:15, having endured cross-examinations from all concerned parties, Barron stepped down. His body ached. Only a few people in the room, Groia among them, knew that he was dying of cancer. It had started in his liver and headed north. Six months of chemotherapy had not affected his appearance noticeably, but it had accomplished little good. His performance before the Commission was his farewell to the business world.

As he walked down the aisle from the witness stand, I asked him what he thought of the proceedings. "I don't think there's any clause you can write that will cover all eventualities," he said. "But all my life I've dealt with honorable people who stood by their word. It was what was *intended* that was important."

"I guess you don't include the Billeses among those honorable people?"

"I wouldn't say that. But you can."

"You weren't trained as a lawyer, were you?"

"No, I don't like to cross and jump across meanings like that," he said. "I like to be straightforward." He paused then. "But if you want a couple of codeine pills, I've got a couple in my pocket. I'm a drug dealer." He opened his left hand. In his palm were three yellow tablets.

I said I hoped he recovered soon.

"Well," he said, "I hope so. But I've got my bride." He smiled at his young wife Beverley then. He had met her, he reminded me, in the old days, when she was Dean Muncaster's secretary. "So you might say it's all in the family." With that he took her arm, and walked out of the room. Eight months later, he was dead.

Down in the lobby of the south tower of the Eaton Centre, Barron's grudging admissions under cross-examination had left Peter Dey feeling very positive. "What we're going to do," he said, "is throw a rope around this corporation."

17

THE HEARING (CONTINUED)

ON THE SECOND DAY of the hearing, its routine established, the spectators took time to look around. All present had changed their clothes, except Barbara, who wore her tattersall jacket again. Alex Barron turned up in a gold corduroy sports jacket. Don Wright changed into a brown suit, and wore his light brown glasses instead of his black ones. Peter Dey sported a bow tie, perhaps in recognition of his new role as culinary advisor to the dealer group. It had been left to him to recommend an appropriate restaurant for his clients, a place for them to convene at day's end. On this occasion the choice had narrowed to three establishments. They could go to Winston's, which was not Dey's preference; or to Il Posto, a fine Italian restaurant in Yorkville, where Dey was an habitué but which many of the dealers had never heard of; or to Auberge Gavroche, for French food. They finally decided tonight would be a Gavroche night. Bob Fung, the dealers' connection at Gordon Capital, had little time for such pleasantries. He seemed to spend half his time in the Commission cloakroom, making important telephone calls on a mobile phone that he carried in a pouch on his shoulder. It looked like something out of a Marvel Comic. Fred Billes, having recovered from his literal brush with the photo scrum, adopted his dormant-volcano pose, a placid island in what was otherwise a tempest of furious note-taking.

A.J. Billes, who had materialized halfway through Barron's testimony the previous afternoon, had abandoned his three-piece suit for a sports jacket, but had moved up from where Fred was sitting, because his double hearing aid wasn't working. The room was full of his friends, ancient Tiremen whose life savings were invested in non-voting shares. They thought the old man looked tired. Ernie Hanson, his old delivery man, chatted with him on the breaks. "I think it'll kill him," Ernie said. "I've already seen a big change in the last three weeks." That was debatable. On breaks in the bathroom A.J. did a creditable Sandy McTire, pulling paper towels out of a dispenser for his dealer friends. "Another?" he would ask, tearing a fresh sheet and proferring it with a smile. "Now," the dealer said, "that's what I call service!" It all seemed quite mad.

The highlight of the second day for Billes watchers occurred mid-afternoon when Martha Gardiner Billes showed up for the first time, surrounded by lawyers. She wore a yellow gabardine dress that showed off her red hair, and a black and tan herringbone mink that she draped across the chair in front of her. She sat on the far side of the room from Fred, a telling reminder that brother and sister no longer spoke to each other.

The bulk of the day was taken up by Robin Law's rambling testimony. Law had been dismissed in 1983 as a director of Canadian Tire, but he still served as the company's secretary and general counsel. Groia dragged Law through the complicated process by which his firm, working with the Billeses' lawyers, had created the coat-tail. It took ages, because Groia lost control of the witness. Trial lawyers have a cardinal rule when questioning a witness: never ask a question to which you don't already know the answer. Law kept muddying his testimony with equivocations. Like Barron, Law maintained that the takeover protection had been created against the backdrop of the family staying together, and that the dealers'

offer was not the sort of deal they expected to slip through the
wording. But, he said, the situation in 1983 was different
from the situation in 1986.

To judge from Groia's evident frustration, that answer was
not entirely helpful to Groia's case. He wanted Law to say that
Tire's takeover protection had been created in 1983 for one
reason and one reason only – to protect the A shareholders.
But Robin Law was himself a first-rate lawyer; he knew how
porous even the most waterproof legal language could be.
More to the point, he knew better than anyone what had
transpired within the executive offices at Canadian Tire
during the fall of 1983. Law had too detailed, too fluid and
comprehensive a sense of what had transpired in 1983 to tell
the simple story Groia required.

Had he been able to speak his piece, what stories Robin Law
might have told! Back in the summer and fall of 1983, after
all, Dean Muncaster and Dick Billes were waging a war with
Fred and A.J. Billes for *control* of the company. The coat-tail
had certainly been created, as Barron maintained, to protect
non-voting shareholders in the event that a *majority* of the
common shares were sold. Barron and Muncaster and their
team owned a lot of non-voting shares themselves. But the
coat-tail's distinction between "majority" and "control" also
served management's secret desires. It would have allowed
Dick Billes (and his cohorts in management) to acquire, say,
Martha's shares, and thereby take firmer hold of Canadian Tire
without buying the non-voting shares he couldn't afford. The
Billeses' finesse of the coat-tail in 1986 was in reality also a
trick management could have pulled off in 1983 as a possible
end run around A.J.'s clan.

But such facts did not serve the Commission's case. Dean
Muncaster and Robin Law and John Kron and Alex Barron were
here in a different capacity – not as clever managers maneuvering for control of a company, but as witnesses for the OSC's
staff, the protector of the downtrodden A shareholders.
Watching both sides pick and choose the evidence that served

their purposes, an observer could only marvel at the sublime flexibility of the law and its practitioners. You take the facts, and out of them you fashion the truth you wish to tell.

SO the hearing went, back and forth, detail after detail. Robin Law compared it to "a bad tennis game." From every witness – Barron, Kron, Law, Wil Matthews (the vice-chairman of Burns Fry), Glorianne Stromberg (Law's partner in drafting the coat-tail at Cassels, Brock & Blackwell) – Groia distilled the same fascinating conclusion: the coat-tail had been created to protect the A shareholders.

And from every witness, Don Wright and Tom Heintzman extracted their own set of admissions: the coat-tail had been accurately described everywhere, had been read correctly by everyone – the witnesses could hardly admit otherwise, in public – and was in no technical way contravened by the dealers' offer.

Together, Heintzman and Wright painted a wonderfully irrational, and thoroughly accurate, picture of the way decisions are made in the stock market. One witness, James Cole, the vice-chairman of Guardian Ruggles Crysdale Incorporated, the Commission's Everyman, proof of how the little investor read the coat-tail – was asked by Heintzman why he hadn't consulted his lawyer before he bought the shares. Cole explained that no one had had time for that.

HEINTZMAN: You were sort of acting as a backroom lawyer as it were?

COLE: Sort of.

HEINTZMAN: Yes. You didn't think of getting in touch with a real one?

COLE: Well, I mentioned earlier that legal opinions vary.

HEINTZMAN: You pay for good ones.

GROIA: [interjecting from his seat, and referring to the dealers' down payment to the Billeses] Sometimes $30 million.

The Billeses' lawyers stayed away from any discussion of the spirit of the coat-tail. If the non-voting shareholders wanted to sue the Billeses for a slice of the premium the dealers had paid for control of Canadian Tire, that was a matter for the courts, where individual wrongs are traditionally addressed. Wright and Heintzman were more than willing to don their frocks and formal collars to appear in court at Osgoode Hall, where the Billeses had strong odds of winning. The rules of evidence are much stricter in a court of law than in an OSC hearing, and intentions – the backbone of the OSC's case – are not admissible evidence. And in court the Billeses' individual right to sell would weigh equally against the non-voting shareholders' right to a cut of the take.

But such subtleties were largely lost on the crowd of sightseers in the Harry Bray Hearing Room, and by the third day of the hearing their interest was lagging. By then it was Saturday, and the streets downtown were abandoned except for Christmas shoppers, who all seemed to be underground. Even the coffee shop on the ground floor was closed, which was a pain, because the weekend security guards made it difficult to re-enter the building.

Somehow the isolation drew the little band together. There was always Fred to watch. Even when he was on his best behavior, Fred was a portable entertainment unit: he could fascinate you just by standing there. Once, during a morning break, Fred encountered a fellow dealer munching on a doughnut. It was a walnut cruller, and it looked especially delicious. "Here's a man still eating his breakfast," Fred said. The dealer offered him a bite, but Fred declined. He was just making conversation. He had a way with small talk, especially where food was involved.

If Fred wasn't acting up, Wright and Groia were. The two lawyers spat objections at each other like cats.

GROIA: I am just struggling along as best I can, Mr. Chairman, to try and get this man's opinion about the effect in the marketplace. If my friend [he meant Don Wright: they always referred to one another as "my friend"] is going to, in my submission, very carefully and craftily get him to comment on the effect of uncertainty, I am entitled to get this man's view about the whole effect in the event this transaction is allowed to proceed.

WRIGHT: Mr. Chairman, I previously objected to my friend characterizing my client and others in the way that he has done by innuendo. I now rise on a personal matter. I do not consider that I behave before this or any other tribunal in what can be properly characterized as a crafty manner, and I ask my friend to withdraw that statement immediately.

THE CHAIRMAN: Well, I think that's right. There is no need for that. Get on with the questions. The hearing is entertaining enough all by itself.

By day's end on Monday, December 22, Groia was only halfway through his list of witnesses, and Beck adjourned the proceedings for Christmas. Joe Groia had a turkey to cook for his father; Christmas Eve would be his first day off since the beginning of December. The betting was still even on who was going to win, but everyone was relieved to have a few days to buy presents.

Martha Billes had already done her Christmas shopping. She was buying two gifts – one for her father, and one for her son. Fred and David were getting nothing from her.

IF there was a single point in the hearing when the evidence turned, it was Monday, January 5, 1987, the day Fred Billes took the stand.

Biff Matthews, Fred's lawyer, whose own evidence had filled an entire day, was particularly solicitous of his client as Fred's trial drew near. Fred had lost fifteen pounds since the hearing started. His daughter at home, he told Matthews, was having to wash her own dishes.

Life was tough all round. Tom Heintzman wore a new tan,

as did Biff Matthews. Fred wore his navy-blue pinstriped suit, and a pair of leaden black shoes with three-quarter inch soles like double-belted tire treads. Barbara was with him, neatly attired in a four-button suit. As soon as she arrived she turfed two spectators out of the chairs she and Fred had occupied before Christmas. "We do have our permanent chairs," she explained. Fred perused the morning's *Globe and Mail* story that summed up the hearing to that point, until Groia finally called him to the stand. Fred lumbered easily to the front of the room.

His testimony, by contrast to the previous witnesses, was surprisingly nimble. Within minutes Groia had asked Fred what everyone wanted to hear: why he had decided to sell his shares.

FRED: Our family was no longer able to operate as a unit in the control of Canadian Tire; and since we could not agree among ourselves, it was thought best to look for someone who would look after Canadian Tire in a proper manner.

GROIA: By, on, or about April first, 1986, were you fairly clear in your own mind about the need to sell your shares?

FRED: Reasonably clear, yes.

GROIA: What about your brother and sister to your knowledge?

FRED: To my knowledge, my brother was of one mind with myself on this. However, my sister, I cannot speak for her. She sometimes seemed to be of one mind and sometimes seemed to be of another.

A nice shot, that. Fred was not slick. No, sir. He referred to Carling O'Keefe as "Carling's," and rounded out his sentences with Fredisms. "Carling's," he said, "intended to buy the company and own it completely, stem to stern." Sometimes, when he tried to talk like a lawyer, he referred to himself in the third person, as in "around September the tenth is about the time that Martha sort of, broke off from David and

Fred and this endeavor." Fred sounded like L'il Abner's Canadian cousin. The 49-percent route around the coat-tail, Fred claimed, "to me it was absolute news." The coat-tail itself was something Dean Muncaster insisted on back in 1983 when "we had absolutely no intention of selling our shares. So the coat-tail was not operative and a non-issue to me." Fred insisted he left most of his big decisions to his lawyers. "I did not worry myself about the coat-tail," he said. "That is why – those sort of things is why I use lawyers – why I go to lawyers to determine whether certain things can be done in certain ways. . . . What I was trying to accomplish was to find a buyer that would look after the company. It had been a family company for years. It is too big for the family to control; it is too complicated. I wanted a buyer who would look after it and keep it going for many years into the future."

He was a careful witness. Whenever Groia pushed him for details of meetings, Fred demurred.

GROIA: Now, Mr. Billes, do you recall being at a meeting with Mr. Sorell on June fifth, 1986?

FRED: Not specifically, but go ahead and ask the question.

GROIA: Do you recall being at a meeting at McCarthy and McCarthy's offices on June fifth, 1986?

FRED: No, I am afraid my recall of these meetings is not what you might like. There were many, many, many meetings at different places, and I do not have that sort of photographic memory that I can recall the date, place, and times, no, I don't.

Fred was not the sort of guy who put a lot of stock in complicated abstractions. He liked to get things down on paper. He thought like a store-keeper. Fred had selected $99.95 as the price he wanted for his shares.

"Sounds like a Canadian Tire deal," Beck commented drily, and wrote it down. Fred only raised his eyebrows in reply.

Some things Fred said surprised everyone. There was the $7.5-million non-refundable down payment he received from the dealers, for instance. Fred insisted it was something he never wanted. Amazing. "Funny as this might sound to you," he told the Commission, "I didn't want $7.5 million or any other amount as a deposit. I don't know exactly where that came from. I think it came from the dealers or Gordon Capital or a combination of them, and the exact terms of it I did not fuss with. That was worked out entirely by the lawyers involved."

That was odd. One of the early lock-up agreements Fred had signed with the dealers was now in evidence before the Commission. It clearly stated that half the deposit was non-refundable; the other half was repayable if the OSC intervened. Fred had signed the agreement himself. Groia wanted to demonstrate that the Billeses and their lawyers made the deposit non-refundable, in the event the deal didn't go through, because they knew the deal was controversial, and might end up in front of the OSC.

GROIA: Did you understand why 7.5 million dollars of it would be refundable?

FRED: Not really.

GROIA: Was there any discussion about there being a concern about the Class A shareholders wanting to take court proceedings or regulatory proceedings?

FRED: I don't believe that that was discussed with me in depth until this thing was pretty well completed. Probably this was signed and over and gone by that time.

GROIA: And what do you recall about those discussions?

FRED: Very briefly, I got a phone call from my lawyer saying that the Securities Commission wanted our file; did I object.

GROIA: Was there any discussion before that, though?

FRED: Well, certainly nothing that impressed me as being terribly important or overpowering or whatever.

GROIA: Did you believe you were treating the class A shareholders unfairly by signing this agreement?

FRED: Well, that's very subjective, isn't it?

GROIA: I would like your subjective comments.

FRED: Well, I can see that the class A shareholders might not be too happy with the situation, but the offer we have here in front of us, I believe, fits within the law and within the policies and within the share conditions, and as such it is certainly not unfair. . . .

GROIA: Did you believe that the coat-tail was a provision intended to share the control premium [with the As] at the time you signed this agreement?

FRED: No, at no point did I ever consider.

GROIA: Sorry, is that your whole answer?

FRED: Well, that's right. The coat-tail had been there for three or four years – three years, been voted for, been proposed by the management. My lawyers told me it was all right, it was okay to go ahead with it. As far as I was concerned it didn't loom terribly large in my mind.

To begin with, we weren't going to sell our shares, so there wasn't going to be any premium. So the coat-tail to us really – as long as it couldn't be triggered accidentally, it really didn't matter, because it was never going to be used. . . .

GROIA: Well, if you didn't think that was the purpose of the coat-tail, what did you believe the purpose of the coat-tail to be?

FRED: I never put my mind to its real purpose. It was something that management wanted. My advisers told me it was fine, it was within keeping, it was a good thing, it was okay. So I went along with it.

Groia was determined to take Fred behind his recitation of when the coat-tail was supposed to operate, to his sense of its moral intention. He was making Fred visibly angry – something Fred's lawyers didn't want to happen. It would not do to have Freddy throw a tantrum in the Harry Bray Hearing Room.

GROIA: Did you form an opinion as a director that the other directors understood how the coat-tail was intended to operate?
FRED: No. I only form my own opinions.

Groia soon finished, and Beck called a break. Martha went into a huddle with John Stransman, and emerged looking less self-assured. Fred went to the bathroom. Barbara was waiting for him when he came out. "Well, gorgeous?" he said, grabbing her hand. She gave him a big smile.

FRED seemed to be feeling cocky when he took the stand again. He was having an easier time as a witness than anyone had anticipated. To prove that he never considered the coat-tail a guarantee to Tire's non-voting shareholders, Fred had claimed he barely thought about the coat-tail. If he hadn't thought about it, he certainly couldn't have formed any opinion as to its intention. So far he was in the clear.

But then Stan Fisher, the lead lawyer for the Shareholders Action Committee, turned Fred's testimony against him. As Fisher cross-examined Fred, it became clear there were a great many details Fred had not put his mind to. The more Fisher pushed him, the more taciturn Fred became. For someone who had served as a director of Canadian Tire for fifteen years, and therefore as someone who tended to his shareholders' interests, Fred was remarkably ignorant of the company's rules and regulations.

FISHER: Mr. Billes, are you familiar with the *Financial Post Survey of Industrials*?
FRED: Not particularly.
FISHER: Well –
FRED: Not at all for this purpose.

FISHER: If that's intended to discourage me, it hasn't, but perhaps you'd like to tell me if you are familiar with that publication, sir? Have you looked at it?

FRED: I have looked at the odd one, but I am not capable of reading it and quoting from it, or I certainly don't put that much store on the *Financial Post*, period.

FISHER: Well, we might be hearing from other people who put, perhaps, a little more store in it.

FRED: Some people make a practice of reading things like that.

Fisher backed off, and redirected Fred's attention to Canadian Tire's board of directors. Earlier in the week the board had publicly denounced the dealers' bid. Fred's own directors were going against his wishes.

FISHER: What was your reaction, sir, when you read this circular?

FRED: I was not very happy with it.

FISHER: Well, I can certainly understand that, but what about the concern that's expressed for the class A non-voting shareholders?

[Fred's face turned scarlet.]

FRED: Mr. Chairman, if I was to talk about my concern for shareholders, class A and others, we could be here for a long, long time. [Here Stan Beck smiled.] I am extremely concerned about these shareholders. Much more concerned that the company falls into the hands of someone who will look after it correctly and give them value for the next bunch of years. Okay? That's my concern in this thing.

I am not concerned in them getting a one-time killing, big profit, once, and then see Canadian Tire go down, down and out. I have dealt with people who have come and offered to buy our shares who would have done exactly that.

Now, I think that I have protected the class A shareholders in a much more meaningful manner by not selling to a fast-buck artist, instead getting someone in there who is going to keep this company running.

[The tirade was over. Fisher dug the needle deeper.]

FISHER: Mr. Billes, the Directors of this company, other than yourself and Mr. Groch, *including your father*, don't share your views; do you agree with me? [italics added]

FRED [huffily]: No.

But, Fisher said, Fred and his siblings stood to make $210 million off the dealers. (Fisher's numbers were a little off, but he was close enough.) "Would you, sir, call that a pretty quick killing?"

FRED: I would call it a fair price for control of a very good company.

FISHER: How much of the equity, sir, are you selling this company for $210 million?

FRED: I don't think that has much to do with the price.

FISHER: You don't?

FRED: No.

That left Jack Geller, Fisher's associate, to drive the point home to the Commission. Of all the counsel for the A Team, Fred seemed to dislike Geller most.

GELLER: Is the takeover protection only window-dressing, Mr. Billes?

FRED: Well, it was one of the negotiated terms that was a part of a re-organization of Canadian Tire. My advisers told me, Mr. Muncaster told me, other people told me that it was fine; that's what was to be there.

I'm not an expert in these things, and as far as I was concerned as long as it was harmless it could be there. It didn't matter to me.

GELLER: As long as it was harmless to who?

FRED: To me.

GELLER: So long as it was harmless to you it could be there?

FRED: That's right.

GELLER: Thank you, Mr. Billes.

Fred's claim that he was protecting the A shareholders from

a "fast-buck artist" by not including them in the dealers' offer was hard for some people to swallow. John Kron found it "pathetic." But Fred's thinking was not difficult to understand. The professional argument being conducted in the Harry Bray Hearing Room was not just about a deal. It was the ageless debate that has always raged at the center of capitalism. Who should own the machinery that produces society's wealth? And how much control over the machine should the owner have? Karl Marx pondered that riddle all his life, but Fred had made up his mind on the question – and once he made up his mind, further discussion was beside the point and irritating to boot.

What incensed Fred, and Barbara, too, was that no one ever talked about their right, as owners, to sell their shares when they wanted. Barbara had a clean, clear, simple view of the world. She figured the non-voting shareholders simply coveted what the Billeses owned. "What we built up over sixty years," Barbara said, "and struggled for, and worked with, eating and sleeping. That's been our problem: too much Canadian Tire." Barbara did her best to keep the company from becoming a family obsession. Down at their twin condos in Florida, where David and Fred and their families gathered for Christmas, anyone who talked about Canadian Tire was "stomped on." But there are some things that can't be made invisible, however much one tries. Fred's family had started the company. Surely his shares were his to sell. Surely that was his due.

Unfortunately, that was not the point at issue. Fred's testimony amounted to a clear implication that the Billeses, with their meagre 4 percent of the company's total equity, expected as a matter of inheritance to do as they pleased – and that included ignoring shareholders' protection when it ceased to be "harmless" to the Billeses' interests.

As soon as Fred stepped off the stand, he made for the door, pausing only to speak briefly with his lawyer, Biff Matthews. Fred was already slipping into his coat, a knee-length, putty-colored parka. He looked like a refrigerator wrapped in movers' quilts, trying to make a fast getaway. Matthews had been nervous about Fred taking the witness stand, but, as he later said, "Fred did well on the stand."

Together, Fred and Barbara headed up Church Street to a restaurant they'd discovered. There you could order a regular dinner and, for $5 or $6 more, turn it into a five-course meal – which of course is precisely what Fred did. He and Barbara got home "the back side of nine o'clock," as Fred put it. But he made sure he wrote down the name of the restaurant. That was a good deal. Tomorrow, at the hearing, he'd tell Biff Matthews about it.

AS it turned out, Alex Barron was not Joe Groia's most important witness. Tommy Kierans was. As the chairman of McLeod Young Weir, one of the largest brokerage firms in Toronto, Kierans was the only independent representative of the investment business that Groia called as a witness. (Groia knew all along that very few investment dealers would have agreed to take the stand to admit that they misread the coat-tail.) Kierans' father, Eric Kierans, the former Liberal cabinet minister, had given him his first lessons in oratory, and his many appearances as a witness in various proceedings made him a formidable force on the stand. Kierans could see the big picture. More importantly, he knew how to read the invisible intent of a lawyer's question, which made it virtually impossible to divert him from his theme.

Kierans was the OSC's secret knockout punch. Ermanno Pascutto had personally asked him to testify. At first Kierans didn't want to. He went scuba diving in the Cayman Islands with his daughter, and returned to discover that his partners at McLeod had volunteered him to the cause.

Kierans gave evidence for most of an entire day, but the nub of his testimony revolved around one phrase he coined early on. From the outset of the hearing, Tom Heintzman and Don Wright maintained investors had to be able to rely on legal language *as it was written*. This was a time-honored argument: once you moved away from the strict meaning of words in a contract, and began to delve into the intentions behind them, you undermined the very foundation of the contract, the law, Canada, western civilization. . . .

William Biggar, Fred's adviser at Merrill Lynch, charged as much in his testimony. A decision by the OSC to cease-trade the deal, Biggar claimed, "could wreak havoc in financial markets to the extent that people read provisions accurately, [and would] suffer financial losses as a result of them [now being] interpreted in other fashions. I think it is paramount with the investors, when they are making an investment decision, that they be entitled to rely upon the attributes of the particular vehicle that they are investing in."

Kierans disagreed – and his was, as Groia would point out, the "independent" voice.

KIERANS: Certainly in the marketplace, it is not common to go behind the articles and the wordings as given and dredge up all the background [behind any coat-tail]. However, in my judgment one cannot review the coat-tail provisions and expect to have a complete understanding of all the possibilities inherent in them. One has to rely on broader principles to assure oneself that the takeover protection actually exists.

GROIA: What do you see those broader principles as?

KIERANS: I think the broader principles are those of fairness and equity [here a banker at the back of the room snapped, "Fairness and equity: bullshit!"] associated with what I regard as the *de facto* contract between the issuer on the one hand and the investor on the other, that the takeover premium will be shared. . . .

GROIA: Do you consider the transaction to be fair?

KIERANS: No, I do not.

GROIA: Why not?

KIERANS: Because the transaction constitutes a violation of what I regard as the *de facto* agreement. . . .

The *de facto agreement*! It was all he needed to say. Stan
Beck wrote it down. Groia wrote it down. Wright and
Heintzman wrote it down. It was news to everyone in the
room, but it had a catchy ring to it – Latin, to boot. For
centuries, business all over the world had been done according to one time-honored precept. "You want to sell, I want to
buy, we both cover our own asses." *Caveat emptor.* It was the
only principle intelligent men could rely on, the ancient
axiom of self-interest. Now, all of a sudden, in the middle of a
room that looks like a waiting room at Pearson International at
five o'clock on the Friday before a holiday weekend, this guy
Kierans pops up with an entirely new motivating principle:
the *de facto* contract! You could almost hear the A Team
lawyers trying it out in their heads: *Hmmm! De facto
contract! I like it! Why didn't I think of that?* Meanwhile the
lawyers on the other side of the room were glaring at Kierans,
their eyes like white-hot lightbulbs. Kierans had just made
legal history.

The B Team couldn't catch Kierans after that. The odd thing
was, he wasn't any more independent a witness than anyone
else in the room. His company, McLeod Young Weir, had, like
most other investment firms in the country, itself recommended Tire's non-voting shares to its clients. (The recommendation was even entered as an exhibit.) The coat-tail was
considered a selling point. But that was then. Now, if the
dealers' offer went through, a lot of Kierans' customers were
going to be upset. As the Billeses' lawyers' pointed out, it was
in Tommy Kierans' interest, too, that the deal be stayed. Of
course Groia and Kierans did not play up that aspect of their
mutual performance. They stuck to the motherhood stuff. It
was, if you will, a *de facto* agreement between them.

AFTER the last witness had testified, the lawyers for both sides
delivered their arguments. For three solid days they filled the
air with selected testimony, facts, legal briefs, precedents,
assertions, and claims. The names of legal cases sang out like

long-lost eccentric friends: Cablecasting, *Farnham* v. *Fingold*, Sombrero Phosphate Company, Goldex Mines, Lacos Land – the obscure bricks of legal scandal by which a nation's economy, its culture of capital, is built up, torn down, restructured. The references were lost on the crowd, which had thinned out dramatically. The stalwarts looked tired and pasty. "When this is all over, and we've been here all this time," Fred allowed, "nothing at all may have happened." He paused. "Or something very great may have happened." He seemed bewildered. The lawyers, Fred said, were making all the money anyway. They certainly were. The hearing had been held by lawyers for lawyers, at the public's and the Billeses' expense.

STAN BECK had refused Groia an extra day to prepare his final arguments, forcing him to get by with two hours' sleep. The sheer weight of the work Groia had done overnight was astonishing, culling conclusions and "quotable quotes" from seventeen hundred pages of testimony, six hundred pages of documentary evidence, and more than thirty exhibits. The dealers' offer, he concluded, was "one of the most abusive transactions of shareholder rights that has ever been perpetrated in this jurisdiction in the name of the law. . . . How Mr. Billes can accept that this is going to be swallowed without a burp by the capital markets is beyond me." The burp crack was an inside joke. Groia had never known a witness to eat as much as Fred Billes did. It drove him crazy.

Groia ended on a ringing note. "Mr. Chairman," he intoned, "we say the message should be this . . . this Commission will not look favorably upon cleverness, avarice and artificial transactions, but rather it will look favorably upon honesty and fairness to shareholders at large."

By the time Groia and Turner finished presenting their argument, the afternoon edition of the *Toronto Star* was on the street. It carried a front page story repeating Groia's claim that the deal was "unfair." Heintzman, Wright, O'Connor, and Dey took another day and a half to present their own version of the facts and the legal precedents of the case. They rode the high road and disdained the public interest. Don Wright put it best. "Mr. Chairman," he said, "as far as this case is concerned, in closing, I would like to paraphrase something that I heard as a young trial lawyer which seems to me to apply very well to my friends' position in this case. It is: if the facts of the case are against you, argue the law. If the law is against you, argue the facts. If both are against you, then ride the horse of the public interest."

At five minutes past four o'clock on the afternoon of Friday, January 9, 1987, everyone went home. All that remained was for Stan Beck and his fellow commissioners to make up their minds. Martha was nursing a cold and longing to be back in Calgary. "Ontario," she said, "is not good for me."

18

THE ETERNAL TRIANGLE

FIVE DAYS PASSED. By half-past three on the afternoon of Wednesday, January 14, 1987, the day the Ontario Securities Commission was due to announce its decision, Joe Groia was feeling so nervous he left the office for a quick tour through the busy Eaton Centre. "I didn't know whether I was a member of the team that had won perhaps the biggest fight in Canadian securities history, or lost it. Careers are won or lost on cases." Did anyone remember the quarterbacks who lost to Joe Namath? That was how Groia saw his position. For lawyers, and particularly for securities lawyers, and especially for trial lawyers, winning is everything. "Saying we played the game well would have been some comfort, but not as much as being able to say that we won and they lost."

When he returned to the Commission's offices, Biff Matthews, Bill Sheridan, and Jack Geller were waiting too. Groia went to the bathroom and collected himself. Five minutes later, the news came down. He had won.

THE Commission had cease-traded the dealers' bid on the grounds that the takeover bid was

> in economic reality, a purchase of all the common shares of Canadian Tire held by the Billeses, although structured as a bid for only 49 percent of their shares, such structure being created by Dealer Holdings in concert with the Billeses in

their capacity as controlling shareholders of Canadian Tire
for the purpose of circumventing the operation of the
take-over bid protection provision applicable to the Class A
non-voting shares of Canadian Tire. . . .

By the careful language of OSC decisions, it was a knockout.

"This is not a press conference," Ermanno Pascutto, the
executive director of the Commission, told a dozen reporters
assembled in the Harry Bray Hearing Room. Then he sat back
and basked in the glory of the moment. The press conference
was Pascutto's show. He looked like a six-year-old at his own
birthday party. He had wanted to have his say in the case since
its outset. During the final days of the hearing, both Groia and
Jim Turner had pleaded with Pascutto not to deliver a speech
of his own during the staff's arguments. Pascutto wanted to
tell Beck and his fellow commissioners to halt the dealers'
bid. Turner convinced him that such a speech would be seen
as political interference on the part of the provincial government, which might then help the other side's case in court. So
Pascutto had been cut out of the case. Groia and Turner threw
him the non-press conference as a bone. Now Pascutto was
chewing on it eagerly.

Already, by half-past four, the trio were referring to the case
as "the most important case in securities regulation in this
decade" because it would send important messages to the
marketplace about the behavior of directors and controlling
shareholders. The gamble had paid off. They were heroes.

They weren't the only ones. At Canadian Tire's head
office, the news of the Commission's decision filled A.J. Billes
with glee.

STAN BECK'S 109-page Reason for Decision was released a
month later. Beck came down hard on everyone involved with
the deal: the Billeses, their lawyers, the dealers, their lawyers.
Beck did not agree with Peter Dey's contention that the OSC
had no right to intervene in the transaction. The dealers' offer
was "a flagrant abuse of the marketplace." To Beck's mind,

the role of the Commission as a knight in white armor was particularly necessary in the financially energetic late innings of the twentieth century, however much such an idea offended old-style Canadian capitalism, where corporate families and their power had been unchallenged for decades. "There are few areas in our public life," Beck wrote, "that are as dynamic and as innovative as our capital markets. For the most part, that dynamism and innovation enure to the benefit of the economy at large and individual investors in particular. But that same dynamism and innovation can, and does, lead to abuse."

He was slapping the wrists of the postwar paper entrepreneurs, lecturing them for their lack of principles and their greed. The evidence was unequivocal, in his view. Fred, David, and Martha Billes made an agreement with Tire's non-voting shareholders. When they wanted to sell, they devised a way around that agreement. The Billeses had no concern for their shareholders, only for themselves and for their fortune. The famous formula was "a device." Beck wrote: "The evidence, and it is clearly the reality, is irrefutable that the transaction was structured to accommodate the desire of the Billeses to sell their entire control position without triggering the coattail [sic]. The Offer is so structured to accomplish that end and, in that sense, may fairly be characterized as artificial. . . ."

In the end, the Billeses had offended the public interest. That was not surprising. The Billeses had lived so long within the walled kingdom of Tire, they had come to believe that their interests were indistinguishable from those of the company and its shareholders. They had little ken of the facts of life beyond Tireland. They could not conceive that they were in the wrong.

But they were. "A transaction such as is proposed here," Beck pointed out, "is bound to have an effect on public confidence in the integrity of our capital markets and on the public confidence in those who are the controllers of our major corporations. If abusive transactions such as the one in issue here, *and this is as grossly abusive a transaction as the Commission has had before it in recent years*, are allowed to proceed, confidence in our capital markets will inevitably suffer and individuals will be less willing to place funds in the equity markets [italics added].'' In so saying, Beck came down firmly against lawyers who believed the law and its meaning ought to remain the exclusive domain of lawyers. ''There always will be occasions where the exercise of private legal rights must give way to broader considerations,'' Beck explained.

Beck's decision was a profound one, and it stuck. On March 12, the Supreme Court of Ontario upheld it; a month later, the Ontario Court of Appeal refused to grant an appeal hearing, despite Tom Heintzman's characterization of the OSC as a ''Big Brother'' of Orwellian proportions. Needless to say, Bay Street's legal community considered the decision controversial. It reduced the power of the lawyers to do as they liked. And it did not distinguish between the intentions of the dealers and the intentions of the Billeses, the buyers and sellers, respectively. Peter Dey found that especially disappointing. The decision was ''unfair to the wrong people,'' he said. ''The real culprits here were the Billeses, the board of directors of Canadian Tire [in 1983], and their legal advisers. . . . And they got off with their $30 million and their reputations intact. And to say it was grossly abusive just was not so.'' But that was a matter of opinion, and now the opinion of a regulatory agency mattered more than the opinion of a top securities lawyer. From now on, anyone who tried to pull a fast one was going to end up in front of the Commission. Indeed, within weeks, the case was being cited in most cases that came before the OSC.

That the Ontario Securities Commission had sided with the financial institutions represented by the Shareholders Action Committee struck Peter Beattie, the head coach of McCarthy & McCarthy's M&A department, as particularly ironic. The institutions had complained in order to grab a piece of the action, Beattie maintained, and they had done everything in their power to raise the specter of the public interest, and make it seem synonymous with their own. That, Beattie believed, was a dangerous development. "I think they were unlucky," Beattie said of Fred and David. "But the people who bitch about this, the institutions, do not need the protection in the marketplace. They knew what they were getting [when they bought A shares]. . . . And if they didn't know, they should have known."

As Beattie observed, "lawyers like to have decisions made that are based on law." If the OSC wanted to change the basis for making its decisions, rejecting the law in favor of something as vague as the "public interest" to make up its mind, fine: but the least the agency could do was change the rules after giving notice, after changing the laws in the legislature. To be persuaded by the so-called intentions of a group of people in 1983, and by what was supposed to have happened based on the recollection of executives who may or may not have meant what they said back then – that, in Beattie's view, was foolish and foggy.

The regulatory environment in which Beattie had grown up and trained was a hard place, but at least everyone knew the rules. Now those rules had been changed, or at least suspended. Beattie was watching a new power struggle, between established interests and the new emerging interests of the public. Beattie did not believe that the interests of the public were any less suspect than those of private organizations. In the old days, the public interest was made up of many sub-interests; but now, thanks to Canadian Tire, the public interest was a whole separate animal, a new breed, and as big as a monster. Beattie knew, for instance, what Stephen Jarislowsky was up to. "Jarislowsky's business," Beattie observed, "is investing funds and making profits. It's long-term profits, but it's also short-term profits. And they want to be the people who control what happens." Until someone else seized Bay Street's zeitgeist anew, people like Stephen Jarislowsky, who could sway public opinion, were now in control of the game. In that too there was a lesson for the callow and the wary: in business, power belongs to no one for long.

AND so Canadian Tire entered limbo, its fate undecided. Life was unpleasant. Everyone was suing everyone else. In April, 1987, Martha brought suit against her brothers for an alleged breach of the Aldamar agreement, which she claimed was intended to keep the Billeses' shares in the family. She wanted Fred and David's shares, or $125 million. In June, Fred and David returned the favor by suing Martha for her shares and $35 million in damages.

The dealers were thinking about suing everyone – Davies, Ward & Beck, Gordon Capital, Osler, Hoskin & Harcourt, the Billeses, you name it. They considered not paying Gordon Capital, claiming they had been ill-advised. Alan Warren was a pariah in Dealerland, and his unappreciative fellow dealers collectively were out $30 million.

The lawsuits served to drive off other potential buyers of the company. Meanwhile, the ownership of the corporation hung in the balance. In the spring of 1987, the A shareholders asked the Billeses to strengthen the coat-tail. A meeting was held in the West Ballroom of the Sheraton Centre in downtown Toronto, and all the old Tiremen were there. Ernie Hanson, Art Arai, Bill Preece, Myrel Pardoe, Mayne Plowman, Fred Sasaki, they all stood in knots and chatted. "This is the way it used to be," Ernie observed. "Everybody happy." But on October 14 the Billeses voted the suggestion down.

By now the A shareholders knew what they were dealing with. The trust J.W. and A.J. Billes had built up within the company over sixty years had suddenly evaporated. In the twelve months after the Ontario Supreme Court's ruling, a special committee of Tire's directors met thirty times with Jarislowsky, the dealers, and various representatives of the A

shareholders, trying to find a compromise that would allow
Fred and David Billes to sell their shares and meet with the
approval of the A shareholders. But Fred still wanted a
premium for his voting shares. He had fought hard for control;
he wasn't about to give it away. By the summer of 1987, a
new proposal had been floated. The Billes boys would swap
each of their common shares for 2.75 A shares, which they
would then sell on the open market. Martha and the dealers
would stay on as common shareholders. The A shareholders would be granted full voting rights. Charles Bronfman
was rumored to be waiting in the wings with takeover money
for all, as were Loblaws, Canadian Pacific, and even Imasco.

On February 19, 1988, Tire's board of directors called a
shareholders' meeting to vote on the new plan. By now,
Jarislowsky's Shareholders Action Committee was split down
the middle; Jarislowsky was willing to vote for the proposal,
but others were not. The A shareholders were adamant: they
wanted what they perceived to be their cut of the action.

The meeting was a rambling nightmare. Fred had a new
haircut, a latter-day Caesar, clipped and combed forward. He
looked like Captain Kangaroo. He ignored shareholders in the
audience who openly suggested a boycott of Canadian Tire.
The dealers in turn shouted the rowdies down. A young
fanatic with red hair unrolled a huge scroll in front of the
directors and called for revolution. They were all part of the
Tire family, and they all seemed quite mad. Hugh Macaulay
was booed. "He's appointed by the Billeses!" someone in the
audience shouted. "They're the ones who ripped us off!"

Yah! Power to the masses! Give us our control premium,
our daily windfall! "Whatever responsibilities we have here,"
Macaulay fired back, "surely our first responsibility is to
courtesy towards one another."

But life at Tire had gone beyond courtesy. "I simply can't
understand," a man in the audience said, "how the princi-
pals, having got the company into that fiasco in Texas, should
now feel they are entitled to a big bonus. They should be

fined, not have a bonus." Whereupon Canadian Tire's non-
voting A shareholders tossed Fred Billes's proposal out on its
ear. Having been abused by the Billeses, the A shareholders
were now going to exact their revenge.

AND so the last phase of the history of Canadian Tire drew to a
close, not with a bang, but a whimper. Limbo prevailed.
    David retreated to Barrie to design engines.
    Martha became more and more involved in the company.
She was approached by Frank Stronach, the chairman of
Magna International, among many others, and Stephen Jarislowsky, but could not find a suitable co-buyer for her
brothers' shares. Suddenly, Dean Groussman had been in
power for three years; his corporate ethos, which had terrified
the dealers into trying to buy the company, continued to
terrify them. The company delivered record performances
anyway. Dean Muncaster's remaining crew moved on one by
one, but Muncaster watched Tire from his small office, where
he ran a bevy of small businesses, with considerable pride.
"It's still the company we built," he pointed out. "As long as
they don't mess with it, it will continue to grow." But
Muncaster's claim grew more tenuous as time passed, and
Martha's grew stronger. She stayed on the board, despite her
father's advice to the contrary. She had never wanted to sell
her shares in the first place; she had been least muddied by
the OSC hearing; she had successfully championed her
father's and Tire's interests. The trial had brought them
closer. Of all the pictures and records she kept in her house
on Lake Simcoe – among all the wedding portraits, marriage
certificates, snapshots, and the surprising number of photographs she kept of her brother Fred – one picture held pride
of place in the dining-room: a picture of Martha and her dad.
Martha knew she had prevailed in the company's time of
greatest hardship: that, if nothing else, would be her legacy.
She was living in the east more and more now, in Barrie and
in a downtown Toronto condominium hideaway. Her son

Owen was working at Arch Brown's store in Barrie. She was enjoying life as a director of Canadian Tire.

In the end, she thought the entire affair had been an education. She still felt betrayed – by Muncaster, by management, and, she admitted, "obviously . . . by my brother. And he'll say he's been betrayed by me. I've been betrayed, shall I say, by the old boys' network." She still seldom missed an opportunity to put Freddy down, whether it was to slight his weight or his habits. But she had found the peace that comes of proving one's worth to others and to oneself. She had proved she could fight it out with the men who never took her seriously, and win. "No matter how adverse something is at the time it's happening," she said one evening in Barrie at her parents' old country place, "it's put there to change things, so you'll come out better. So you'll come out improved. Between the summer of 1978 to the summer of 1988, I think I've become a much bigger, stronger person. I figure I can carry on to accomplish a lot more. I've had some terrific experience." Her only concern was her father. "He's seen that first child of his destroyed by the family, by management, by the fiasco of management," she admitted.

Martha hesitated then. She planted Duchess, one of her Lakeland terriers, in her lap. "I don't think I betrayed myself," she added at last. She looked the dog in the eye. "I think I've been true to my principles. So we can sleep at night, can't we? Mmm-hmmm."

FRED remained philosophical. By the spring of 1988, he was out of Tire in all but name. He still owned his shares, and was still a director, but those connections were technicalities. He and Barbara sold their big fat house on High Point Road; sold a couple of thousand A shares; resigned their Toronto club memberships; and took up formal residence in the Cayman Islands, one of the world's great tax havens. The Caymans became their new winter home. The roads were the only letdown, smaller than Fred expected, and he was forced to buy a small imported car to navigate them. (Martha wondered aloud how he managed to get into it.) For summer living he and Barbara preferred their magnificent new home on the American side of the Thousand Islands district in eastern Ontario. No, there was no doubt about it: Freddy was out. In many ways he was the one who had suffered most in the aftermath of the OSC ruling, but his philosophical detachment from the hard reality of life beyond Tire protected him from serious upset. If he sold his shares, he sold them. If he didn't, he didn't. At least he was out of the rat race now. He had never cared much about his reputation. He would undoubtedly have dismissed the theories of William Allen, the leader of the Shareholders Action Committee, as bunk. Allen saw Fred's defeat by the OSC as a conscious act by the Toronto Establishment to teach Fred and other apostates a lesson. "One hears about this fascinating term called the Establishment," Allen insisted. "The Establishment is self-defeating. If someone gets into the Establishment by virtue of wealth or control, and if they don't conduct themselves in a way that is becoming, they become an embarrassment to the Establishment. And I'm sure the Establishment would like to get rid of them. It's not easy to stay in the Establishment. If you are prone to excessive greed and the acquisition of power and wealth at any cost, you become a pariah, an outcast. And that's as it should be."

Allen's theory was popular with those who liked to believe the business world was capable of moral enlightenment. In truth, however, capitalism isn't given to moralizing. The shareholders' reform movement of 1988, touted by the press as the harbinger of "people's capitalism," had grown out of the greedfest of the 1980s, and in turn would mutate into something else. Fred seemed to understand that. Fred had simply tried to sell his shares. He had been raised to think of the family company as his own. If he tried to manipulate the situation in which he found himself to his own advantage – and he did – he seemed no different from William Allen and Stephen Jarislowsky and the lawyers and the dealers, all of whom did exactly the same thing. Fred Billes had taken control of a company with other people's money; was that so different from the non-voting shareholders trying to grab a slice of a control premium they never intended to own when they bought their shares in 1983, when the Billeses said they were in Tire for life? Was it so different from the lawyers using the Tire case to establish their firms as hotshots in the legal community? Was it so different from the dealers trying to use Tire to elbow their way into the corporate big-leagues? In the corporate world, everyone uses everyone else. If anything, Fred was the shrewdest of the lot. What had he suffered? He earned $7.5 million for putting his shares up for sale, and he still owned his shares.

Fred, too, had proved something to himself, and to the world. He proved that he was not a stupid man, that he could play the big-league game, even if his father had denied him the chairmanship or the presidency of Canadian Tire. Fred's lawyers were the first to admit that. They suspected Fred's reputation had a great deal to do with his weight. It made him an easy target. "I think it's so unfortunate that he's so large," a lawyer involved in the takeover observed. "If you're fat and get a lot of money and are controversial, then the community goes after you. I thought in that regard they were very unlucky. Because I think people look at someone who's that large and think he's not very bright."

As for the Establishment, well, the Establishment could think what it wanted. Fred had no time for little clubs of like-minded men protecting their interests of the moment. He didn't care for reputation the way Martha or Dick Billes did. Seen in the light of capitalism's omnivorous opportunism, Fred's transgression was not in taking advantage of the little man; Fred's transgression was not in taking advantage of someone else; Fred's sin, if it was a sin, was to be caught trying to do so. It was for that, if anything, that the Establishment resented and belittled him. He had given away a secret, and made it harder for other controlling shareholders to take advantage of their trusting publics.

OF all the people whose lives had been formed and affected by Canadian Tire, however, there was one to whom my thoughts turned most often in the months following the hearing, and that was A.J. Billes. As the passage of time diluted the events of the fall of 1986, A.J. had grown frail and weak. Despite all that I knew of him and his devious ways, I had come to think of him as a peculiarly Canadian hero. Maybe he was; maybe he wasn't. But now I knew what his friends meant when they said that he touched everyone who met him.

At first I thought the infectiousness of his spirit had something to do with his energy, his ceaseless enthusiasm for the enterprise he and his brother had created. Gradually, however, it became clear that his power derived from something far more mysterious. The source of A.J.'s charisma and drive was his need. He had never hidden the fact that he needed others, sometimes desperately, to bring his vision of Canadian Tire to life. This need drew people to him, made them want to do his will. This great longing was never satisfied, in large part because he was never fully conscious of it. It drove him in the same way a writer is driven to write, a painter is driven to paint, an athlete is driven to perform. It completed some missing part of him, even if he never consciously understood the mechanics of whatever internal engine it was that drove him. Sometimes I found myself astonished by the magnitude of his accomplishment; by the fortunes he had created for thousands of people; by the pleasure and the sense of family he had engendered for so many Canadian children of the Depression. At other times, however – and far more often – I sensed his loneliness, his isolation. Maybe it is as noble to create a first-class organization as it is to paint a beautiful picture, or to write a profound novel. Perhaps the result is just as ephemeral.

Or maybe he was just an old man in his eighties, relishing

and regretting his life while he still had time to do so. One evening near the end of it all, I visited him at his penthouse apartment a block north of Sheppard Avenue off Yonge Street, up among the immigrants and the ordinary people to whom A.J. felt so close. By then his age was beginning to affect him: he moved in and out of awareness like a man who doesn't want to listen. But whenever he talked about the past of his company, his memory was as sharp as a new knife.

The post-Billes Canadian Tire did not please A.J. Groussman and Macaulay never seemed to listen to him anymore. He couldn't squeeze any information out of them. He prayed for the future of the fifty-fifty plan, but he held out little hope. More than anything else, however, A.J. regretted having given his shares to his children. He had "gifted them," had given them something they ought to have worked for, and now he realized the errors of his ways. He considered his own sons greedy, and said so, though he never lost his good spirits: for he knew his name was written in the history of Canadian business. Still, it was hard for A.J. to give up control once and for all, even from a distance.

It was late that evening when Marjorie, his wife, came into the living-room to poke the fire. A.J. watched her.

"You know," he said, after a pause, "Grannie's a bit of an incendiary."

That was strange. For a moment, he thought I was his grandson. He had forgotten who his children were; or perhaps, more accurately, he thought everyone was his child. He paused again, and watched her leave the room. "You know," he said then, suddenly aware, "we could get away from all this trouble. One single stroke. Castrate all the men. But leave me alone, of course."

This is the thing: if you grow up entirely within a self-enclosed world, such as the one that held Canadian Tire together between 1928 and 1988, the real world comes as a surprise, sometimes a pleasant one. But the price of your old comfort is old bonds, and true escape from the old world is seldom, if ever, possible: the mother system grasps you, no matter how far away you flee. You can move to Calgary, the Cayman Islands, Pompano, a penthouse, an engine design company in Barrie, anywhere you like. But you cannot snip the ties of past compromises, past loyalties. In this way it is possible to love a corporation, especially a company of one's own making, as much as it is possible to love another human being; and sometimes, as is the case with human beings, it is impossible to stop loving the corporation, no matter how hard you try.

Years earlier, during Dean Muncaster's reign as the steward of Canadian Tire, while the Billes children were still in the background, a consulting company had advised Canadian Tire to change its logo. A triangle standing on its apex was "unstable," the consultants said. But instability is its own stability, and even in disarray the triangle held the Billes family within its strange power. None of them could leave it behind. "That's been our problem," Barbara Billes had observed. "Too much Canadian Tire." She and her husband had tried to break free, but the floating scarlet triangle decided to keep them in its thrall a little longer.

A.J. knew that. It was his symbol, after all, the result of his doodling. He didn't regret his invention, this vast, deep corporate experiment dedicated to the adornment and adulation of his own middle-class mores. But he did regret his weakness. "To give something away, and not get value out of it," A.J. said, "is a sin. You don't give somebody something they don't want. And they have to know why they want it." Suddenly King Lear was living in a condo in north Toronto.

The old man stood up then and walked to the window of his penthouse on the verge of the city, where everything was clean and proper and modest and in its place. "You can see the lake, on a clear day," he said. "I can't. But others can." We had been talking about J.W. and the boys on the boat, the good times, years ago. His eyes were failing him, and he groped a hand ahead of himself. He stood at his window looking south, toward Head Office, the deep heart of his life's one dream. From the window he could see all the world that lay before him. It was not a huge view, but it was enough. He looked frail and weightless against the black window of the night. "There's Sheppard Avenue," he said, pointing to a ribbon of dotted lights. "And there's the 401. Can you see the cars going by?"